The Latin Tinge

John Storm Roberts

The Latin Tinge

The Impact of
Latin American Music
on the United States

New York   Oxford
OXFORD UNIVERSITY PRESS
1979

Library of Congress Cataloging in Publication Data

Roberts, John S.
  The Latin tinge.

  Discography: p.
  Bibliography: p.
  1. Music, Popular (Songs, etc.)—United States—History and criticism.
2. Music, Popular (Songs, etc.)—Latin America—History and criticism.
I. Title. ML3558.R6   780′.42   78-26534
ISBN 0-19-502564-4

Printed in the United States of America

Contents

Acknowledgments

The musicians who have provided information for this book—as well as the music that inspired it—are too many to mention individually, but three, Mario Bauza, Willie Colon, and Charlie Palmieri, are owed a particular debt.

I am grateful to Mr. Samie Kiamie, who shared his reminiscences of the 1930s New York Latin scene; to Mr. Raul Azpiazú, who made available the scrapbook of his aunt, Marion Sunshine; and to Lou Stevens, for his valuable 78 records.

Valuable pointers were given by Mr. Martin Williams, of the Smithsonian Institute; Mr. Richard Allen, of the Hogan Jazz Archive at Tulane University; and Mr. Russell Sanjek, of Broadcast Music, Inc.

The revision work on the book was helped by a grant from Mr. Jerry Masucci, of Fania Records.

Photographers David Haas and Johan Elbers were part of my exploration of contemporary Latin music, besides contributing photographs to this book.

Mr. Robert Christgau and Mr. Richard Goldstein, of the *Village Voice*, were among the first in musical journalism to understand the importance of New York salsa. Another was Mr. James Goodfriend, music editor of *Stereo Review*, who commissioned my first published article on the subject.

Lastly, mention should be made of the continuing documentation of Latin music's past and present in *Latin New York* magazine, and above all, of the interviews and articles by Max Salazar therein.

Introduction

Over the past century, Latin music has been the greatest outside influence on the popular music styles of the United States, and by a very wide margin indeed. Virtually all of the major popular forms—Tin Pan Alley, stage and film music, jazz, rhythm-and-blues, country music, rock—have been affected throughout their development by the idioms of Brazil, Cuba, or Mexico. Moreover, these Latin ingredients have gained in strength over the years: not only does the standard repertory contain a significant representation of tunes of Latin-American origin or inspiration, but the whole rhythmic basis of U.S. popular music has become to some extent Latinized.

Aside from the successive specifically Latin styles that have swept the country ever since the late-19th-century *habanera*, both Latin-Caribbean and Mexican idioms have become indigenous to the United States through Puerto Rico and the Chicano Southwest. Since the 1930s, they have been joined by a U.S. Latin dance music that developed principally in New York, and has come to be called *salsa*. Lastly, the enduring importance of the hybrid called Latin-jazz has been only slightly less underestimated than the overall Latin tinge in U.S. music.

Though all this is not only true but obvious, more information is available on the music of the Matto Grosso Indians than on this major element in American popular culture. Why this should be so is not within the scope of this book, though racism and xenophobia, together with other kinds of historically based stereotypes about Latin America, clearly enter in.

Two possible additional causes are inherent in the history of the subject itself. First, overtly foreign elements of many sorts have always been used as a seasoning by Tin Pan Alley, and though "Latin" music has long been a United States sub-style, just like jazz or country music (whose roots are equally alien), it is still thought of as foreign, and therefore presumably ephemeral. Second, many Latin styes—the tango, rumba, conga, samba, bossa nova—have arrived surrounded by the tinsel panoply that attends all massive fads, and have given rise to fairly frivolous and nonsensical spinoffs that have obscured both their importance and their dignity. In the words of the Cuban musicologist Emilio Grenet, writing at the end of the 1930s:

> What is now presented . . . as something new, capable of pro-ducing new thrills, is not something which has been improvised as a tourist attraction, but a spiritual achievement of a people that has struggled during four centuries to find a medium of expression.

The very success of Latin idioms at the mass level guaranteed their downgrading by critics and commentators confused by irrelevant criteria of "serious" and "popular" music. Jazz enthusiasts—myself among them—clung to a new and misleading dichotomy between jazz and "commercial" styles, though in fact the tension between personal vision and popular taste has created as many masterpieces as it has spoiled, in *all* idioms.

This book is a first attempt to start putting the record straight, and, like all introductions, it is necessarily superficial. I have no doubt that, as the previously unresearched areas (which comprise perhaps three quarters of the whole) are further explored, it will prove to be wrong in many major and minor respects. Somebody has remarked that you can tell an expert by how aware he is of his own ignorance. By that criterion, working on this book has made me an expert indeed.

For several reasons I have made no attempt to write a classically balanced study. Much that is relatively trivial belonged in it for the record. Much that is profoundly important needed amplification. Certain significant and forgotten historical figures deserved added detail.

Problems of vocabulary also cropped up. The rest of the continent's objections to the co-option of the word "American" to mean "United States" are well known. I have tried, not always successfully, to avoid it. On the other hand, I have adopted the Latin musicians' usage of "American" music as opposed to "Latin" music. I have also tried to distinguish among the various senses of the word "Latin" by referring to people as "Latino." As for more technical vocabulary, I have provided an informal glossary. I also coined the term "American-Latin" to cover various Tin Pan Alley imitations and parodies.

I hope that this book's obvious imperfections will at last stimulate the adequately supported research into American popular culture's last major unexplored facet that is so long overdue. It is, of course, dedicated to the invisible men and women of American music: the Latin musicians.

The Latin Tinge

ONE

The Roots

The music of Latin America is fully as varied as one would expect of an area containing almost thirty countries and encompassing both tropical and temperate climes. It makes use of two European languages, embraces three cultures—European, African, and Amerindian—and within each of these subdivisions, there are further variations. Brazil's main European culture is Portuguese; the rest of Latin America's is Spanish. Both French and Italian music were also highly influential in the 19th century, and American in the 20th; and even countries sharing common musical influences made use of them in different ways.

The resulting unity-in-diversity is extraordinary. Even the smallest country has its own clearly identifiable musical culture, ranging from the simplest folk idioms to national conservatory styles. Yet from another perspective, all represent versions of one cultural mix, even though not all its elements are equal, or even present, in every country: Cuban and other Latin-Caribbean music have no discernible Amerindian survivals, for example, and the styles of some Andean nations have few overtly African ingredients.

Despite this great musical richness, relatively few Latin styles affected the music of the United States, and most of those that did were big-city popular forms. The enduring influences came from four countries: Cuba, Brazil, Argentina, and Mexico.

Of these, the impact of Cuban music, not only directly but through its effects on most of the others, has been much the greatest, most varied, and most long lasting.

Taken as a whole, Cuban music presents a more equal balance of African and Spanish ingredients than that of any other Latin country except Brazilian. Spanish folklore enriched the music of the countryside, of the city, and of the salon. At the same time—aided by an illicit slave trade that continued right through the 19th century—the pure African strain remained stronger in Cuba than anywhere else. Yoruba and Congolese religious cults, and the Abakwá secret society, which is of eastern Nigerian origin, remained powerful almost everywhere. As a result, western African melody and drumming—and even the Yoruba language—were brought cheek by jowl with country music based on Spanish ten-line *decima* verses and southern Spanish melody. The co-existence of European and African rhythmic, melodic, and harmonic procedures led, of course, to their blending, and that blending took place at the most profound level.

The basic building block of Cuban music is *clave*, a 3-2, (occasionally 2–3) rhythmic pattern, which covers two measures that are treated as if only one. This is so fundamental that, as Cuban musicologist Emilio Grenet put it, to play out of clave "produces such a notorious discrepancy between the melody and the rhythm that it becomes unbearable to ears accustomed to our music."

Clave, which has a strong first part and an answering second part, like the call-and-response structure common in African and Afro-American music, appears to be a way of incorporating into European measure-patterns the basic western African rhythmic pattern of eight notes and rests, usually built up of combinations of two and three beats.

Almost all the Cuban styles that influenced music in the U.S. displayed this blend of European and African elements, in varying proportions and degrees of homogenization. The first style—and in the long run probably the most influential of all—was the *habanera,* which was one root of the Argentinian tango (itself a major influence on U.S. music) and also affected jazz directly, besides feeding into Mexican styles that were to travel north.

Most Latin musical forms are remarkably resistant to being pinned down, since they usually involve a rhythm, a dance, a style or styles of playing, typical tempi and even subject matter. Moreover, their origins are often unclear and they frequently change greatly over a period.

The mid-19th century song form called the habanera is no exception. Cuban musical historian Emilio Grenet called it "perhaps the most universal of our musical genres," citing examples from Sebastian Yradier's "La Paloma" to the habanera in Bizet's *Carmen.* Yet "La Paloma" was written by a Spaniard stationed in Havana and may have come to the U.S. via Mexico, where it is often taken for a local song, and Grenet remarks that Bizet's habanera is "more or less a Spanish tango."

The habanera's immediate ancestor was the *contradanza,* a Spanish version of a line dance thought to derive from the English "country dance," and which came to the Americas via Spain. The contradanza was well established in Cuba by the early 19th century (the earliest surviving example, a composition called *San Pascual Bailón,* dates from 1803). The form that swept the island wasn't the Spanish "contradanza," however, but its French counterpart, the *contredanse,* introduced somewhat later by French refugees from the Haitian revolution. In Cuba it soon developed two (closely related) time-signatures, 6/8 and 2/4, both of which influenced later dances.

From its earliest days, the Cuban contradanza took on African-derived elements. Though whites and blacks played the same numbers, blacks added a "lift," as Cuban historian and critic, Alejo Carpentier put it—a certain swing. It was presumably black musicians who began to syncopate the contradanza's rhythm. A so-called *ritmo de tango,* extremely similar to the Argentinian tango, became a feature of Cuban contradanzas, and spread into many other local forms. So (probably via the French contradanza) did the *cinquillo,* a fast five-beat throb that is basic to Puerto Rican music and the Dominican and Haitian merengue. Both patterns appear to have become fundamental to the *contra-*

danza habanera by the very early 19th century. Black musicians further syncopated the beat of this ritmo de tango. An 1856 contradanza called "Tu Madre Es Conga" (Your mother is Congolese—an interesting title in the circumstances) introduces a held first note with an effect identical with the Afro-Cuban *conga.*

The habanera, in fact, seems to have got its name from abbreviating the phrase contradanza habanera, the "Havanese contradanza," and its nature from an Africanization of a widespread European dance. This despite the fact that, so Carpentier remarks, it was not a purely Havanese style—and was never called the habanera by the people who created it!

The habanera had one very important characteristic that helped it to be absorbed into U.S. music. Though it preserves an element of African call-and-response in a strong first part and a weaker "answer," its rhythmic pattern is contained in a single measure. Another factor was perhaps equally important, given that in the 19th century the most effective way in which any new form could spread was by way of sheet-music: the early use of the habanera bass in piano compositions—the earliest known piano version being a piece called "La Pimienta," written in 1836.

The international influence of Latin idioms has often rested on individual compositions, and the habanera was no exception. "La Paloma" seems to have been the first, and in a sense crucial, habanera to have been exported. Written before 1865, it was extremely influential in Mexico by twenty years later, became a nationally known standard in the the U.S., and had a similar impact in Europe.

Another important individual work was Eduardo Sanchez de Fuentes's 1890 habanera "Tu", which, in Carpentier's words, "erased the memory of earlier habaneras." "Tu" was originally slower than earlier habaneras, having what the Mexicans called a "hammock rhythm." It was republished as a *tango habanera* in Paris, and became very popular in Buenos Aires because it was close to Argentinian music in feeling.

The Cuban style that had the most direct impact on U.S. music was very different from the habanera. The *son,* the basis of the 1930s *rumba* craze, has been described as the first rhythm *invented* by Cubans. It began as an Afro-Cuban rural form that was originally accompanied by percussion. It made use of widespread Afro-Latin rhythmic patterns, including the anticipated bass and the ritmo de tango; its revolutionary quality, according to Carpentier, was a "sense of polyrhythm subjected to a unity of tempo." It also had another highly African characteristic: its melody had no rhythmic connection with the underlying percussion.

When the son arrived in Havana around 1920, it was typically performed by voices, a nine-stringed guitar called a *tres,* a bass instrument (derived from an African finger-piano) called a marimbula, maraccas, claves, and bongó. Soon afterward a trumpet was added to form the style know as *septeto,* and during the 1920s, the sones groups developed recognized stars like Ignacio Pineiro's Septeto Nacional. The septeto trumpet style combined echoes of 19th-century cornet, the bull ring, and jazz, and still lives in the solo work of veteran Chocolate Armenteros.

A few sones by conservatory composers like Alejandro Garcia Caturla were published in New York by New Music Editions. But the real impact of 20th-century Cuban music, which was huge, came from popular composers like Moises Simons (author of "The Peanut Vendor") and composers who straddled conservatory and popular music.

One of the most important, from the U.S. viewpoint, was Ernesto Lecuona. Born in 1896, Lecuona, a child-prodigy pianist, was composing dance pieces at the age of eleven and teaching piano and singing at fifteen. He appeared in concert in New York's Aeolian Hall at seventeen, toured Europe and the Americas, organized the Havana Orchestra, and composed cantatas, operettas, and musical comedies. In 1943 he became Cuba's honorary cultural attaché in the U.S.

Though he ran a "rumba" band, the Lecuona Cuban Boys, which recorded for Columbia during the 1930s, most of Lecuona's musical activity was in "national" music, and his main influence on U.S. Latin music was through the huge popularity of compositions like "Siboney," "Maria La O," and "Para Vigo Me

Voy" (Say Si Si), as well as more ambitious semi-classical pieces of the kind Carpentier disapprovingly calls *morceaux de genre*, of which "Malagueña" and "Andalucia" are perhaps the best known.

The habanera, the son, and the immensely popular romantic works of Lecuona and people like him fed directly into mainstream American popular music. But equally important were the Cuban ingredients in the hot, creative blends of Latin and American idioms that developed in U.S. Latin communities.

The Latin elements in the hot U.S. Latin substyle that has come to be called salsa and its antecedents were very largely Cuban. They included basic structural elements like clave, and other aspects to be dealt with in their due place. U.S. Latin groups were also modeled on the various Cuban types of ensemble: the string quartets and trumpet-led septets that performed sones in the 1930s; brass-and-sax orchestras adapted from jazz, which mostly played the big Havana hotels; the trumpets-and-percussion *conjuntos*, and the flute-and-fiddle *charangas*.

These various types of groups were associated with different styles and even rhythms. During the early 1870s, a couple dance called the *danzón*—a descendant of the *contradanza* and thus distantly related to the habanera—became popular.

Up to around 1916, danzones were played outdoors by so-called *orquestas típicas*—cornet-led bands supported by clarinets and trombone, with tympani predominant in the percussion. Grenet describes their sound lyrically as a "picture of blinding luminosity which brought our most remote sensuality to the surface."

Indoors, the same danzones were played by groups known as *charangas francesas* (French orchestras), or charangas for short, in which violins backed a flute lead, and the tympani were replaced by the smaller *timbales*.

By the 1930s orquestas típicas were rare in Cuba. Charangas, by contrast, came in all sizes, from the famous aggregation of Antonio Maria Romeu, with its touches of Liszt and Friml and its aura of white gloves and potted palms, to small típico charangas with a far earthier sound.

The danzón and the charangas that played it were essentially bourgeois and petty-bourgeois, given to arrangements of popular classics (Romeu's orchestra was full of members of the Havana Conservatory) and separate from black street music and the sones of the septetos.

Toward the end of the 1930s, a new type of band, based on the black carnival parade groups, called conjuntos, began to be popular. These groups consisted of trumpets, voices, and conga drums, and—like the earliest New Orleans jazz groups—added piano and bass when they came indoors.

The conjuntos differed from the charangas in many ways. While charangas characteristically used two voices singing in harmony, flute, violins, and timbales, the dance-hall conjunto style united a frequently more African singing style with two or three trumpets, and a style stronger and more percussive than the more delicate charanga developed. The conjuntos rarely if ever played danzones, but a rowdier and blacker music.

The most important name in the development of the conjunto was that of a blind Afro-Cuban, Arsenio Rodriguez. Rodriguez was a percussionist and a master of the Cuban tres, whose smoky chords he used to offset the brass-and-percussion conjunto sound. He is also credited with bringing the *mambo* rhythm into the dance-halls from the Congolese-derived religious groups. Rodriguez, who lived in the United States from 1950 onward (and died there in late 1970), was a major influence on the New York band-leaders of the 1960s tipico revival, and his compositions are part of every salsa group's repertoire.

Though the raucous conjunto sound was at first no more popular in polite society than New Orleans jazz had been in its first days, the conjuntos very soon affected the charangas, by way of the group run by flutist Arcaño, whose bass-player, Israel "Cachao" Lopez, is credited by some with being the real originator of the dance-hall mambo.

"Cachao," who wrote many of the band's arrangements, introduced several elements of the mambo into danzones that he composed for Arcano. After six months of boycott by an irately conservative public, Arcaño y Sus Maravillas became enormously popular. The danzón-mambo mix added to the grace and elegance of the charanga sound a remarkably original and intoxicating swing, hot but light. As a result the charangas adapted gradually to the general Africanization of Cuban music, unlike U.S. ragtime orchestras, which were overwhelmed by New Orleans jazz. The charanga was, in fact, to be the origin of the *chachachá* (a descendant of the danzón) in the 1950s, and remain a force in both Cuban and U.S. music through the 1970s.

Nor were the charanga and the conjunto the only forms of orchestra to have a direct or indirect influence on Latin music in the U.S. The Cuban trumpet style, which still survives—though much altered by jazz influences—owed much of its beginnings to the small military bands, usually cornet-led, that played in Cuban city parks during the 19th century; and, with the timbales drums, it also provided dance music. The large dance orchestras of the big Cuban hotels, with their frontlines of brass, reeds, and violin, played arrangements of popular Cuban music that began the process whence the New York big-band sound of the 1940s was eventually to develop.

Though the music of both Puerto Rico and the Dominican Republic stem from much the same mix as Cuban music, the differences are substantial. That of the Dominican Republic is rich in both Hispanic and African styles, but the only form that made a mark in the United States was the *merengue,* a country dance with a marked—sometimes almost polka-like—2/4 to which the cinquillo adds a syncopated pulse.

The basic country merengue group consists of accordion, a distinctive metal *güiro* scraper, and a double-ended barrel-shaped drum called a *tambora,* played with a stick and muted with one hand. A saxophone—usually C-Melody—was also common, played in a somewhat manic style reminiscent of New Orleans creole clarinet playing. Merengues are also played, along with Cuban numbers, by bigger brass-fronted urban dance-bands. But the tambora, the characteristic cinquillo pulse, and the sax style are standard.

Though Puerto Rican musicians have played an enormous role in U.S. Latin music, Puerto Rico's music has been a good deal less influential than Cuba's. The idioms that have been lastingly important have come from both ends of Puerto Rico's cultural spectrum: the Spanish and the African.

The bomba is a dance and musical style of strongly African nature. Though an account of 1778 describes it as performed by guitar and drum, it came under heavy Haitian influence during the early 19th century, and in the form in which it still survives in the Puerto Rican village of Loiza Aldea, it is performed on two or three drums with a distinct counter-rhythm tapped out on the side of one of them.

The role of the bomba's drums was and is extremely close to the traditional western African two- or three-drum corps, in which a lead drum exhorts the dancers and improvises along with them while the other provides the ground bass. Moreover, the strongly syncopated three-note pattern typical of the bomba is more clearly African than most of the rhythmic patterns that came into the dance halls, almost all of which were Cuban.

The plena, a song form variously said to have come from Ponce or San Juan, is somewhat like the Trinidadian calypso in history and role, though not in sound. Plenas are commonly topical, often satirical and political. Though they were originally accompanied by percussion, their form is usually European verse-and-refrain, unlike Dominican merengues, which use a great deal of call-and-response. At various times they have been accompanied by accordion, Cuban septeto-style trumpet, and clarinet; dance-bands were playing them in New York by the 1930s.

Puerto Rico also has an extremely rich Hispanic rural tradition, usually called *jibaro* music (*jibaros* being the island's small landholders), which survives in a relatively undiluted form. New York salsa musicians have sometimes made use of the Christmas songs called *aguinaldos,* but jibaro music's most consistent influence is in certain vocal inflections and phrasings used by *soneros* of Puerto Rican descent.

Though Cuba's claim to the richest of Afro-American traditions is matched by Brazil's—whose Afro-Iberian mix is markedly dif-

ferent because its main European ingredients are Portuguese—
the Brazilian influence on American and international popular
music has been much more intermittent than Cuba's, perhaps for
geographical reasons. In any event, most of Brazil's musical
riches are irrelevant to the story of Latin music in the U.S.
Nevertheless, some of its basic qualities have become part of the
U.S. musical landscape.

Perhaps the most obvious and striking difference between
Brazilian and Cuban music of most sorts, to the casual listener, is
that while Cuban music has a driving, "hard" quality, virtually all
Brazilian styles have an indefinably laid-back beat even at their
most ebullient. While some Brazilian singing has a nasal quality
that comes from the country's Amerindian tradition, Brazilian
melodies are characteristically limpid, flowing, gentle, and full of
offbeat accents—qualities inherent in the gentle and elided
nature of the Portuguese language itself, as well as of the
Portuguese folk and popular music that Brazil inherited.

Something of this also seems to have infused even strongly
Afro-American percussion. The drumming styles of the black
Rio carnival organizations called *scolas da samba*—made familiar to
many Americans through the film, *Black Orpheus*—have a spring-
ing quality very different from Cuban and Cuban-derived drumming, which is always *pa'lante*—"straight-ahead." The difference
is one of accentuation, and is obvious in comparing Brazilian and
Cuban versions of the same rhythmic patterns. Though there is
no proving the point, this, too, seems to stem from differences
between Spanish and Portuguese music.

With the popularization of the samba, and even more importantly of the bossa nova, Brazilian music began to infuse
American music. But Brazilian percussion has been quite as important as melody to more contemporary U.S. styles. While esti-
mates of their number vary wildly, there can be little doubt that
Brazil has more percussion instruments than any other Afro-
American country, by a very wide margin, though many of them
correspond to Cuban and other drums and rattles. Brazil—perhaps because of its size—has developed far more variations in
every category than has Cuba.

Two percussion instruments in particular have recently traveled north. One is the *cuica,* a form of friction drum. The *cuica* looks like an ordinary small drum, but it has a tube attached to the head on the inside, and sound is produced by rubbing that tube. The effect—a squeaky, almost vocal sound as surprising as it is variable—plays a role in Brazilian carnival marching music, and in the large number of popular songs patterned after it.

The cuica, which is found in most parts of Brazil, is thought to be of Congo-Angolan origin. So is the *berimbau*—a musical bow, with an open sounding-gourd held against the chest. The string is tapped with a stick, and a soft sound is produced which, while capable of more than one note, is essentially percussive.

Though both the cuica and berimbau have recently become part of North American music, more important than either is the fact that a number of Brazilian percussionists have revolutionized U.S. attitudes to percussion playing as a whole, particularly in opening up attitudes to the function of percussion.

In contrast to Cuban music, which has given the U.S. several dances, only three Brazilian rhythms have caught on in the United States, the maxixe, the samba, and the bossa nova. The first was the *maxixe,* of which Brazilian ethnomusicologist Oneida Alvarenga has commented that "the European polka gave it its movement, the Cuban habanera its rhythm, and Afro-Brazilian music added its syncopations." It derived from a habanera-influenced version of an earlier Afro-Brazilian dance, the lundú.

But by far the most influential Brazilian dance was, of course, the *samba.* The word "samba" itself, which is probably Congo-Angolan, is used for many different dances, found in many parts of Brazil. The version known overseas is the so-called "carioca" form of Rio de Janeiro. This originally developed from the Afro-Brazilian ring-dance form still danced in the Rio slums to a battery of percussion, also the basis of most carnival dancing.

The modern urban samba dance is thought to have derived from the maxixe. Its music gradually became the most characteristic popular form in Brazil, slowly edging out the many regional idioms that had preceded it. By the 1940s, the samba dominated Brazilian popular music, giving birth to various allied forms like the slow, often sentimental samba-cançao, (song-samba), usually performed in international-pop style, as well as faster danced versions.

The popular samba singers of the 1940s were highly influenced by U.S. and other music. Groups like the Banda do Lua (best known as accompanists to singer Carmen Miranda) or the Anjos do Inferno used harmonies that owed as much to the Ink Spots or the Andrews Sisters as to Brazilian tradition; and while others rang the changes of Brazilian guitar styles and percussion, these were not, on the whole, the artists whose influences were felt overseas. Typical were the recordings of the Bando do Lua, which blended tight close-harmony with Brazilian melodies and fairly brisk percussion.

Not surprisingly, the increasingly bland popular scene of the late 1940s provoked a reaction. This initially took the form of a return to the "typical," folk-popular vein. The *baião,* a jaunty dance from the northeast of Brazil, became popular, and with it a simpler instrumentation of more traditional type. One of the most popular of all baião singer-composers was Luis Gonzaga, an accordionist who introduced several regional percussion instruments into Rio's popular music scene.

The national impact of the baião was relatively short-lived—though not as short-lived as it was in the U.S., where an attempt was made to popularize it. It was followed by a swing in quite the opposite direction, in the form of the bossa nova.

Unlike the samba and baião, the *bossa nova,* which reached the States very soon after it developed in Brazil, was not directly a folk-popular form. On the contrary, it was a deliberate creation by jazz-minded musicians and poets during the 1950s. According to singer Flora Purim;

At that time, what was popular was very conservative. The bossa nova was like an oasis . . . very mellow, full of harmonies and melodies, a lot of influence from progressive jazz. The real beginners were João Gilberto, Ton [Antonio] Jobim, João Donato, and a bunch of avant garde poets. They would write poetry for the musicians and the music was being written for the poets. It was like a renaissance. . . .

The bossa nova schematized and simplified Afro-Brazilian elements into something that could be played and understood by non-Brazilians. With the exception of guitarist Djalma de Andrade, "Bola Sete," most of its creators were white, and many were middle class.

Typical enough was one of the most significant of the bossa nova's creative figures, João Gilberto. Gilberto, a white guitarist from the strongly Afro-Brazilian city of Bahia, was experimenting with mixtures of samba and a West Coast cool-jazz feeling by the mid-1950s. His attempts to interest the Rio de Janeiro music business in this style went nowhere until the better known Jobim took him to Odeon, where they recorded a single and a 1958 album, *Chega de Saudade,* both of which were substantial hits.

Ironically, the first really mass rage in the U.S. for a Latin style emanated came from a country that was musically much less developed than either Cuba or Brazil: Argentina. The origins of the Argentine tango, like those of most New World popular music, provide an ethnomusicological dueling ground on which the "European origins" and "African roots" factions battle with double-edged fragments of ambiguous evidence. The name, "tango," is found everywhere in the Latin world, from the gypsy music of Spain to the Cuban *tango congo* (Congolese tango) as well as the habanera. Argentinian experts mostly agree that the modern tango grew from the influence of the habanera on one or other earlier Buenos Aires dance, probably the *milonga.* But the habanera's Cuban *ritmo de tango* is close enough to patterns found everywhere in the Latin world to believe that the similarities may be coincidental.

Like many other vital American forms that developed in the late 19th century, from jazz to calypso, the Argentinian tango was originally associated with the demi-monde. Though its most famous exponent, Carlos Gardel, was a singer, it began as a strictly dance form, with an instrumentation of violin, flute, guitar, and the German accordion called a bandoneon. By 1910 it was sweeping the cafés of Buenos Aires, and in 1912 it was accepted into café society as the centerpiece of a ball organized by one Baron Antonio de Marchi. It also began to be recorded about this time. Up to this point the tango had been a flashy exhibition dance. As it became more popular it was adapted to the talents of ordinary dancers.

The vocal tango, sometimes called a *tango-balada*, was developed around 1917, largely by Carlos Gardel, the son of French immigrants. Gardel sang the popular "Mi Noche" in theater style at the Emerald Theatre, and from then on became the personification of the tango, and a film star whose recordings still sell throughout Latin America more than forty years after his death in an air crash in 1936.

Even though Argentina now has almost no black citizens, their musical influence during the 19th century was strong, and the tango was a blend of European and African elements. But the non-Spanish influences that were a small part of Cuban development were much more important in Argentina with its large proportion of Italian immigrants. The result has never been better summed up than by Argentinian tenor saxist Gato Barbieri: "The tango is very European harmonically, and the melodies are almost operatic. The rhythm, sure, that was born in Buenos Aires. The tango rhythm is very special with that four-four."

Different as it is in most respects, Mexican music is like Argentinian in that its African influence was relatively weak and non-Spanish European elements relatively stronger. Moreover, more northern Spanish immigrants reached Mexico than the Caribbean islands, bringing with them a folk music with closer links to other European folk music than to the part-Moorish styles of Andalusia.

As happened in New Orleans (though for different reasons), France was largely replacing Spain as the lodestone for Mexican taste by the late 18th century. This is probably why the waltz (still widespread as a folk form throughout the Caribbean) became so major a part of Mexican music. By 1815 it was being denounced by a church official as a "corrupt importation from degenerate France."

Once arrived, the waltz encountered several other 3/4 (and 6/8) forms. The *jota* of Navarre and León was one, which soon blended with the waltz into a local form called the *sandunga*. The waltz remained the salon dance *per excellence* during most of the 19th century and, since 19th-century salon dances remain part of the folk idiom throughout the Caribbean, it is not surprising that 3/4 time is one of the most common in Mexico.

The strength of the polka (which was also widespread in the Caribbean) is only slightly more unexpected. It is unclear whether it reached Mexico from Paris in the 1860s, when French influence was at its height, or from the U.S. in the 1840s. In any event, its staccato 2/4 time soon became established, even more firmly in rural than in city areas; it is still a major folk and popular rhythm, especially in the north.

The waltz and other 3/4 rhythms, and the polka, are only rivaled by the far more complex *huapangos* of Jalisco region, which juxtapose several meters in mixed Amerindian and African cross-rhythms known to North Americans from "La Bamba" and other perennials.

From about the middle of the 19th century, Mexican music became increasingly Cubanized. The habanera was extremely popular by the late 1860s, and as was the case in the U.S., one of the earliest songs to popularize it was Yradier's "La Paloma".

"La Paloma," in fact, was eventually considered by many Mexicans as an example of the mid-century sentimental drawing room ballads known as *canciones mexicanas,* and it did in fact inspire many Mexican composers. From around 1870, "La Paloma" and other songs using the habanera rhythm were known as danzas in Mexico, and they became extremely popular in Mexico—which, as we shall see, was to prove ironically significant in at least one area of the United States.

The cross-fertilization of Mexican music by Cuban was a continuing process. A troupe from Havana playing Mexico City in 1884 presented various black-influenced numbers, and by the end of the century the Cuban danzón was the most popular dance of urban Mexico, though the earlier rhythm continued fashionable as a "habanera de café," a slow or moderately slow 2/4 version possibly modeled on Sanchez de Fuentes's "Tu."

Cuba's influence on Mexican urban popular music continued strong in the 20th century. Ironically, though Aaron Copland named his 1937 tribute to Mexico "El Salon de Mexico," the bands at that leading Mexico City dance-hall played mostly danzones, and many of their musicians—including the rhythm section that played the opening night in 1920—were Cuban. The leader of a danzón orchestra still popular in the mid-1970s also came from the island, and all the currently famous Cuban groups play Mexico City from time to time.

Various Mexican song forms influenced the United States, most importantly perhaps the *corrido* and *ranchera*. Corridos are long ballads, mostly with rather declamatory melodies whose last lines are stretched by their singers in a very distinctive manner. They can be in polka, waltz, or march time; conventionally, 2/4 is used for upbeat topics and waltz time for all others (a dashing waltz may carry a tragic narrative). They are very frequently sung in duet with one voice slightly dominating, often in parallel thirds and sixths—the most basic Spanish-derived harmonic approach.

The corrido began to develop from an earlier form called a romance during the early 19th century, and became a major form during the mid-century Mexican civil war (1846–48), the entire history of which is preserved in corrido texts. Other corridos cover events ranging from the coming of the railroads to romantic entanglements and bank heists. Their style is extremely detailed, replete with dates, names, and everything a cub reporter is exhorted to provide for a news story. Though the corrido's subject matter is melodramatic, it preserves the deadpan language and performance style of most folk styles. Ranchera singers, by contrast, display an emotionalism that most Anglo-Saxons would avoid even when singing in the bath.

Strictly speaking, rancheras are "ranch songs." They were sung in the theater as interludes between the acts of nationalist plays around 1910, and if they were ever genuinely folk music they soon became commercial songs performed mostly by urban singers. In fact, they probably helped the decline of Mexican regional styles. From the 1930s onward they became an important part of Mexican films, several of which—such as *Alla en el Rancho Grande*—were built around well-known songs.

Like the corridos, rancheras tend to straight-forward lyrics, and their singers draw out the final notes to lines or stanzas. But the ranchera singers add a glissando that has become "typically Mexican" in American eyes, and is a powerful vehicle of sentiment or sentimentality. Like corridos, rancheras can be accompanied by different types of instrumental groups.

Several types of Mexican folk popular groups—and their sound—are probably as familiar to many North Americans as any but the best-known individual tunes. Above all is surely the trumpet-led *mariachi*—a newcomer to Mexican music. Mariachis (the word probably comes from the French *mariage*, since they are usually played at weddings) were originally string orchestras led by a harp or fiddle. The trumpet was added in the 1940s because the sound of harp-led mariachis was thought too thin for broadcasting. Commercial mariachis soon became standardized at two or three trumpets, two or three violins, guitar, and *guitarrón* (a four or five-string bass-guitar).

Marimba groups, which also became popular, and stereotyped, in the U.S., are centuries old in the Mexican states of Chiapas, Oaxaca, and Tabasco. (The instrument itself is said to be pre Columbian, though the name derives from Africa.) Marimba groups began showing up in Mexico City in the 1920s. Before the arrival of motion pictures, they used to accompany silent films, but their popularity eventually faded except as a tourist attraction.

A third type of aggregation, the orquesta típica, had an early effect on U.S. perceptions of Mexican music. The word "típico" (typical) has important though rather imprecise connotations in Latin music, to which the nearest English equivalent is perhaps "down home." But there was nothing down home about the first Mexican orquesta típica, which was formed in 1884 out of National Conservatory teachers and students to play habaneras, pasodobles, mazurkas, polkas, waltzes, and light overtures. This group made a highly publicized tour of the U.S. A second orquesta típica, formed by Juan Torre Blanca, toured Germany in the 1890s; a third, founded by Miguel Lerdo de Tejada, performed in the U.S. This was a so-called *típica tipo de concierto* (such contradictions in terms never fazed "educated" musicians who got their hands on the folk tradition).

The orquestas típicas were apparently based on 19th-century village dance bands, which mixed strings and wind instruments, and in turn probably developed from the military bands maintained by various Mexican regiments, playing both light classical music and popular Mexican tunes.

A good deal of the Mexican music that was popular in the U.S. was not folk material, but written by well-known composers. Like their Cuban counterparts, many of these moved between popular and salon music. A good example is Manuel M. Ponce, who published collections of conservatory style *canciones mexicanas* for piano during the early part of the 1910 revolution, and in 1909 wrote "Estrellita," an early and enduring Mexican hit in the U.S. Closer to the popular tradition we have Lorenzo Barcelata, who emerged from the folk music revival in the 1920s and specialized in the huapangos of his native Veracruz—besides writing the music for a film, *Maria Elena,* whose title song did well in the States.

Most of the songs that became major successes in the U.S. were not particularly Mexican in style. Ponce's "Estrellita," as musicologist Claes af Geierstam remarks, "owes much to its model, Schumann's 'Träumerei.'" The very first international success by a Mexican composer, Juventino Rosas's 19th-century waltz, "Sobre las Olas," was so Viennese in spirit that Europeans simply didn't believe it was written in Latin America.

Even songs thought to be traditional are not always what they seem. The original "Cielito Lindo" is a traditional son going back at least to the 18th century, and still popular in the Gerrero and Huasteca area. The version popular in the U.S. uses the same text; but the music is a waltz-canción quite unlike the original tune, claimed by several composers but believed by one Mexican musicologist to be Spanish in origin.

"La Bamba" may in fact be one of the few authentic folk tunes widely known to Americans. It was performed at the Coliseo de Mexico in 1775, and virtuoso 19th-century huapango dancers of Veracruz performed what the report calls a "danza de la banda," which may simply have been a misprint. The same dance was performed by the Ballet Folklorico de Mexico to "La Bamba," itself a huapango that arrived in Mexico City in 1945. Mexican music's relatively familiar rhythms and strong external influences may be reasons why it has consistently melted into U.S. popular styles as an often unidentifiable seasoning, where Antillian and Brazilian music has tended to preserve at least some of its identity. But the presence of Mexican music in the southwestern United States also made it one of the ingredients of the western U.S. folk ethos from the start.

The dominant Latin musical area in the Southwest is Texas, whose flourishing culture not only preserved Mexican forms but developed an indigenous Mexican-American style, Chicano or *norteño* music.

Strictly speaking, the word *"norteño"* is applied to an ensemble, consisting of an accordion lead, a guitar and/or *bajo sexto* (a type of 12-string guitar), and sometimes a double bass. The music played by these groups leans heavily on corridos and on dances like the polka, waltz, and schottische. It seems to have originated on both sides of the border. *Canciones norteñas* were originally accompanied by the guitar-like *vihuela*, but harps and psalteries were in use by the mid-19th century. Canciones norteñas became popular throughout Mexico in the 1920s, as part of the ranchera movement.

Contemporary norteño music, however, appears to be a fruit of U.S. cultural crossover. Chicano accordionists believe their instrument was introduced to the area by the German Bohemian and Czech engineers building the railroads between San Antonio and Monterrey, Laredo and Corpus Christi, as well as in the mines of Monterrey. The only instrument said to have been sold by the local commissaries was the accordion, and a modern Chicano musician, José Morante, has said, "When these German bands played the polkas it was the same polkas as we play, so it's really a German polka—but we give it a little different taste!"

It is true that the playing of Texas norteño groups shows clear Central European influences. Since the polka was popular throughout Mexico during the 19th century, however, this influence may in reality not stem entirely from 1890s Texas. Another remarkable example of crossover, a group of schottisches with strongly Gaelic melodies recorded by Texan accordionist Narciso Martinez in the 1930s, presumably does not attest to a Scots tinge in Texas but to the fact that the schottische (spelt *chotis*) became virtually the typical dance of Madrid!

In any event, Mexican-American versions of Mexican forms soon took on a specifically Chicano cast. Corridos on specifically Chicano themes—often involving political and cultural clashes—have been composed since the 19th century, and still continue to be produced. The earliest known complete U.S. corrido, "El Corrido de Kiansas," tells of the cattle drives to Kansas in the late 1860s and early 1870s, and is known to have been sung in the Brownsville area by 1870.

Aside from norteño music and corridos, which properly belong elsewhere in this book, older forms of Spanish music were still easy to find in the U.S. Southwest as late as the 1950s, though the ten-line decimas that are the backbone of most Spanish-American folk music were by then dying out with the old men who still remembered them. A 1946 recording issued on Folkways includes a New Mexican "Corrido de Elena" which is a version of an ancient song known throughout Latin America as well as in Spain. The same album documents the fact that Mexican popular music was a continuing influence in the north by including a huapango that the singer had learned in Slater, Wyoming, from a group of Texans!

Though all of these Mexican styles—including Chicano music—did influence U.S. popular music to a greater or a lesser degree, ironically enough few of the most popular songs of Mexican origin—"Besame Mucho," "Cuando Calienta el Sol," "Granada"—are particularly Mexican in nature. With a few exceptions like "La Bamba," almost all are examples of a more or less "international" idiom in which Latin American popular music has blended its local differences into a generalized Latinity as phonographs and radios greatly speeded up a cross-fertilization that had been going on—as we've seen—ever since the mid-19th century.

Two of the composers whose works are most popular in the U.S. became famous at a time when this process was well advanced. Agustin Lara (1900–1970), the composer of "Granada," was a self-taught musician who worked in a "cosmopolitan" style that represented the realities of Mexican popular music at the time. Though many of his works (not the ones best known abroad) were Mexican in spirit, Lara regarded himself as being as much Spanish as Mexican.

So did Maria Grever, whose life and work both exemplified the "international" tendency. Grever was born of Mexican parents en route to Spain and was never a Mexican citizen, though she regarded Mexico as her homeland. Grever's most famous song, "Cuando Vuelva a Tu Lado"—known to most Americans as "What a Difference a Day Made"—began its life, typically enough, as a tango.

"International Latin" was essentially a ballad style, spread by the guitar trios that proliferated all over Latin America during the 1920s and 1930s; Colombian trios might sing a few local *pasillos* and Puerto Rican trios an occasional aguinaldo, but the romantic Cuban *boleros* were their stock in trade. The best known of these—the Mexican-style Trio los Panchos, which formed under that name in New York in 1944—early dropped rancheras and huapangos in favor of the ubiquitous boleros in line with this universal trend in romantic Latin music. The Trio los Panchos, in fact, may not have been very Mexican, but they were—as their many recordings still available illustrate—entirely "Latin."

In reality, the issue of "authenticity" is largely irrelevant in popular music. Not only have the various Latin countries consistently influenced each other, but some of their most "typical" styles are the result of cross-fertilization from overseas. The often denounced influence of the United States is also far more of a two-way affair than is usually recognized, since long-term examination of any area's music suggests an ebb and flow between indigenous and foreign influences. Even in the ethnomusicological field, "purity" can only be asserted by admitting as acceptable any influence more than a century old.

In any event, cross-fertilization has been at the heart of the Latin experience in the United States for more than a hundred years.

two

The Foundations

By the second half of the 19th century, U.S. music was already coming under significant Latin influences. During the 1850s and 1860s, Louisiana composer Louis Moreau Gottschalk made extensive use of Cuban elements. Latin music was part of the cultural mix in New Orleans, and one of the ingredients in black music very early on. It was also beginning to have an effect on Tin Pan Alley and Broadway.

What was to be the United States' first independent Latin idiom was already acquiring a separate identity during the early part of the 19th century. The first corrido-like song documented in what was to become part of the United States was "La Batalla de los Tulares," a narrative ballad, dating from 1824, that recounted an uprising by the Indians of Santa Barbara, California, against the Spanish. An early example of a typical corrido lyric, "El Condenado a Muerte," was also discovered in New Mexico. This lamented the author's coming execution for an unstated crime, and with typical precision gave the exact date: Wednesday, July 20, 1832. What may be the earliest Texan corrido, the "Corrido de Leandro Rivera," dates from 1841. [Though the corrido ballad form was found in many parts of Mexico, its development was very different in the north.]

Texan scholar Americo Paredes has called the period from 1836 to late 1930s the "corrido century" on the lower border.

Picking on 1836 because civil war, Indian raids, and English-speaking invasions all took place in that year, he has speculated that Indian raids, the attempt to set up the Republic of Rio Grande, and guerilla warfare against Zachary Taylor all featured in local corridos. Certainly, old residents of the area have been witness to now-forgotten ballads about the local Indian fighter Antonio Zapata and the Federalist anti-Taylor guerilla, Antonio Canales.

The earliest specifically north-of-the-border corrido hero of whom we can be certain was Juan Nepomuceno Cortina. In 1859, Cortina shot a Brownsville, Texas, city marshal who had been mistreating a servant of his mother, and with his followers briefly occupied the town before fleeing across the border.

Similar ballads continued to be produced in the early 20th century. Some of them became an enduring part of what is still a living tradition. Such were the corridos about Gregorio Cortez, wanted on a false charge of horse theft. Cortez killed a sheriff in what appears to have been an accident. He escaped, and during his time on the run killed another sheriff leading a posse sent to take him. In 1905, Cortez was found not guilty of the first murder but guilty of the second, imprisoned, and pardoned after eight years. There are probably more corridos about Cortez in Mexican-American tradition than about any other single figure. One of them, recorded in the 1930s by Pedro Rocha and Lupe Martinez, a duet from San Antonio, has been reissued on a Folklyric album. It shows the pure rural style, with an uneven 3/4 rhythm, a skeletal guitar accompaniment using runs quite similar to Anglo-American guitar playing, and almost no pauses between verses.

The corrido form was an intensely serious one; not merely a record of passing events for a people hardly served by newspapers, but the repository of myth and history for a culture to some extent cut loose from its roots. The ethos of the early Chicano corridos has never been better expressed than by Professor Paredes. In his book, *With His Pistol in His Hand,* he remarks that they tell of "men who lived by the phrase, 'I will break before I bend,'" and their performers "sing with deadly serious faces, throwing out the words of the song like a challenge, tearing savagely with their stiff, callused hands at the strings of the guitars." A couplet in "Gregorio Cortez," "No corran rinches cobardes/Con un solo mexicano" (Cowardly Rangers, don't run from a single Mexican), is typical.

How much the songs of the Mexican-Americans of the Southwest influenced, or were influenced by, their Anglo-American counterparts is not clear. Both ballad styles shared a number of elements: a dead-pan quality, a liking for detail apparently regardless of significance, and other devices that give a sometimes startling immediacy to the songs. Many themes are also similar: the cowboy ballad of "The Texas Rangers" is a mirror-image corrido, and so is the Texas version of "The Buffalo Skinners."

Given that so many later versions of these songs—Woody Guthrie's for example—tend to use corrido-like 3/4 and 2/4 guitar accompaniments, the surface case for a strong Mexican influence—or a strong mutual influence—appears attractive. But the reality is not so straightforward. First, "The Buffalo Skinners" is not an original theme, but an adaptation of an adaptation. It derived from a Maine lumberjack's song that was itself based on an English love song, and was well known in Pennsylvania under the name of "Colley's Run-I-O," where it had an extremely Anglo-American 3/4 melody.

From Pennsylvania, "Colley's Run-I-O" moved into the Midwest and down into Texas. There, it certainly underwent changes, acquiring a corrido-like bleakness and violence—"We left old Crego's bones to bleach on the range of the buffalo." Though it also seems corrido-like in its detail—"It happened in Jacksboro in the year of seventy three, a man by the name of Crego came stepping up to me"—that verse (including the date) is carried over from the eastern version. Moreover, the whole incident appears to be fictional, unlike most corridos.

Nor are the apparent Mexicanisms of style quite so straightforward as they might seem. In 1941, collector John A. Lomax recorded a Texas version of "The Buffalo Skinners" learned many years before. This is still clearly Anglo-American in style, with strong Irish elements. Though two verses include bent notes, these are at least as akin to British and Anglo-American vocal ornamentation as to corrido or ranchera singing. The song's best known version, by Woody Gutherie, certainly draws out many phrases' final lines, and may well owe some of its performance details to Mexican balladry. But these may well have come from Guthrie's own early experience, which included time spent in Texas, rather than a more general cross-fertilization.

Nevertheless, when two styles meet, each is frequently affected by a reinforcement of ingredients shared by both. The Mexican corridos and Anglo-American ballads (which both, in the very long run, stem from a common European stock) may well have reinforced each other. Certainly the two styles must have crossed paths often enough. Mexican wagon trains traveling from Chihuahua or moving up the Santa Fe Trail to New Mexico commonly carried corrido singers known as *trovadores*. When two trains met and camped together, the trovadores from each would set up a song contest. Though Mexican and Anglo-American cowhands were often at loggerheads, it seems improbable that there was no crossover during the entire period.

Outside the Southwest, the infiltration of Latin music in the U.S. seems to have been largely confined to the last quarter of the 19th century, perhaps both because contact with Latin America was relatively sparse until then, and because the music of both northern and southern America was in a state of formative flux.

That Cuban music was heard in the U.S.—or at least was available in sheet form—by the 1850s is suggested by an anecdote in an early book on Cuba. Its author, José Maria de la Torre, mentions an Italian professor of music in New York "who greatly loved the Cuban Contradanzas and who used to urge us to play them constantly. He himself played them with admirable taste and perfection without ever having been in Cuba."

But the most celebrated and well-documented mid-century example of Latin influence on American music is the work of Louis Moreau Gottschalk (1829–1869), a composer with claims to have been the first U.S. piano virtuoso.

Gottschalk, who studied in Paris and was friendly with Chopin, Saint-Saëns, and Offenbach, began composing works on popular themes from his first composition, a "polka de salon." In

1848 he wrote two famous pieces based on his memories of New Orleans creole music, "Bamboula" and "La Savanne, Ballade Creole."

Gottschalk returned to the U.S. in 1853, and a year later went to Cuba for professional and health reasons. Within a month of his arrival he had produced his first Cuban-influenced work, an impromptu based on an Afro-Cuban dance called "El Cocoye," which he played at his first Havana concert on March 13. Besides performing all over Cuba, Gottschalk spent a period recuperating from malaria on a plantation near Cienfuegos, where he talks in his diary of spending nights listening to the slaves singing.

In 1855, Gottschalk left Cuba for New Orleans, where he presented in concert a number called "Maria La O" whose origin, according to the program notes, was the singing of "a band of revelling Negroes." Local critics called "Maria La O" more mature and stronger than "Bamboula," but it aroused so little interest outside New Orleans that it was never published.

Gottschalk returned to Cuba in 1857, giving several successful concerts before embarking on a tour with Adelina Patti and her father, which included the Puerto Rican cities of San Juan and Ponce, as well as Haiti and Jamaica. Moving on to South America, he performed in Caracas, Venezuela, and the Guianas, before traveling south down the Brazilian coast of Para, as far as Belém.

In early February, Gottschalk spent several months in Martinique and Guadeloupe, during which he wrote a number of Latin- and Caribbean-inspired compositions. These included a "Marche des Gibaros," thought to have been based on a Puerto Rican folk song, and one of his finest short piano pieces, a Cuban dance called "Ojos Criollos." He also composed a two-movement symphony called *Nuit des Tropiques,* apparently based on French Antillean creole music, with rhythms in the second movement very similar to the 20th century *biguine.*

In early 1860, Gottschalk returned to Havana in style, giving a concert in February for an orchestra of more than six hundred, a drum corps of fifty, some eighty trumpets, and a chorus of one hundred voices strong. Among the works he played were the *Nuit des Tropiques* and *Escenas Campestres Cubanas,* a suite for voices and orchestra. In April he gave an even larger concert which included no less than thirty-nine pianos playing "Ojos Criollos" and another work of Cuban inspiration, "Ay Pompillo, no me Mates." Gottschalk returned to the U.S. from 1862 to 1865, when he left California after a scandal, and traveled to Panama, Peru, and—in 1866—Chile. In 1867 he was in Buenos Aires, and Uruguay. In 1868 he went to Rio de Janeiro, where he played several pieces for the Brazilian court, including "Ojos Criollos" and a fantasy on the Brazilian national anthem. A series of huge festival concerts in Rio for 800 performers came to a premature end when he collapsed at the piano after playing the first few bars of the second concert, dying of peritonitis on December 18, 1869.

Gottschalk was very much a composer of his age, and his works were also affected by his need to attract paying pupils by displays of piano virtuosity. Nevertheless, many of his Cuban-inspired pieces are remarkable, in part no doubt because of the close relationship between the music of Louisiana and that of the Caribbean islands, with their common mix of Spanish, French and African elements.

The Parisian *Journal des Débats* summed up one of Gottschalk's great strengths in a review on April 3, 1851, when it remarked, "He knows the limit beyond which the liberties taken with rhythm lead only to disorder and confusion, and this liberty he never transcends." It also commented on "the charming ease with which he renders simple things."

That ease was at its height in his Cuban-inspired works, especially his small piano pieces. *Escenas Campestres*, for soprano, tenor, baritone, bass and orchestra, owes more to operatic than to Cuban singing—Gottschalk made no use of the typical Cuban harmonizing in thirds and sixths—and some of the most effective instrumental passages are based on almost Rossini-esque string writing. But many of the melodies have a strong Cuban feel, and he frequently used the habanera rhythm, notably in the piece's climactic measures.

Among the piano works, "La Gallina," written very early in Gottschalk's Cuban stay, sounds like any light classical piece "inspired" by a folk music that the composer only superficially understands. But "Ojos Criollos" is a very different matter. As

Gilbert Chase points out in *America's Music,* the habanera rhythm and the rhythm of the 19th century black U.S. cakewalk, the basis of much ragtime phrasing, are extremely similar. Gottschalk interweaves both versions in an extraordinarily beguiling piece like a very ornate piece of Scott Joplin except that "Ojos Criollos" was written forty years before ragtime appeared. For a North American, Gottschalk's Latin inspiration was unique at its time. But somewhat similar semi-classical works by Cuban composers were also available in the United States. Nicolas Ruiz Espadero (1832–1890), a Romantic composer whom Gottschalk befriended while he was in Cuba, published a number of pieces in New York including a nocturne, a reverie, and other evidences of Parisian yearnings, as well as a contradanza.

How much any of this work reached American ears is by no means clear. Even if Americans did listen to Espadero's works, they were being exposed to nothing any more Cuban than—or even as Cuban as—much of Gottschalk's work.

Latin-American musical contacts with the U.S. increased considerably during the 1870s. Many of them were evidence of a growth of Latin-American interest in European classical music rather than of Latin influence in the U.S. In 1862, for example, the nine-year-old Venezuelan piano virtuoso Teresa Carreno made her debut at the Irving Hall in New York; and in 1875 the Mexican Juvenile Opera Company performed Offenbach's *Grand Dutchess of Gerolstein* and *Robinson Crusoe* at the Fifth Avenue Theater. (American audiences apparently liked their virtuosi young: the prima donna was one Nina Carmen y Morón, aged eight.)

Ignacio Cervantes Kawanagh, whom Alejo Carpentier calls "the most important Cuban musician of the 19th century," took refuge in the U.S. in 1875, during a rebellion against the Spanish. He lived there for four years, giving artistically and financially successful concerts.

The fact that relatively little popular performance of Latin music in the U.S. was documented in the press of the time tells us only what the papers thought worthy of comment, not what was actually happening. In any event, by the late 1870s, the United States had certainly been exposed to the habanera rhythm, in the form of Sebastian Yradier's "La Paloma" the first major Latin hit in U.S. popular music, and an important influence in its own right.

"La Paloma" was published by G. Schirmer in New York in 1877, under the title of "La Colombe" (its English lyrics were not written until 1907, by the Rev. Henry G. Chapman), and gained public performance around the same time. A publication by White and Goullaud in Boston of the same period is inscribed: "As sung by the Zavitowski Sisters in the Burlesque of Robin Hood." This edition is rather cryptically called a "canción americana," but makes use of the habanera bass throughout.

Various ostensibly Latin groups were also touring the country at about the same period, as is shown by an 1886 sheet of "Melodias Mexicanas," also rather confusingly labeled as "Aztec Fair, Ancient and Modern Mexico para piano solo executed by the Fandango Minstrels at Orrin Bros. and Nichols." On the other hand, as an anecdote told by black bandleader and composer W. C. Handy makes clear, "Latin" performers were not always what they seemed. In a letter to Handy, George L. Moxley, the mulatto interlocutor of Mahara's Minstrel Men, wrote that in the 1870s "the public knew me as George L. Moxley, the 'Cuban Tenor Solo Singer,' and considered me as white as any foreigner is expected to be. This made it possible for me to get in all shows."

By this time, scattered compositions by Americans were beginning to show signs of Latin influence. An example is a song called "The Danza," by G. W. Chadwick, published in Boston. This does not make use of a habanera bass but of a rather unusual version in 3/8 time; however, the lyric's fervent references to a "creole maiden" called Inez prove that it was evoked by Caribbean rather than Spanish sources.

The number of 19th century publications or Latin-inspired music lying forgotten in archives may reach the hundreds. Even casual searches turn up enough to prove that Latin inflections were permanently in the air from this period on.

Many of these inflections were Mexican, in part because of close contact between the two countries and partly because Mexican composers often wrote dance forms already popular in the U.S. Examples like the mazurka, "Un Beso," published in

1890, or the collection of banjo selections by D. Emerson, including at least two Latin-inspired pieces, a "Mazurka Mexicana" and "Rita Polka," can be reduplicated many times. In the 1890s, a number of marches with more or less Latin inspirations also appeared, among them "La Fiesta," by Alfred Roncovieri, and John Philip Sousa's "New Mexico," which interwove Indian, military and Mexican elements.

While the rise of interest in Latin music had begun much earlier, the Spanish-American War of 1898 no doubt helped sustain it. From around 1895, when another rebellion broke out, Hearst newspaper agitation helped make the U.S. Cuba-conscious. Moreover, several black regiments fought in the brief war, and presumably gained some firsthand experience of Cuban music. The whole affair also fomented a brief flurry of patriotic numbers, like the 1898 "The Cuban Flag," written by Frank J. Herron to the tune of "The Bonnie Blue Flag," and "dedicated to the Cuban nation," and "The Havana Patrol," by Albert F. Huntington.

A far more significant event for the long-term future of American-Latin music came with the peace treaty: the cession of Puerto Rico to the United States. But the effects of the transfer on the United States were not to be felt for another twenty-five years or so. During the early part of the 20th century, Mexican music—in its internationalized form—continued to be the dominant influence, notably through the 1909 publication of Manuel M. Ponce's "Estrellita," which—though not so influential as "La Paloma"—was to become a permanent presence on the American music scene, with revivals in the 1920s, 1940s and 1950s, and be recorded by such unlikely artists as Jascha Heifetz!

One important factor in Mexican music's consolidation was the beginning of tours by groups that at least approximated authentic Latin styles. Though it was to be a long time before Americans heard real Cuban music, such Mexican groups as the Orquesta Típica of Miguel Lerdo de Tejada (which played at the 1901 Pan-American Exhibition in Buffalo, New York) were becoming familiar. And while this was a long way from folklore, or street-popular styles, it was Mexican music as conceived of by Mexicans.

At least notionally Latin themes were also showing up in the theater before the turn of the century. John Philip Sousa's *El Capitán*, written in 1895 and presented in 1896, was his most successful operetta (his march of the same name became equally famous.) The following year, the enormously successful light composer, Victor Herbert, included a number called "Cuban Song" in his musical comedy, *The Idol's Eye.* Since this was set in India, the logic involved was presumably that of fashion. In any event, his lyricist, Harry B. Smith, provided early examples of two major stereotypes that were to haunt American-Latin compositions for half a century. His lines opened,

> In the isle of Cuba, fair Havana
> There I raise the coconut and the banana,

and later continued,

> Oh, the eyes of Cuban girls they go right through you.
> They pursue you and they woo you and they undo you!

"Cuban Song" was the beginning of a Broadway flirtation with Latin themes that was to last for half a century. Most of them were longer on exoticism than musical authenticity. In 1904, a long-running musical comedy, *The Yankee Consul*, opened at the Broadway Theater. Its stars were two popular artists, Raymond Hitchcock and Eva Davenport. Its plot concerned the adventurers of "a bibulous young fellow, Abijah Booze." Despite song titles like "My Santo Domingo Maid," the score—by Alfred G. Robyn, of St. Louis—was not noticeably Dominican.

A second south of the border plot surfaced two years later. This was *Mexicana*, set in "Mexico—land of the Montezumas, beyond the Sea of Darkness," as the original program notes rather cryptically put it. *Mexicana's* characters included one Johnny Rocks, a Wall Street broker, and various revolutionaries. Despite the cultural confusion suggested by a number called "Lorelei," the composer Raymond Hubbell (best known for the song "Poor Butterfly") did at least attempt something a little more authentic in a piece called "The Bolero"—certainly one of this rhythm's earliest appearances in the United States.

Cuba's turn came two years later, with a musical comedy called *Havana* that ran over 250 performances at the Casino. Like *The Yankee Consul*, this starred Eva Davenport, one of the period's most successful comediennes, as well as James T. Powers. The music was by an Englishman, Leslie Steward (whose real name was Thomas Barrett).

Tin Pan Alley and Broadway's way with Latin styles was always eclectic, and usually trivial. It was, nevertheless, part of the process by which U.S. idioms absorbed Latin ingredients. There is an inevitable conflict between "authenticity" and this absorption process, which necessarily involved the breaking down and "Americanizing" of foreign ingredients. Though the level of artistic achievement may have been higher, the process was not too different in the areas where Latin styles had the most significant impact: black music.

Black American music has frequently been the channel by which the Latin tinge entered mass-popular styles, and the process was underway even before the formative years of jazz and ragtime. Nineteenth-century New Orleans had a particularly important Latin influence, though in such a polyglot musical culture, the Latin strands are often difficult to disentangle with any certainty. First, New Orleans creole music itself was sufficiently similar to cause problems. Second, the jazzmen who provided most of the information often referred to both Spaniards and Latinos as "Spanish" (just as many people, Latino and non-Latino, still do). Nevertheless, the Latin influence was certainly there; as Alan Lomax put it in *Mister Jelly Roll,*

French opera and popular song and Neapolitan music, African drumming . . . Haitian rhythm and Cuban melody . . . creole satirical ditties, American spirituals and blues, the ragtime and the popular music of the day—all these sounded side by side in the streets of New Orleans.

Scattered reports of musical contact with Cuba date back to the early part of the 19th century. One of New Orleans's first classical impresarios, John Davis, was a French refugee from Haiti who came to the city from Cuba. A Spanish troupe from Havana performed at the St. Philip Theater in 1824. In 1827 the first violinist of the Havana Opera toured the U.S. with a New Orleans opera performed at the St. Charles Theater. These classical contacts were the only type likely to be reported, but it is certain that there were many more at the popular level. New Orleans was sympathetic to Cuban aspirations long before the Spanish-American War. An international incident blew up over the treatment of New Orleans citizens who had fought for the Cuban filibusterer, Narciso Lopez, in 1849–51, and in 1869, a local publishing house published a piece in the Spanish 6/8 *paso doble* rhythm called "Viva Cuba" and dedicated to the Cuban leader in the Ten Years' war, General Carlos Manuel Cespedes.

Yet, ironically, the most clear and major episode of Cuban musical influence in New Orleans came by way of Mexico, where, as we have seen, the habanera rhythm became extremely popular during the 1870s. In 1884–85, New Orleans hosted the World's Industrial and Cotton Centennial Exposition. Many countries took part, but none so lavishly as Mexico, whose exhibit rivaled that of the U.S. itself. As part of its contribution, the Mexican government sent over the band of the Eighth Regiment of Mexican Cavalry. This band, which has been variously estimated as sixty and ninety strong, was the hit of the fair. It played at the opening, and at all major functions, and in the words of *Century* magazine, "has enlivened the fair throughout all its stages, furnishing music on every ceremonial occasion with never-failing courtesy and good nature," playing "Dixie" or Mozart, or "singing the songs of love and patriotism of their own country." Contemporary newspaper reports give the names of a number of these Mexican numbers. They included waltzes, schottisches, as well as danzas, which were, as we have seen, Mexicanizations of the habanera!

That the "Mexican band," as it came to be called, was highly important to New Orleans music is beyond doubt. Within a year of its stay, local publishing houses had issued sheet music of many of its most popular numbers, many of them arranged for piano by a New Orleans composer, W. T. Francis. The most prolific of these publishers, Junius Hart, also continued to issue other Mexican and Mexican-inspired numbers, many of them strongly influenced by the Cuban habanera. Of thirty-five examples published by Hart, ten were mazurkas, seven waltzes, four schottisches, one a danzón (also identified as a danza) and seven danzas. All the danzas whose sheet music has survived show the typical habanera rhythm.

Given that the numbers played by the Mexican band sold thousands of copies of sheet music, it is clear that Cuban music, introduced via Mexico, was a significant part of New Orleans musical life in the pre-jazz period.

But the Latin strain in New Orleans went further than that. Several members of the Mexican band remained in the city, among them one Joe Viscara or Vascaro, a saxist of whom Jack "Papa" Laine, leader of one of the earliest white jazz groups in the city, has said, "He could hardly speak American, but that son of a bitch could handle a horn!"

Just how important this Latin-American strain was in the growth of jazz is not clear. But it is not necessary to subscribe to views like the one quoted in *New Orleans* magazine, that the word "'jazz' is a corruption of the Mexican 'Musica de jarabe,'" or New Orleans author Al Rose's speculation that ragtime bands were the result of black musicians trying to play Mexican music, in order to realize that it was of real significance.

Nor was the "Mexican band" an isolated phenomenon. Several important early musicians whom jazz writers have casually labeled "creole" were in fact of Mexican origin. Among these are clarinetist Lorenzo Tio, Sr., whose father was a clarinetist and saxist from Tampico, another branch of whose family came from Veracruz, and whose son taught many of the major New Orleans clarinetists. Other Mexicans were Tio's brother, Luis, and Florenzo Ramos, another veteran of the "Mexican band." Further musicians of Latin background included Alcide "Yellow" Nunez, who played for a while with the original Dixieland Jazz Band. Nunez's father was Mexican, and one of his uncles came to New Orleans with the Eighth Cavalry Band. He was also part

Cuban, since he was related to Jack "Papa" Laine's wife, herself a Cuban.

Interviews and other evidence show that at least two dozen musicians with Spanish surnames feature regularly in the reminiscences of early jazzmen. Some of these were undoubtedly Spanish, but others were Latin. Nor did they all play with white or creole groups. Some played with black bands even before an 1894 amendment to the Black Code which greatly tightened segregation in the city. Among them were Perlops Nunez, who is said to have run one of the first black bands in New Orleans, in the 1880s, and Jimmy "Spriggs" Palau, who played with the legendary jazzman Buddy Bolden. It is entirely probable that (as happened in New York until the 1940s) Latin musicians went along with local patterns of discrimination, thus disseminating more widely their common musical heritage.

Certainly the music of many early black bands was not inimical to Latin influence. They included many string groups playing waltzes, mazurkas, schottisches, and almost certainly numbers introduced by the "Mexican band"; and even Buddy Bolden's group—often regarded as the first true jazz band—played polkas, mazurkas, and similar dances on appropriate occasions.

Some New Orleans musicians may even have had direct experience of Cuban or Mexican music. There were also plenty of opportunities to hear the real thing in New Orleans itself, since the city had not only a number of Latin musicians but even a Latin section, or sections, in the French Quarter. This has been described by "Chink" Martin, another veteran of Papa Laine's band, whose parents were Mexican and Spanish, and who learned guitar from a man named Francisco Quiñones, who was himself either Mexican or Spanish.

Martin has told interviewers that the stretch of Royal Street between Dumaine and Esplanade, as well as several other blocks, was inhabited mostly by Mexicans and Spaniards. He has also testified that Latin music was common in the French Quarter in the early part of the 20th century. He himself used to accompany Mexican and Spanish serenading (he mentions specifically "La Paloma," "La Golondrina," and a Puerto Rican song called

"Cuba"). Martin also performed in a Mexican band in seamen's joints on Decatur Street, and played violin in a trio with a Puerto Rican guitarist named Tafoya and a bassist called Frank Otera.

It is difficult to gauge the effect New Orleans's considerable Latin tinge had upon early jazz, but it may well be that much that has been labeled "creole" is either Cuban or syncretized with Cuban music. The rhythm of "Mo' Pa' Lemé Ca," as played by clarinetist Albert Nicholas and other creole jazz musicians in the 1940s, is almost identical to the habanera rhythm, played fast and hot. While individual examples from a later period do not in any sense constitute proof, the available evidence does suggest that the Latin ingredients in early New Orleans jazz are more important than has been realized.

That is certainly the impression given by a very wide range of scattered comments by many jazzmen. Guitarist Danny Barker (a creole of the Barbarin family) talked of times when ". . . the rhythm . . . would play that mixture of African and Spanish syncopation—with a beat—and with just the rhythm going." Here, Spanish almost certainly has to mean Latin. The whole passage suggests the passages for percussion called *rumbones* that are still part of salsa today, and accounts of New Orleans at the end of the 19th century are full of such references. Pianist Jelly Roll Morton called New Orleans the stomping ground for all the country's greatest pianists. "We had Spanish, we had coloured, we had white. . . ."

Morton himself was considerably influenced by Latin music. Aside from converting "La Paloma" into a "ragtime tango," he wrote several unpublished Latin-bass pieces: "Creepy Feeling," "Mama 'Nita," "The Crave," "Spanish Swat," among them. (His recorded version of "Jelly Roll Blues" has a more genuinely Spanish rhythm.) Though some of these may have come from the later tango era, at least one of his works did not. "Now in one of my earliest tunes, "New Orleans Blues," you can notice the Spanish tinge," he told Alan Lomax thirty-five years later. "This 'New Orleans Blues' comes from around 1902. I wrote it with the help of Frank Richards, a great piano player in the ragtime style. All the bands in the city played it at that time." "That time" was eleven years before the nationwide tango craze.

Jelly Roll Morton went so far as to claim that the "Spanish tinge" was the essential ingredient that differentiated jazz from ragtime. "In fact if you can't manage to put tinges of Spanish in your tunes, you will never be able to get the right seasoning, I call it, for jazz."

Morton used "La Paloma" to demonstrate the process to Lomax.

I heard a lot of Spanish tunes, and I tried to play them in correct tempo, but I personally didn't believe they were really perfected in the tempos. Now take "La Paloma," which I transformed in New Orleans style. You leave the left hand just the same. The difference comes in the right hand—in the syncopation, which gives it an entirely different color that really changes the color from red to blue.

Despite Morton's theories, the "Spanish tinge" was by no means missing from ragtime. It has already been pointed out that the habanera's ritmo de tango was virtually identical with the cakewalk rhythm—and in fact, both are versions of a rhythmic motif common in a wide range of Afro-American music. If ragtime pianists had used the kind of held notes in their left hand that converted the ritmo de tango into an early version of the conga, that might have given their playing an apparent but misleading Latin flavor. But ragtime's bass-patterns were kept very pure. So when Eubie Blake says that pianist Jesse Pickett used a habanera rhythm for this composition "The Dream" in the 1880s, it is virtually certain that it was in fact a habanera, not a direct development from the cakewalk.

Pickett was one of a semi-legendary generation of late 19th-century black musicians. According to Blake, "some say he was from Philadelphia," but he mostly played in "The Jungle," near Hell's Kitchen on New York's West Side. That pre-ragtime black piano and Latin elements were already interweaving by the 1880s is further confirmed by the fact that Pickett used "The Dream" to teach Eubie Blake to play ragtime! Interestingly, he gave it two parts—first fast, then slow-drag with blues—that were a kind of reversal of the Cuban contradanza's common two-part form. And the blending with blues is significant of the way in which Latin ingredients have always melted into U.S. music.

"The Dream" itself became part of the jazz repertoire, losing its original Latin bass in the process. In 1926, Fats Waller recorded an organ version called the "Digah's Dream," and in 1939 James P. Johnson led a small band version for Asch Records. (Interestingly, both men were virtuoso pianists and major figures in the New York stride piano style, of which Pickett and his like were early forerunners. The habanera influence may have been part of what freed black music from ragtime's European bass.)

The habanera was also part of other black New York musicians' arsenal by the 1890s. William H. Tyers was to become a founder-member of ASCAP, and composer of the jazz standard, "Panama," itself important in black-Latin crossover in the early 20th century. Fifteen years before "Panama," in 1896, Tyers published a "Cuban Dance," called "La Trocha," with the now familiar habanera bass.

Black/Latin musical crossover increased as more black musicians came in contact with Cuban music. In 1900, W.C. Handy's band traveled to Cuba and, while he was there, he bought a copy of the national anthem, the "Hymno Bayames" and arranged it for the group. Handy was particularly struck by the small bands playing in the backstreets.

These fascinated me because they were playing a strange native air, new and interesting to me. More than thirty years later I heard that rhythm again. By then it had gained respectability in New York and had acquired a name—the Rumba.

(If Handy was correctly identifying his rhythm, this suggests that the son had arrived in Havana by the turn of the century, not at the end of World War I as is usually said.)

Handy's autobiography contains a particularly telling anecdote about the impact of Latin music on black Americans. In 1906 or thereabouts, he says, at a black carnival site called Dixie Park, in Memphis (a town well clear of any confusing creole tinge), he was playing an early Latin-influenced work, W.H. Tyers's "Maori." "When we . . . came to the habanera rhythm, containing the beat of the tango, I observed that there was a sudden, proud and graceful reaction to the rhythm. . . . White dancers, as I had observed them, took the number in stride. . . ."

Handy's memory was at fault in some minor details— "Maori" ("A Samoan Dance") was published in 1908, and rather than a habanera rhythm, it used (even more interestingly) a syncopated 2/4 bass vaguely reminiscent of the rumba. But the broad lines of the story ring true, and the follow-up is even more interesting. Suspecting some kind of ethnic response, Handy had the band play "La Paloma" as a kind of check, and created exactly the same reaction among black dancers. It was this incident, he says, that led him to introduce the rhythm (which for some reason he called a "tangana") into the "St. Louis Blues," the instrumental piano version of "Memphis Blues," the chorus of "Beale St. Blues," and several other compositions.

In isolation, this anecdote would prove very little. But it is not in isolation. Latin music has evoked similar responses on the part of black Americans to the present day, and Latin rhythms have been absorbed into black American styles far more consistently than into white popular music, despite Latin music's popularity among whites.

The role of Latin music in ragtime during the early 20th century is—as was ragtime itself—interwoven with the history of commercial music publishing. This fact, together with a tendency to disapproval of perceived threats to a loved style, may explain why the Latin tinge in ragtime has been so little remarked upon. The characteristic attitude was expressed by Samuel Charters and Leonard Kunstadt, in their 1966 book, *Jazz: a History of the New York Scene*. Commenting on young black New York composers' supposed commercialism, they wrote: "When tangos were popular they wrote tangos, when blues were popular they wrote blues."

It seems likely that the perception of ragtime as a classical form corrupted by commercial music, rather than as a style with varying wings of is own, has distorted the total picture. First, it is not true that the black New York composers *only* used tango forms when tangos were popular (though there seems no reason why they should not have done so). Tyers's "La Trocha" was written long before the tango era. Moreover, while William J.

Schafer and Johannes Riedel quote Charters and Kunstadt approvingly in the *The Art of Ragtime,* they mention several examples of highly effective ragtime/Latin blends. One was "Temptation Rag," by Henry Lodge, whose work they describe as more "rhythmically explosive and vital than those of any of the big three—Scott Joplin, James Scott and Joseph Lamb." Another was the "Pastime Rags" of Artie Matthews, an obscure player whom Jelly Roll Morton called the best in St. Louis in his time, and whom Schafer and Riedel dignify with the adjective of "genuine."

The role and effect of the habanera in the prehistory and early history of ragtime, and the tango in its later years, have— like almost every aspect of Latin music in the United States—still to be studied. But it was clearly a continuing one, in ragtime as in early jazz. Other Latin elements were rarer. An interesting work by Scott Joplin appeared in 1909 (the year in which "Estrellita" was published). This was "Solace," a slow piece described by its composer as a "Mexican serenade."

Rudi Blesh, in *They All Played Ragtime,* called "Solace" "a most unusual tango for the period: it avoids the minor mode, and its melodies are rather anticipatory of those of the Brazilian maxixe, which was to be introduced a few years later." In reality, "Solace" had little more to do with the tango than it did with the maxixe or—in any precise sense—a Mexican *serenada.* It is an agreeable mood piece with a mostly habanera bass, whose connections with Mexican music are more a matter of feeling than either imitation or recreation.

"Solace" was, in fact, an example of Latin-influenced American music: not Mexican, but a side of Scott Joplin that Mexican music brought out. Like "Ojos Criollos," half a century earlier, it demonstrates that the consistency of the Latin tinge in American popular music is no coincidence. Many Afro-U.S. rhythmic patterns are similar to Afro-Latin rhythms, for the very good reason of a common heritage, even though the Anglo-Saxon element in the black U.S. music mostly forced those rhythms into the four-square context of common time.

Ragtime's rhythmic impetus was largely due to the cross-rhythms that the tango-like cakewalk patterns produced when set against that 4/4 beat. In "Solace," they blend with a perfectly compatible left hand. The result is, in a sense, far more "natural" than the usual ragtime cross-rhythms, though it also shows by contrast how essential the northern European rhythmic approach was to the peculiar tension of black-U.S. swing.

The fate of W.H. Tyers's 1911 "Panama" illustrates this process of absorption. Tyers's original piano score used the habanera bass, and so did the orchestral arrangement played by the New Orleans society ragtime orchestra of Armand J. Piron. A version of this on a limited-edition recording played by the New Leviathan Oriental Foxtrot Orchestra shows it to have been a somewhat lumpy hybrid, with the held first note heavily emphasized by the tuba.

"Panama" was widely played both as a rag and as a march. Most jazz groups dropped the habanera rhythm, but it can still be detected in a recording of the Olympia Brass Band of New Orleans. A long passage for marching drums, which is virtually identical to common conga patterns, leads to several final choruses in which the habanera and march-band rhythms are fused in an interesting demonstration of a halfway stage in the habanera's absorption.

William H. Tyers was an important member of the first generation of black musicians to make a *personal* impact on Tin Pan Alley. Besides conducting dance orchestras, Tyers worked as a staff arranger for various music publishers, later became assistant conductor of Will Marion Cook's New York Syncopated Orchestra. As a man prominent in "respectable" New York dance-band circles and an arranger for Tin Pan Alley, he certainly played a significant role in Latinizing the popular music of his time. But by the time he wrote "Panama," the Latin tinge was well established in a wide range of American popular styles, and that tinge itself ranged from the more or less overt presence of Mexican melodies to an underlying Cuban rhythmic strain. On Tin Pan Alley, these Latinisms were still only a seasoning, hardly more important than Italian music and much less so than Irish. But thirty years of preparation had readied the country for its first really massive Latin invasion.

THREE

The Tango Rage

The tango reached the U.S. from Buenos Aires by way of Paris and Broadway. Paul Reuben's musical comedy *The Sunshine Girl*, which opened at the Knickerbocker Theatre on February 3, 1913, introduced a new singing star, Julia Sanderson; a new husband-and-wife dancing team, Vernon and Irene Castle; and the first massive nationwide Latin fad. In the words of the *Variety Music Cavalcade*, the Castles' dancing of the turkey trot and Vernon's tango with Julia Sanderson "eliminated the waltz from the musical comedy stage and substituted a vogue for dances of Western origin."

The Castles were, on the face of it, unlikely vehicles for this kind of revolution. An Englishman whose real name was Vernon Blyth, Castle had begun his stage career virtually by accident, as a boy in Lew Fields's *Girl Behind the Counter*. Irene, who came from New Rochelle, had been rejected as a stage dancer for being "awkward." Stranded on tour in Paris, the couple nearly starved before catching on at the Café de Paris and returning to New York at ten times their previous U.S. salary, bearing the tango with them.

Within a year, the Castles were almost an institution. The Castle House School of Dancing was the leader in its field. Its orchestra—which was conducted by Will H. Tyers at one point, as well as by another famous black New York composer/orchestra leader, James Reese Europe (who wrote several pieces for them, including maxixes, and presumably tangos)—was in constant demand for society balls. Castle Tango Palaces opened up all over the U.S.

Though they popularized a number of American dances—including the turkey trot—the tango, which they danced again in the 1914 revue, *Watch Your Step*, was the Castles' semi-permanent gift to American music. They also introduced another Latin dance, the Brazilian maxixe. This was close enough to its more popular cousin to have been called a "tango brésilien" at times, but it did not have the same success. For one thing, it lacked the tango's panache. The Castle's 1914 book, *The Modern Dance*, called it "a very quiet and pretty dance," and "a development of the most attractive kind of folk dancing . . . an exquisite expression of joyousness and of youthful spontaneity," but their instructions made it seem a good deal more complex than the tango, which may have been one reason for its lack of success.

The enormous success of the Castles is impossible to exaggerate. Their influence reached beyond social dance—Irene Castle was the first woman in New York to bob her hair—but it was as dancers that they shone. Their fee for an appearance was reputed to be $1,000, in 1914! Their only real rivals were Maurice Mouvet and Florence Walton, who danced under the name of Maurice and Walton.

E.B. Marks—himself by far the largest publisher of Latin music in the U.S.—summed up the qualities of the two couples in his autobiography, *They All Sung*.

Miss Walton's beauty was more sultry and voluptuous than Irene's, but less individualized. Maurice, dancing at first with the insolence of the bal musette, acquired the polish of a master. The Castles were a sprite and a steel spring; Maurice and Walton were a tiger and a woman.

In its heyday, the tango was particularly popular in the restaurants and clubs specializing in *thés dansants:* Louis Martin's Café de l'Opera at 1457 Broadway; Reisenweber's on Eighth Avenue near Columbus Circle; Murray's, on West 42nd Street; and Bustanoby's Domino Room, on 39th and 6th, where Rudolf Valentino was a *danseur mondain* (or less politely, gigolo) and Sigmund Romberg played paino in the house orchestra.

That the tango and *thé dansant* were associated very early is shown by a splendidly forgettable 1913 song by Cecil Macklin, "Tango Is the Dance for Me," whose opening lines ran: "Tango is the dance for me, I trip it merrily, Then have a cup of tea,

And dance some more—Whee!" Interestingly, this song was described as "adapted to" Sigmund Romberg's 1912 "Très Moutarde," which was originally a turkey trot but was hurriedly coopted in a 1913 edition with the words, printed in red, "or Tango." In reality, the *thés dansants* were a rather more worldly phenomenon than "Tango Is the Dance for Me" makes them sound. As Marks put it, cocktails, some of which were named after popular dancers, were the "typical tango tea drinks."

The dance craze revolutionized for a while the polite social scene. New hotels like the McAlpin and Sherry's were the first to cater to it. Older places held back, but in 1914 the fashionable Waldorf gave in. People even danced between courses at meals, "to the indignation of chefs and maitres d'hotel," in Marks's words.

Anything so popular was bound to generate a press coverage that escalated that popularity. The tango was reported variously as bad for the spine and as good for all sorts of ailments. A Mrs. Ethel Fitch Conger broke her leg dancing it and told reporters she was going to seek legislation banning a step called the dip. A high school student died in a trolley car after dancing for seven hours, and the headlines read "Death Attributed to Tango." In 1914, Yale made the front pages by banning the tango from its Junior Prom—and Harvard made them in double column by saying it *would* tango.

Nor did the moralists ignore it. The New York *Mail* referred to "the tango which appals lovers of sound manners and morals is an immodest and basely suggestive exercise tending to lewdness and immorality," and Bishop Schrembs, of Toledo, denounced "the nauseating revels and dances of the brothel." Protestants were more cautious, mostly warning against excess. One Episcopalian bishop even felt that "the tendency is more and more toward stately walking dances and will eventually bring back the minuet."

Whether by coincidence or not, the same tack was taken by the rather defensive introduction to the Castles' *Modern Dance:*

> The much-misunderstood Tango becomes an evolution of the eighteenth century Minuet . . . when the Tango degenerates into an acrobatic display or into salacious sensation it is the fault of the dancers and not of the dance. The Castle Tango is courtly and artistic.

Cynics might feel that the dance's salacious reputation took it further than any possible minuet-like qualities. In any event, of course, it triumphed. Even Mrs. Stuyvesant found that she needed an exhibition dance to draw guests to her affairs. She asked the Castles to invent a desensualized tango, and they came up with the Innovation, a version performed without touching. The mayor of New York, John Purroy Mitchell, invented a step called the Twinkle. Senator Hoke Smith of Georgia and Secretary of the Treasury William Gibbs McAdoo were rivals for tango honors on Capitol Hill. And the rest of America tangoed along behind them.

Much of the music to which they did so was only marginally Latin, though one of the earliest hits of the period, A. G. Villoldo's "El Choclo"—published by Schirmer in 1913—was Argentinian. But the tango did affect American music profoundly in several ways. Not the least was the interest of E. B. Marks's publishing house. Marks had a part-time salesman in South America, Milton Cohen, who also "traveled in trunks" in South America. On his wanderings, Cohen sold Marks's publications, and also bought all the local sheet music he could find. "His shipments of Argentine tangos and Brazilian maxixes enabled us to present something new to the American public," Marks later wrote. They also laid the foundation for an involvement with Latin music that made Marks by far the largest U.S. publisher of authentic and ersatz Latin material for many decades.

From the point of view of U.S. popular music history, the local imitations of Latin music were in any case as important as the relatively few examples of the real thing. Critics have tended to treat "commercial" popular music as a nefarious influence on supposedly pure forms. Characteristic is a comment in *The Art of Ragtime,* to the effect that Tin Pan Alley composers wrote rags in all sorts of popular forms but that "ragtime itself was strong enough to absorb and transmute all the influences around it, all attempts to reorganize *or corrupt* it [my italics]."

In reality, like all music, ragtime always borrowed from and lent to other forms; the pejorative and, in the context, essentially meaningless, concept of corruption betrays a basic misapprehension of musical evolution. Certainly, nobody could accuse

Tin Pan Alley of pedantry ("Otchi Tchernaya" was once mar-
keted as a "famous Russian tango"). But pedantry is not necessarily an appropriate reaction to the hybrids that soon went on
sale. In the first place, they were part of a blending process that
added important new ingredients to the popular songwriter's
vocabulary. In the second, while a number like J. Rosamund
Johnson's maxixe, "The New Maurice Brazilian Tango," may
have been an ephemeral piece written for commercial reasons,
the maxixe and the tango were close to U.S. black music in their
roots and therefore good fusion material. Looked at without
prejudice, many of these compositions were as healthy as hybrids commonly are.

The Castles themselves frequently worked with black
musicians. Will Tyers directed their New York orchestra for a
while, as did James Reese Europe, who also accompanied them
on a European tour. (Jelly Roll Morton later claimed that he had
been offered the post but was too busy to go, and so "they
featured "Jelly Roll Blues" all across the continent.")

The popularity of ragtime had already established black
music as an important ingredient in Tin Pan Alley. The tango's
popularity brought in its wake a number of "ragtime tangos"
that prolonged an association of the rag style with the ritmo de
tango in a new guise. At least three were published in 1914. Abe
Olman's archetypally named "Tango Rag" was one. Another
was "Everybody Tango," by Paul Pratt, a white pianist from
Indianapolis, published by McKinley Music in Chicago, which
suggests the tango had already caught on outside New York;
and the dean of ragtime publishing, John Stark, published a
"Chicken Tango" written by his son, Etilmon J. Stark, a practicing "legitimate" musician.

Tin Pan Alley ragtime was not the only music to feel the
effect of the tango. It followed the habanera into the post-
ragtime New York jazz style of piano called stride. One of stride
piano's greatest exponents, Luckey Roberts, composed a superb
tango called "Spanish Venus" (he returned to the Latin vein in
the 1930s in a symphonic work). But the most famous jazz
tango of all is also one of the most famous jazz numbers of all
time: W. C. Handy's "St. Louis Blues," published in 1916.

"St. Louis Blues" introduced a format that has become

traditional in jazz-Latin fusions: an introduction or first theme in a tango rhythm, followed by a section in jazz 4/4. There is an amusing parallel between Dizzy Gillespie's bebop classic, "Night in Tunisia," and a 1916 jazz tango called "Egyptian Fantasy," both of which adopted this same dual rhythmic pattern, and used North African titles to exotic effect.

"Egyptian Fantasy" is an interesting example of the critically neglected Latin thread in early jazz. The only known recording— a 1941 version by Sidney Bechet, with Red Allen and J. C. Higginbotham—is a singularly beguiling composition, with real solidity under its eclectic exoticism. The low-register opening to Bechet's version is apparently fairly close to the original, first played by his mentor, George Baquet.

Though it soon fell into obscurity, "Egyptian Fantasy" was the theme used by the Original Creole Band of New Orleans to introduce their vaudeville act. This group was the remains of the band run by the great early trumpeter, Freddy Keppard, which had been taken over by its bassist, Bill Johnson. The Original Creole Band made a tour of the U.S. on the Pantages vaudeville circuit, doing so well at the Palace in New York (coincidentally the theater where the great "rumba" craze of the 1930s was to begin) that, in Jelly Roll Morton's words, whereas "it was known that no act played the Palace Theatre . . . for more than one week. . . . the Original Creoles played for weeks to standing room only." "Egyptian Fantasy," in other words, traveled extensively.

Aside from the tango, which continued popular, the Latin tinge was at best intermittent for the rest of the decade, despite occasional songs like the 1917 "In San Domingo." Things were not much different on Broadway, which was to become an important vehicle for the spread of American-Latin music in the 1930s. In 1916, Sigmund Romberg was involved in a rather unsuccessful musical comedy called *The Girl from Brazil*, which included at least one song of vaguely Latin inspiration, "My Señorita." The following year, Cuban impresarios confused the issue with a show called *The Land of Joy*, which opened at the Park Theatre.

Though this was billed as a Spanish-American review, it was composed by Quinito Valverde, "the Victor Herbert of

Spain," and the dances were Spanish fandangos, seguidillas, and
so forth. It was, in fact, not "Spanish-American" but Spanish
and American. Its music and dancing were, however, nearer to
authentic Latin sounds than most Broadway productions, and a
report in the *Evening Mail* commented that the audience for the
first night of *The Land of Joy* was mostly Latin-American, which
suggests a fairly large Latin colony in the city. (The *Mail* headline, "In 'The Land of Joy' Spanish Dancers are Lovely, but
American Comedians Awful," pretty much sums up a problem
that was to beset Latin music for the next sixty years. One
reason why it has been taken less seriously than any other
popular form is that excellent Latin bands have so often appeared with awful comedians when they reached a mass audience.)

In many respects the main importance of the war period
was as a transition era between the beginnings of Latin influence
in the U.S., and its establishment as a major presence. In the
long term, by far the most important event of relevance to this
process was not musical but political. On March 17, 1917, Puerto
Ricans were granted U.S. citizenship. Almost immediately, mi-
gration from the island to New York got under way. The earliest
immigrants mostly settled in the Red Hook area of Brooklyn,
but others began moving into the then Jewish and Italian area of
East Harlem. These new arrivals were to lay the foundation for
the development, little more than ten years later, of an indigenous urban Latin sytle.

In a sense the 1920s simply continued the process of consolidation, bridging the tango era—the first major wave of Latin
influence—and the "rumba years", which began in 1930 and
formed the early period of development of a truly American-
Latin substyle. During the 1920s, also, the enduring pattern
was established by which genuine and imitation Latin songs
both competed and reinforced each other, many of them becoming permanent parts of the popular repertoire in the process.

The spread of Latin music during this period was continuing
and rapid, though less spectacular than the spread of black music.
But the one facilitated the other. Some of the era's dances (the
Charleston and the Black Bottom) were based on cakewalk-like

rhythms, and thus resembled a speeded-up basic tango; and more generally, acceptance of the relatively hard rhythms of jazz—and indeed the whole notion of "rhythm" as an almost self-subsistent, and certainly self-validating, element in music—laid the groundwork for Latin versions of the Afro-American synthesis.

The 1920s might more accurately have been called the Dancing Age, rather than the Jazz Age; besides dancing at almost all social occasions, a husband and wife might roll back the rug and dance to the radio or phonograph after supper.

Like jazz, Latin music often travelled on the back of social dance. The tango, especially, did what relatively few dances have done: it moved from a fad to a near-permanent part of the social dance repertoire.

Many things contributed to the tango's continuing strength long after its companion in *The Sunshine Girls*, the turkey trot, had vanished. One was the scene in the film *The Four Horsemen of the Apocalypse* in which that former Bustanoby's *danseur mondain*, Rudolf Valentino, danced a tango in an Argentinian dive in full dude-gaucho rig. The contribution of a silent film to a *musical* style is necessarily limited. But the scene gave thousands of cinema pianists—including many jazz pianists—a further chance to work on the blending of American and Latin music, and hundreds of thousands of cinema-goers a further opportunity to discover it.

Interlinked with social dance was Tin Pan Alley. Until now the Latin-American influence in popular music had remained little more than an exotic flavoring. But by 1920, when John Alden published "La Veeda," it had become the strongest of the exotica, overshadowing Italian, German, Jewish, and the others.

"La Veeda" was typical of the rather tentative approach to Latin music that was still common in the early 1920s, even to the misspelling (as late as 1925, the International Novelty Orchestra felt the need to spell "Mi Niña" as "Mee Neenyah"). Like many American-latin compositions as late as the 1940s, "La Veeda" was labelled a foxtrot, but though its melody was not particularly Latin (or for that matter unLatin) its rhythm, at least as played on an early 1920 recording by the Columbia Saxophone Sextette, was essentially a brisk Americanized tango.

During the first years of the decade, things Latin were suddenly "in the air." In March 1920, Ted Lewis's Jazz Band recorded an Irving Berlin song called "I'll See You in C-U-B-A," whose style—under the period charm and bird-whistling—showed no Latinisms at all. Two years later, the Columbians' recording of "Just Like a Doll" used a quotation from Sigmund Romberg's "In Brazil" (from the musical comedy, *Springtime of Youth*) as its introduction. Neither thing was strictly a "Latin influence" in the musical sense, but that both reflected the growing viability of Latin references in popular music is born out by the fact that several specifically Latin or Latin-inspired songs were published in 1922. One was Mexican composer Alfonso Esparza Oteo's canción mexicana, "Mi Viejo Amor," which was to become particularly popular in 1926, and was also republished in 1940. Another was perhaps the first of the enduring U.S.–Latin standards, a piece that, while part of U.S. popular balladry, owes its existence to the presence of Mexican music in the U.S. This was the 1922 "Rose of the Rio Grande," with words by Edgar Leslie and music by Harry Warren and Ross Gorman, which jazz musicians kept alive for several decades.

The following year saw at least three major Mexican-influenced compositions. One was "Cielito Lindo," with its traditional text set to a Cuban-influenced canción melody in waltz time. A second was a revival of Manuel Ponce's "Estrellita"—a song with a remarkable shelf-life—revived in an arrangement by Frank LaForge. The third was the pseudo-Latin "Mexicali Rose," a "waltz-ballad" by Jack Tenney and Helen Stone* that was recorded at least four times that year and featured by Ralph Pollock's dance orchestra, before being revived a decade later, this time under the patronage of Xavier Cugat. The upswing of interest in Latin numbers that year was strong enough to impel The Columbian's dance band to revive Victor Herbert's 1913 "Marcheta," a piece with a somewhat tango-ish feel which they enhanced with a loud castanet part during the introduction.

It is important to distinguish at this point between Latin or Latin-inspired melodies and rhythms on the one hand and Latin styles of playing on the other. Most Americans heard all these compositions in highly American versions. "Mi Viejo Amor," for example, was recorded by Max Dolin, a popular violinist of the time, fronting what was essentially a section of the Victor Records house orchestra, led by Nat Shilkret. The tango rhythm and Oteo's melody were strongly featured, but the only other stylistic concession to the piece's origin was an anachronistic set of castanets. Otherwise, the writing, for trumpet and fiddle lead, contrasted with sections for violins and saxophones, was standard sweet dance-band fare.

The Victor house orchestra made a large number of similar recordings during the early and mid-1920s, both under Max Dolin and as the International Novelty Orchestra. One of the earliest, under Dolin's name, was a 1921 version of "La Golondrina" and a "bolero cubano" called "Si Llego a Besarte." "La Golondrina," in which a muted trombone played a counter-melody, was not unlike the style of late 19th century and early 20th century sweet dance groups in Cuba, Mexico, and Puerto Rico. Nor was the group altogether committed to mass-popular numbers. The backing to their 1921 "Cielito Lindo" was a danzón, "Telefono a Larga Distancia."

Their version of "Quiereme Mucho" and "Morena Mia," to a larger extent than any of their earlier recordings, showed how Latin rhythms could become absorbed into an American style of playing. The former in particular is a strongly Latin-inflected piece, yet entirely within the U.S. dance-band canon of the time. "Quiereme Mucho" also contained a passage for marimba, an instrument of great antiquity in Mexico and Guatemala that became extremely popular in the U.S. for a while.

The marimba groups playing in the United States during the 1920s provided an early example of the Americanizing process at a stylistic level. Several of them included Mexicans and Guatemalans whose knowledge of the root styles was thorough. The Hurtado Brothers of Guatemala—fairly characteristic of Central American marimba groups down to the fact of being siblings—were among the best known.

In its concentration on popular hits of the day, in its mix of non-Latin and Latin repertoire, and in its blend of U.S. and Latin stylistic elements, the Hurtado Brothers' music was not unlike the music of future groups like those run by Xavier Cugat. But the Hurtado Brothers were playing at an earlier stage in the acceptance of Latin music, when the idiom's stylistic traits were to all intents and purposes totally unknown. As a result, their balance of ingredients was tipped far more toward Tin Pan Alley. An early recording of two one-steps, "Fletita" and "Catalina," was fairly representative. "Fletita" is in a fast 1920s vaudeville style with no discernible Latin elements. The strongly Central American melody of "Catalina" is developed by the marimbas (with backing that includes trumpet, possibly saxophone and piano) in more or less purely popular vein, with overtones of player-piano ragtime.

The Hurtados were quite active in the recording studio. Celso Hurtado played with, and sometimes led, a series of interlocking groups throughout the second half of the 1920s, some of them at the same time: the Miami Marimba Band from 1924 to 1928, the Mexican Marimba Band in 1926, and the Dixie Marimba Players, which played almost entirely American tunes, from 1926 to 1930.

The music of the early marimba groups was yet another illustration of a highly important point about the interrelationship of Latin and American music. Despite what one might expect, this does not proceed from the importation of something fairly genuine through a progressive watering-down. The early stages involve highly diluted Latinisms. Then, as Latin music and its various substyles have become familiar, they have become stronger—not necessarily moving toward "authenticity" in terms of their origins, though that has frequently happened, but establishing themselves as healthy U.S.–Latin forms.

The groundwork of this part of the process was being laid by the mid-1920s. One important aspect was that an increasing percentage of the Latin numbers published in the U.S. were by Latin composers. In 1924, Joseph M. LaCalle published "Amapola" ("Little Poppy"), another of those songs that, first appearing with no great fanfare—though (like almost every tune composed, it sometimes seems) it was recorded by Victor's International Novelty Orchestra—was to re-emerge several times as a major success.

Another example of the same process was G. H. Matos Rodriguez's "La Cumparsita," originally published without words in Milan, in a tango version that first became known in the U.S. in 1926, then republished in the 1930s by E. B. Marks, as a rumba with words by Carol Raven. Most of these compositions were in the "international" style prevalent at the time. Maria Grever's "Jurame" ("Promise, Love") appeared in the same year as "La Cumparsita." The "tango tzigane" "Jalousie," another composition with enormous staying power, followed in 1927. The same year came Wolfe Gilbert's "Ramona," in connection with the film of the same name. And in 1928, thirty years after it had revolutionized Mexican music, Eduardo Sanchez de Fuentes's habanera, "Tu," was published in Boston by Oliver Ditson, with a Yankee understatement to the effect that it had been "published earlier in Havana."

Though E. B. Marks was still by far the largest publisher of Latin music in the U.S., Ditson was indicative of a growing interest among other publishers. That same year, the firm brought out another Sanchez de Fuentes composition, "Mirame Asi" (taken over by Marks in 1931 and given English words by Carol Raven), and Jose Padilla's tango, "Princesita," which had been published in Paris two years before.

The following year, a work was published that was far more significant than any of these, both in its own right and as a harbinger of what was to come. This was "Siboney" by Ernesto Lecuona, undoubtedly the most famous of all Cuban composers. Its U.S. publisher, Leo Feist, issued "Siboney" (advertised in the August 1929 issue of *Metronome* as "That Quaint Melody All Havana Dances To") with a fairly typical schizophrenia, both in a standard foxtrot-tango arrangement and as a "danzón cubano." In one form or another it was to become one of the best known of all Latin numbers.

While Latin and pseudo-Latin songs appeared in a steady trickle throughout the 1920s, Broadway was also increasingly turning to Latin America, either for its themes or its actual material. A couple of early examples of what was to become a fairly standard practice—the inclusion of a humorous, romantic, or satirical song of Latin inspiration in a revue or musical comedy—occurred in 1922. Sigmund Romberg wrote a song for the musical comedy *Springtime of Youth* called "In Brazil," using the familiar habanera bass. Its lyrics reflected the common confusion and clichés: they referred to "Natives dancing gay fandangoes in Brazil," and part of the chorus was in Spanish! George Gershwin's "Argentina," sung by Dolores Costello in *George White's Scandals of 1922*, was, believe it or not, not a tango but a bolero.

Gershwin was to return to Latin themes in the future. So— to an even greater extent—was Richard Rodgers, who wrote a Cuban-influenced number, "Havana," for the 1926 musical, *Peggy-Ann*. The same year, *Rio Rita* set a romantic narrative about Captain Jim Stewart, a Texas Ranger who falls in love with a Mexican girl, to music by Harry Tierney. *Rio Rita,* which produced a couple of popular hits—the title song itself and "The Ranger's Song"—was successful enough to be filmed three years later, starring John Boles and Bebe Daniels. In 1931, *Metronome* was still carrying advertisements for the sheet music, and a mention of John Boles in the same year referred to him as "featured in *Rio Rita.*"

In true musical comedy fashion, *Rio Rita* made light entertainment out of a rather grimmer reality. In Texas and the other areas where Mexican- and Anglo-Americans rubbed shoulders, friction was generated more often than romance. Chicano singers often dealt with themes involving Mexicans and the Texas Rangers, "los Rinches," in a very different vein from *Rio Rita.* Tex-Mex corridos dealt with problems between Chicanos and white law officials even more often—perhaps because of the semi-epic form of the corrido—than the blues.

A later corrido, "Los Rinches de Texas" (The Texas Rangers) is typical:

Es una triste verdad	It is sad but true
De unos pobres campesinos	about the poor farm workers
Que brutalmente golpearon	who were brutally beaten
Eses Rinches asesinos.	By those murdering Rangers.

In the late 1920s, Okeh, Victor, and other labels began to issue norteño records, just as they did country music, blues, and almost every American ethnic style. The first Chicano commercial recordings were mostly by performers who appealed to wealthier Texas-Mexicans, who could afford the luxury of buying records. These usually featured "trained" musicians with piano or orchestral backing. Though many corridos were recorded, they tended to be nostalgic "classics" about figures prominent in the 1910 Mexican Revolution.

In this, as in every other aspect of Latin music in the U.S., the 1920s were, in a sense, a preparation for a revolution that took place in the early 1930s.

By 1929, in fact, Latin music was operating on two levels. The patterns that had been established since the beginning of the decade continued. Broadway still used Latin America as a source of romantic drama of dubious authenticity, though even *Nina Rosa*, with music by Sigmund Romberg, which was set in a Peruvian tin mine, and ran 137 performances at the Majestic, showed one important new pattern: the employment of Latin artists, "Armida" and Cortez and Betty.

Meanwhile, even on Broadway, the real thing—or an approximation—was beginning to be heard. Miguel Lerdo de Tejada's Mexican orquesta típica came to Broadway in March 1928, on the same bill as vaudeville star Marion Sunshine at Keith's RKO Palace Theatre. According to *Variety*, it scored a "rousing success," despite an attempt at crossover: a jazz number that the paper's reviewer recommended the group "should eliminate at once."

The old patterns continued. The tango, for instance, was still in vogue. In the words of the manager of the Roseland ballroom, Charles F. Burgess, "The tango goes well here. True, few dance it, but . . . the others crowd up to watch and you have a free vaudeville show." But far more important—though still less obvious—than the old patterns was what lay behind the new ones: the development of El Barrio (East Harlem) into a major Latin district.

The presence of a large Latin community in New York—and later in other U.S. cities—provided a demand for authenticity, a place for musicians to play undiluted Latin styles, and, perhaps most important, a doorway for innovations from Cuba and other Latin countries.

The first sign that El Barrio was becoming a separate musical market was the establishment of a Latin music store—the Almacenes Hernandes, on Madison Avenue between 113th St. and 114th St., by Puerto Rican composer Rafael Hernandez (who was to lead a well-known string quartet in the 1930s) and his sister. In 1929, Hernandez wrote what was perhaps one of the first, and certainly one of the most famous, compositions expressing an emigré's nostalgia for his country: "Lamento Borincano." He did so, it is said, on the sidewalk outside his store.

Many important musicians arrived during the 1920s. San Juan-born valve-trombonist Juan Tizol, who was to give Duke Ellington's early Latin experiments—notably "Caravan"—such a distinctive sound, came to Washington around 1920, in an orchestra that played the black TOBA vaudeville circuit. As Ellington tells it, in *Music Is My Mistress:*—

> He was with the band from Puerto Rico that Marie Lucas brought back to play in the pit at the Howard. We had to acknowledge that was a hell-fired band, all the musicians could switch instruments, and at that time, that was extraordinary.

But individual Latin musicians had been coming to the U.S. for decades. What was new was that by the late 1920s, New York had bands made up of Latin musicians resident in, not merely touring, the States, and playing for Latins, not Americans. Many of the Latin musicians in New York were finding regular employment, with Columbia recording the enormous amount of tunes that were issued for sale in southern America. Joseph LaCalle was in charge of this department, and Nilo Melendez and Alberto Socarrás were among the musicians who were earning up to $150 a week in the studio.

But by the late 1920s some of them were also playing for a new Latin public. One was pianist Nilo Melendez, who in 1929 wrote the enduring composition, "Aquellos Ojos Verdes" (Green Eyes). Another band, headed by Cuban Vicente Sigler, who had been working in New York for at least a decade, played the midtown hotels like the McAlpin, the Waldorf Astoria, and the Astor. Sigler's group served as a talent incubator, like other famous bands to follow. It also provided one condition for the development of a New York Latin style—a mix of Cuban and Puerto Rican musicians. Among them were three who would lead bands in the 1930s: Cuban flutist Alberto Socarrás; violinist

Alberto Iznaga; and Puerto Rican trumpeter Augusto Coen. Cuban flutist Alberto Socarrás is typical of Latin musicians whose contributions are as unsung as they are substantial. Arriving in New York in 1928, he made within a few weeks what is said to be the first recorded flute solo in jazz, on a version of "Have You Ever Felt That Way?" by Clarence Williams (on which he also played sax). The same year he worked as a studio musician for Columbia Records, besides also playing Cuban shows at the Harlem Opera House with Nilo Melendez's band. Late that year he quit Columbia and became a featured soloist (along with Augusto Coen) in *Blackbirds Revue* and *Rhapsody in Black*, with which he toured Europe.

Socarrás was one of a small number of Latin musicians who were establishing the beginnings of an authentic Latin sound on American soil—something that had so far been lacking in popular music. But other musicians who played in the 1920s were important in the 1930s Latin flowering because they hired other Latin musicians (often fine ones) to play a hybrid music which familiarized Americans with elements of Latin music in an easily digested form.

By far the most famous was Xavier Cugat, a Spaniard born in Gerona on January 1, 1900. Various versions of Cugat's life contain many contradictions. His family emigrated to Cuba when he was five. According to his account to a Spanish journalist, he was playing the violin in Havana cafés by the time he was seven or eight, and also in a pit trio at a silent movie house that included the famous Moises Simons (composer of the "Peanut Vendor") on piano. He also played violin with the Havana Symphony, and according to his interview was taken up by Caruso (who set him on his secondary career as a cartoonist.)

As Cugat told it, he set off for New York, arriving on the day of Caruso's death, which took place in 1921. (Another version gave Cugat's arrival as 1915.) He got a job in a café on 57th and 7th Avenue, but finding that he was not a good enough classical violinist to shine in the U.S., became a cartoonist for the Los Angeles Times.

In Los Angeles, he got to know Rudolf Valentino, who encouraged him to form a tango orchestra, Xavier Cugat and

His Gigolos, which, Cugat has said, opened at the Coconut Grove in Los Angeles on the night of Bing Crosby's debut. Crosby sang some tangos with the group, the beginning of a long acquaintanceship.

Cugat once claimed that his group tested for Warner Brothers even before the appearance of *The Jazz Singer*—that is, in 1927 or earlier. Whether or not this is true, his band certainly got onto film early.

The advent of sound brought about an amazing number of short musical movies, many of them produced by Vitaphone. During the company's 1927–1928 season, Cugat made at least two, both of them with a characteristic mix of Latin and non-Latin numbers. The first, simply titled X. *Cugat and his Gigolos*, and set in a Spanish courtyard, presented "El Relicario," "Estrellita," "Mighty Lak a Rose," "Spanish Dance," and "Y Como Le Va." The second, called *By the Camp Fire*, credited to X. Cugat and Company, included Carmen Castillo—who sang with Cugat for several years—and two dancers, Nanette Vallon and Margarita Duval. This film featured "Cielito Lindo" both as background and sung by Carmen Costello, and Cugat playing "The Old Refrain" and "Zigeunerweisen" on the violin!

Meanwhile, another Spaniard, also a violinist—and also Catalonian—was having a similar success in New York. This was Enrique Madriguera (his first name was often spelled Enric). Four years younger than Cugat, Madriguera toured the U.S. as a concert artist at the age of fourteen, studied under Leopold Auer, and became the conductor of the Havana Philharmonic. Switching to popular music, he played the Havana Casino before going to the Embassy Club and Pierre's in New York.

Like Cugat, Madriguera played tangos, show tunes, and "dinner music." Like Cugat, also, he had already begun to build a base from which to profit more greatly from the coming Cuban wave than the musician who was to be largely responsible for it.

Ernesto Lecuona, composer of many of the Cuban songs best known in the United States.
BMI Archives

João Gilberto, a major creator of the Brazilian bossa nova.
BMI Archives

Arsenio Rodriguez, father of the modern Cuban trumpet-based conjunto sound.
Cariño Records

19th-century New Orleans composer Louis Moreau Gottschalk based both major and minor works on Cuban styles.

Among many early Latin influences on New Orleans was the band of the Eighth Regiment of Mexican Cavalry, seen here in a drawing from an 1885 Century *magazine.*

As a result of the success of "the Mexican Band," New Orleans publishers issued many Mexican compositions during the 1880s and 1890s.

Irene and Vernon Castle introduced the tango to the U.S. via Broadway in 1913.
BMI Archives

*Largely responsible for the 1930s
rumba craze was Don Azpiazú's
Havana Casino Orchestra.*
Courtesy Raul Azpiazú

Society bandleader Paul White-
man's recordings of numbers like
"Cuban Love Song" were an
important part of Cuban music's
spread during the early 1930s.
BMI Archives

Among the growing number of
Cubans playing with New York
jazzmen was bandleader/flutist
Alberto Socarrás.
Courtesy Alberto Socarrás

Narciso Martinez, father of Chicano accordion style.
Courtesy Chris Strachwitz, Arhoolie Records

Lydia Mendoza, an early success among recorded Chicano singers.
Courtesy Chris Strachwitz, Arhoolie Records

Desi Arnaz and his conga took Broadway by storm in 1939.
BMI Archives

Among American singers to flirt with Latin music was the young Dinah Shore, who recorded with Xavier Cugat in 1939 and 1940.
BMI Archives

In the early 1940s, Jimmy Dorsey (left) with Helen O'Connell and Bob Eberly, had major hits with "Amapola," "Green Eyes," and other Latin compositions.
BMI Archives

*Mainstays of the 1940s surge of Latin film musicals were Xavier Cugat and
Carmen Miranda.*
BMI Archives

Pianist Noro Morales, a major name of the 1940s.
RCA Victor Records

*Machito's Afro-Cubans were the most important Latin band bar none. Seen in the mid-1940s at La Conga nightclub, Machito (**left**), singer Graciela, and musical director Mario Bauza.*
Courtesy Graciela Perez

Conga-player/composer Chano Pozo's brief stint with the Dizzy Gillespie big band made him a hero of the early Cubop movement.

BMI Archives

A major name in 1940s and 1950s Latin-jazz was West Coast bandleader Stan Kenton.
BMI Archives

Among many hugely popular artists with an affection for Cuban music was Nat "King" Cole.
BMI Archives

FOUR

The 1930s:
The Rumba Era

On the afternoon of Saturday, April 26, 1930, a full house filed back after the intermission at New York's Palace Theater. The curtain rose, and the course of Latin music in the United States was changed.

The first Broadway appearance of Don Azpiazú's Havana Casino Orchestra was important less for what was played than for how it was played. Don Azpiazú brought American audiences, for the first time, authentic Cuban dance music, complete with the maraccas, claves, güiros, bongós, congas, and timbales that were to become so widespread that their Cuban origin is now almost forgotten.

As Don Azpiazú's group broke into what might be called the earliest piece of salsa heard on Broadway, the classic "Mama Inez," a Cuban dance team strutted on stage in the first exhibition rumba ever staged in the U.S. Then, with their third number they introduced what was to be the best known of all Cuban tunes in the United States: "El Manicero"—"The Peanut Vendor."

It did not happen overnight. In May 1930, Don Azpiazú recorded "The Peanut Vendor" for RCA Victor. The record was not released until November, after considerable nagging, because Victor was afraid it would be too strange for American ears. Nor were leading dance musicians more ecstatic. Guy Lombardo predicted that "The Peanut Vendor" never could be made into a popular dance number, and its rhythms at first defeated American bandleaders. But the public had no such problem, and by early 1931 "The Peanut Vendor" was a national hit.

Marks solved the bandleader's problem by issuing a "simplified version in 4/4 time" (regardless of the fact that all Cuban music is basically in four-four time), and in January 1931, *Metronome* reported that the tune was being played at Earl Carroll's Vanities, the Cotton Club, the Hollywood Restaurant, and in an orchestral version by Major Bowes and cellist Yasha Bunchuk at New York's Capitol Theater.

"The Peanut Vendor" had its detractors. Walter Winchell claimed that it was based on Ravel's "Bolero" (which was in fact composed four years later.) And one reviewer commented: "The melody—if that is what it is—is a plaintive whine, and the rhythm is simple"(!) But nationally, Peanut Fever reigned: among its excesses, a "Peanut Vendor" sundae sold at the Melody Lane Fountain of the Belasco Theatre, Los Angeles (and, ironically, made with pecans).

"The Peanut Vendor" received powerful impetus when Will Rogers, one of the country's leading syndicated columnists, mentioned it, and it stayed in the bestseller lists until June. Much of the tune's success was based on its vaudeville trappings. An overture version by Phil Fabiello, orchestra leader of the RKO Coliseum Theater, included cocktail shakers filled with shot and used as maraccas, and Azpiazú's own lead singer, Antonio Machín, came on stage pushing a peanut stand. Nonetheless, Don Azpiazú's version was a polished but authentically Cuban piece: a type of son called a *pregón* derived from the chants of Havana street vendors, and played with a good rhythm section, under lyrical septeto-style trumpet. (Virtually all of the pieces known to the U.S. as rumbas were in fact something else. "Mama Inez" was a tango conga, and "Siboney" began life as a danzón, but the majority were sones.)

Azpiazú's "Peanut Vendor" was a ground-breaking recording in more than one sense. In those days, at least when recording, Cuban orchestras repeated the sung melody in unison between verses. According to Azpiazú's son Raul, one of the band's two trumpeters "was fooling around in the studio, playing variations. My father told him, 'why don't you put that in the record?'" The resulting improvisations were a major part of the record's success and perhaps the first Cuban *inspiraciones* to be recorded.

Azpiazú was not the only musician behind "The Peanut Vendor's" success. The 1930 sheet music calls it "A New Cuban Melody Made Famous by Major Bowes' Capitol Theatre Radio Library. Yasha Bunchuk and His Band Will Serve It Piping Hot," and Azpiazú himself wrote later that "within a week there existed a Havana Royal Orchestra, a Havana Novelty Orchestra, and a Havana God Knows-What."

There was, of course, nothing new about Cuban tunes becoming popular in highly Americanized versions. Azpiazú's success was important because his band's style was far more Latin than Americans were used to; it raised the level of American awareness of the Latin idiom across the country.

"The Peanut Vendor" might have been a nine-day wonder. That it was not may be due to Don Azpiazú's sister-in-law, Marion Sunshine, who was a remarkable woman in her own right. After a successful vaudeville career in the 1920s, as one half of the Tempest and Sunshine team, she became heavily involved in Latin music, acting as a link between Tin Pan Alley and its more authentic wings. It was she and her husband, Eusebio Azpiazú (whose professional name was Don Antobal) who engineered Don Azpiazú's first tour, and she sang "The Peanut Vendor" from coast to coast with the band on its 1931 tour.

Throughout the 1930s, Sunshine supplied the English lyrics to many Latin songs, including "Amor, Doce Veneno," which was to become the first samba widely popular in the U.S. under the title "Brazilian Night," and what may have been the first conga to reach the U.S., "La Conga," as well as writing jazz-oriented numbers for Chick Webb (who called her "The Rumba Lady"); Ella Fitzgerald recorded her "I Got a Guy" and three other songs.

It is quite possible that the rumba would have swept the country without the success of "The Peanut Vendor;" certainly more Cuban music was already being published than had appeared during the 1920s. But Azpiazú's authenticity, coming at a time when El Barrio was beginning to develop as an alternate Latin center, ensured that Cuban styles, and not just Cuban melodies and rhythms, would become part of American music.

Azpiazú returned to the Palace Theater in April 1931. In the same month, Gretsch advertised a "full rumba line" of "native instruments." These were Casa-Coleta brand güiros, claves, maracas and bongós (which Gretsch described as tom-toms). In April, too, the New York *Daily Mirror* organized a "Cuban Fiesta" benefit for Radio Hospital with Azpiazú; Marion Sunshine; Yasha Bunchuk, playing "an extraordinary cello rumba number"; and perhaps the first crossover between the music of El Barrio and what was to be the midtown Latin scene, an act from the San José Theatre on 110th Street and Fifth Avenue.

The success of "The Peanut Vendor" led, of course, to a flood of other Cuban tunes. Many of them were significant compositions. Eliseo Grenet has called "Mama Inez," which soon became almost equally popular, "A symbol of our most noble and unquestionable past." (*Metronome* called it "the most famous of all rhumbas and the Cuban equivalent to a lowdown 'hot' number.") The romantic side of Cuban music was also strongly represented by "Marta," which was to become the signature tune of "The Street Singer," Arthur Tracey, and was the first popular song recorded by Benjamino Gigli, and by Lecuona's "Maria La O" (Maria My Own).

When the Cuban boom began, E. B. Marks had a huge jump on the opposition, but other publishers soon began to compete. Southern Music started a rumba sheet music club with a number that was to become a permanent part of the American music scene, Melendez' "Aquellos Ojos Verdes" (Green Eyes), of which Azpiazú's recording, on which he used American singer Chick Bullock, was only the first of many versions.

Almost immediately, American popular composers began to produce Cuban-influenced works. Not all of them were ordinary songsmiths. George Gerswin wrote a "Cuban Overture" that is almost a textbook case of how not to use an exotic influence. He clearly did not understand Cuban music, and his composition neither resembles it, nor transmutes it into the kind of successful hybrid of which Louis Moreau Gottschalk was capable. The Cubanisms are no more than a banal garnish to a work both bland and pompous.

Though the success of "The Peanut Vendor" established Cuban music in a dominant position during the 1930s, other Latin forms continued to flourish, and the tango's slow decline in popularity was certainly not apparent at the beginning of the decade. By September 1932, E. B. Marks had almost 600 Latin-American songs in its catalog. Though the bulk was Cuban, they included a Venezuelan pasillo, "Anhelos," a samba, "Batente," examples of another Brazilian rhythm called a *chôro*, and other relatively unusual items, along with many tangos and Mexican compositions. Throughout the decade, in fact, a steady flow of Mexican numbers, and an increasing number of Brazilian and Brazilian-styled tunes, accompanied the flood of Cuban inspired compositions. Aside from "Adios Muchachos," 1932 saw the publication of a so-called "Japanese tango," "Tcho-Tcho-San," an all-time candidate for silliest song.

Among the songs that appeared in 1933 were classic compositions like the Cuban "La Negra Quirina," as well as Marion Sunshine's ephemeral attempt at a follow up to "The Peanut Vendor," a son-pregón called "The Ice Cream Man" featured by her husband, Don Antobal. Lorenzo Barcelata's "Maria Elena"— a ballad that was to give its name to a Mexican film and become a major success of the 1940s—was also published in 1933. The following year saw the appearance of Mitya Stillman's "A Touch of Carioca," presumably under the influence of the successful film, *Flying Down to Rio*.

But 1934 was most notable for three Mexican songs: "Alla en El Rancho Grande," Maria Grever's "Cuando Vuelva a Tu Lado," and the traditional "La Cucuracha." Between them, these typify the varying Mexican styles influential in the United States. "Alla en el Rancho Grande" started life as a fairly typical ranchera. "Cuando Vuelva a Tu Lado," an example of Mexican "international" Latin music, became so much better known in the U.S. under its English title, "What a Difference a Day Made," that few non-Latins have any idea of its origin. The opposite fate awaited the one authentic Mexican folksong in the trio. "La Cucuracha" became so universally known that it is difficult to shake off the irritation of over-familiarity and discover the authenticity beneath. Yet authentic it is, and enough of a folk theme to have produced endless variants.

One of the great Cuban perennials, Lecuona's "Para Vigo Me Voy" ("Say Si Si") appeared in 1933 (and was immediately recorded in an elegant version by Xavier Cugat). In 1936, the indefatigable Marion Sunshine wrote both words and music to a fairly durable minor hit called "Hot Tamales," and the following year she collaborated with Alberto Socarrás on two pieces, "Virgen" (In a Cuban Garden), and "No Se Puede" (Said the Monkey), which spanned both major American stereotypes of Latin music—romantic and risque.

A Mexican "international" piece, "A Gay Ranchero," was published in 1938, as was a Mexican folk tune that was to prove a good deal more durable. This was "Chiapanecas," a waltz that was a favorite among marimba bands of the Chiapas region, and appeared in the U.S. under the title of "While There's Music There's Romance." Marie Grever's "Ti-Pi-Tin" had a moment of popularity the same year—as did "Doce Veneno" (with English lyrics by Marion Sunshine and the English title of "Brazilian Night"), one of the first sambas to attract any attention in the United States.

Another Brazilian composition, one that was to become one of the most enduring of U.S. Latin standards, appeared in 1939. This was Ary Barroso's "Aquarela do Brasil" ("Brazil"), which was to undergo several major revivals in years to come. Other publications of the same year included one of the most successful of homogenized "international" compositions, Alberto Dominguez's "Frenesí," and a prophetic example of a new Cuban rhythm that had begun to reach the U.S. during the late 1930s—Eliseo Grenet's "Viene la Conga" (The Conga is Coming).

The conga dance, with its long line that might eventually sweep in everybody in the place, and the kick on the fourth beat of every measure accentuated by the percussion, combined simplicity and panache. Though it was a Cuban carnival tradition, it became firmly associated in the U.S. with the name of one man: Desi Arnaz. Arnaz himself has claimed to have introduced it to the U.S. In his autobiography, "A Book," he gives a long and fairly convincing account of introducing it in Miami Beach because his non-Latin musicians couldn't play anything more complicated.

The story is a good one, but it doesn't stand up. Arnaz's version covers the week of New Year, 1937–1938. By that time, Eliseo Grenet's "La Conga" had been published in the U.S. under the title "Havana Is Calling Me." Another conga had been composed fully two years earlier in 1935, by a British "Latin" musician called Maurice Burman.

Even if Arnaz's specific claim that "the conga had never been done in the United States" had referred to the dance—and the context makes clear that he is also talking about the music— *Variety,* a full year earlier, commented about a show at the Roxy: "The versatile Foster girls shake their maracas to rumba, tango, *conga* and son-foxtrot tempos [italics mine]."

In reality, Arnaz had little solid connection with Latin music. His brief stint with Xavier Cugat came at a period when Cugat was already very much a part of "American show business." Arnaz joined the band in Cleveland where it was playing Billy Rose's Aquacade and spent a few months at the Waldorf, before going back to Miami Beach.

Like Cugat, Arnaz was an important popularizer. Unlike Cugat, he knew relatively little about the music he was hybridizing. But he had looks, charm, chutzpah, and the great advantage over most important Latin musicians of being both upper-class (the son of a former mayor of Santiago de Cuba) and pure white. He also had a talent for meeting useful people, encountering Bing Crosby while he was with Cugat, and Sonja Henie and Joe E. Smith in Miami.

In reality, Arnaz was not a musician but an entertainer. In 1939, while playing opposite Pancho's tango group at New York's La Conga, he came to the attention of the famous songwriting team, Richard Rodgers and Lorenz Hart, who were looking for a Latin male lead for a new musical. His successful appearance in the 1939 *Too Many Girls* was part of the culmination of a decade of increasing Broadway interest in Latin idioms. During the 1930s, Broadway fed off the immense success of Latin music, satirized it, and—particularly toward the end of the decade—contributed to it. Sigmund Romberg's 1930 *Nina Rosa* was something of a leftover from earlier styles. But Broadway soon picked up on the new rumba. The *Third Little Show*, which opened in June 1931, contained a piece sung by Walter O'Keefe entitled "When Yuba Plays the Rumba on His Tuba" that became a hit in its own right, being recorded by Rudy Vallee and the Connecticut Yankees as well as several lesser bands. 1930s Broadway also nurtured one of the most striking examples of pervasive Latin influence in the work of a major American popular composer: the underlying rumba rhythm that, as popular music historian Sigmund Spaeth once pointed out, was a Cole Porter trademark. It is most familiar in Porter's "Begin the Beguine," which originated in the 1935 musical, *Jubilee*, though it did not make much of a mark until Artie Shaw recorded it in the late 1930s. But "Begin the Beguine," which had little connection with the biguine of Martinique, a jaunty dance closer to the creole rhythms of New Orleans than to Latin music (it might more accurately have been called "Begin the Bolero") was not Porter's first Latin experiment: he had included a so-called biguine-rumba, "The Gypsy in Me," in the 1934 *Anything Goes*.

Broadway's most significant contribution to the Latin tinge came in 1939, when several shows with Latin elements were running simultaneously. The most important was *On the Streets of Paris*, a revue starring Abbott and Costello and French singer, Jean Sablon. One of its turns was a song and dance number that made an instant star of a tiny Brazilian singer-dancer called Maria de Carmo Miranda de Cunha.

Carmen Miranda (1909–1955) was already a radio and recording star in her own country, and had made four films in Rio between 1934 and 1938. In *The Streets of Paris* she sang "South American Way" as the first act finale, wearing six-inch heels and the fruited headdress that were to become her trademarks. "South American Way" drew the almost immediate compliment of a parody—Imogene Coca's takeoff called "Soused American Way" in *The Straw Hat Revue*—and within a year it had made Carmen Miranda a star both on Broadway and in Hollywood.

Almost as important as *The Streets of Paris* was Rodgers and Hart's *Too Many Girls*, which brought Desi Arnaz to fame. *Too Many Girls*, which opened in October 1939, concerned the sex life of a South American football player at a U.S. college. As originally conceived, its Latin content was peripheral, but when Arnaz got the part of the hero, Manolito, his nightclub conga dance was written into the first act finale. Also in the cast was Diosa Costello, a Puerto Rican dancer well known in the Latin scene of the 1940s.

Aside from Arnaz's conga number, *Too Many Girls* included "All Dressed Up Spic and Spanish" sung by Diosa Costello, and "She Could Shake the Maraccas," sung by Costello and Arnaz. All this reinforced an image of Latin music as "fun," lightweight, and essentially trivial that has become a crushing stereotype. But it also undoubtedly helped to further the spread of Latin components into U.S. styles.

Meanwhile, the cinema was also discovering Latin music as a source of material. As we have seen, it began to get onto film almost as soon as sound was introduced. Vitaphone, Paramount, and other makers of shorts continued to film live performances. Don Azpiazú, for example, filmed "The Peanut Vendor" and "Siboney" in 1931. He also made a version of "Por Tus Ojos Negros" with the enormously popular tango singer, Carlos Gardel, who went on to make other films in 1934, including *Tango on Broadway*. (Gardel's U.S. experience was not altogether happy. He canceled his option with NBC after appearing in New York, because he was not allowed to sing with his usual guitarists.)

"The Peanut Vendor" was also emphasized almost too extensively in the 1931 *Cuban Love Song* which featured Ernesto Lecuona's Palau Brothers Cuban Orchestra, and starred Jimmy Durante, operatic baritone Lawrence Tibbett, and Broadway star Lupe Velez. The title song became a hit in its own right, recorded by—among others—Paul Whiteman in waltz form.

Both Tibbett and Lupe Velez made other musicals with at least a Latin tinge. Velez—a film as well as stage star ever since she played opposite Douglas Fairbanks, Sr., in *The Gaucho* in 1925— appeared in the musical, *The Girl from Mexico,* and Tibbett went on to appear in Otto Preminger's 1936 *Under Your Spell,* which included a song called "Amigo."

Most active musicians were marginal in films. But one, Xavier Cugat, was not. Cugat, in fact, has been said to have appeared on more film footage than any other American band-leader. As we have seen, he had already appeared in shorts in the 1920s. By 1930 he was already working in feature films, ap-pearing with Ramon Novarro in *In Gay Madrid;* the next year he provided music for *Ten Cents a Dance,* which starred Barbara Stanwyck and Ricardo Cortez. He also appeared in the 1937 *Go West, Young Man.*

Another Latin to appear regularly in film was Tito Guizar, who—like Lawrence Tibbett—had started out as an operatic singer before having considerable success with popular Mexican songs in New York. Guizar became a regular in Hollywood musicals, playing in the 1935 *Under the Pampas Moon,* with Rita Hayworth, and the 1938 *St. Louis Blues,* with Dorothy Lamour. Throughout the 1930s, Hollywood kept up a trickle of movies with Latin themes or aspects, mostly sentimental or frothy romances. Don Ameche made the film of *Ramona* in 1935, and John Boles—who had gone on from the stage version of *Rio Rita* to become a matinee idol—filmed both *Rio Rita* and a well-forgotten *Rose of the Rancho.*

This persistent but marginal Latin element was typical of 1930s films. But some major careers also began in 1930s Latin vehicles. Most notable were Ginger Rogers and Fred Astaire, who were first paired in the most successful of all 1930s Holly-wood musicals with Latin themes, the 1933 *Flying Down to Rio.* This contained Vincent Youmans's song "Carioca," the earliest samba-based number to have substantial success in the U.S. (danced as a swirling-skirted production number without much Latin content.) It also amusingly parodied U.S. attitudes to Latin music. The visiting American orchestra is condescendingly amused at a bunch of mañana-ish musicians dozing on the stand of a local nightclub where they will be appearing; but the samba the Brazilians play wipes the superiority off the New Yorkers' faces.

Rogers and Astaire were not the only major stars to have played in Latin musical films early in their careers. George Raft, then known as a dancer, appeared with Ann Sheridan in two baldly titled movies, the 1934 *Bolero*, in which he danced Ravel's "Bolero," and a follow-up the next year called *Rumba*. And many films without a Latin theme used a Latin number for color, like the 1938 *Girl of the Golden West*, starring Nelson Eddy and Jeannette MacDonald (said to have been the most successful singing partnership in film), which included a song called "Mariachie" [*sic*.]

All the activity in popular music publishing, stage shows, and films were essentially no more than intensifications of a Latin tinge that had been steadily increasing for almost fifty years. What was new, and made the 1930s the crucial period for Latin music in the United States, was the sudden development of a music scene that was *stylistically* Latin.

This had two wings. One, "downtown," was centered on the fashionable hotels and nightclubs, catered to Americans, and resulted largely from the success of Don Azpiazú's authentically Cuban arrangements. The other, "uptown," catered to Latins and was the result of the growth of East Harlem as a Latin barrio.

Both styles were important in the gradual Latinization of American music. Though the "downtown" groups have customarily been dismissed as sweet commercial bands of no musical interest, the truth is a little more complex. The major 1930s downtown groups—notably Xavier Cugat's orchestra—frequently reacted creatively to the tension between authenticity and commercial demands. Cugat's band in particular sometimes played a fusion music that had importance.

When Cugat traveled to New York from Los Angeles to open the new Waldorf Astoria and then became the hotel's resident group, he began rather subtly and gradually to alter his style. His orchestra, which contained both Latin and non-Latin musicians and consisted of three or four violins, trumpet, piano,

accordion, marimba, guitar, and American drumkit, was hired
to play international light concert music: "None but the Lonely
Heart," a Strauss waltz, a Latin standard like "Cielito Lindo,"
perhaps eight American show or light concert pieces, then a
tango or a well-known number like Lecuona's "Comparsa." As
he gained popularity, he gradually increased the ratio of Latin to
American numbers until he was presenting a largely Latin
bill.

Cugat, who—as a Spaniard—had no deep commitment to
Cuban music, was always very clear about his tactics. In the
1950s he described them to a Spanish interviewer: "Americans
know nothing about Latin music. They neither understand nor
feel it. So they have to be given music more for the eyes than
the ears. Eighty percent visual, the rest aural." One of his first
decisions was to put a pretty woman in front of the band.
Among his earlier finds was Rita Hayworth, then thirteen; later
he hired the Spanish dancers Rosario and Antonio.

"To succeed in America I gave the Americans a Latin music
that had nothing authentic about it," Cugat added. "Then I
began to change the music and play more legitimately."

Cugat's music was not "Cuban." It was, in fact, an example
of fairly thorough-going fusion. Even his somewhat peculiar
instrumentation served a purpose. Though it came to be considered part of the Cugat sound, the marimba was there originally because his years as a bandleader began in the late 1920s,
when the instrument was popular. He included an accordion as
a major component of a reasonably authentic tango.

Cugat's music was, in fact—at least for the first fifteen
years or so—a deliberate, ingenious and frequently highly successful attempt to combine the various Latin elements popular
at the time. The result, in the 1930s and early 1940s, was an
original and at times excellent synthesis. His first recording, in
1933, which included his famous signature tune, "Ombo," was
a relatively tame beginning, despite its Cuban orquesta típica
clarinets, septeto trumpet, and Argentinian accordion. But he
soon developed a strong sense of style. His tangos—such as the
1934 "Love What Are You Doing to My Heart"—retain a great
deal of charm almost half a century later. Cugat began using

American singers early (as had Azpiazú, be it remembered): his 1935 "The Lady in Red" blends an attractively extrovert introduction for acoustic guitar and percussion, septeto-style trumpet, a somewhat rowdy chorus, and an attractive piano solo, all taken at a clip that leaves singer Don Reid sounding rather breathless.

How well Cugat's hybrids could work at their best was shown by his Victor version of "Las Palmeras," which mixed strong bongó playing, acoustic guitar in bolero style, an attractive vocal by Pedro Berrios, a female duo in the vein of the Cuban Marti sisters, and a *montuno* that included a good septetostyle trumpet solo. The canny Cugat backed "Las Palmeras" with a tango, "Inspiracion," replete with accordion, violin and Heavenly Choir harmonizing. "Inspiracion" has period charm, but "Las Palmeras" has a good deal more than that.

A very important counterbalance to the downtown groups like Cugat's was provided by the bands playing in El Barrio. Without a corrective, the fusions played by Cugat and the like might well have degenerated into a totally bland flavoring as happened in Britain, which had no Latin community. East Harlem served as a source of new musicians, a gateway for innovation from Cuba and elsewhere, a place where more purely Latin styles were played, and a workshop for fusions of a very different nature from the Tin-Pan-Alley, mass–popularoriented downtown versions.

By 1930, East Harlem had already developed much of the infrastructure for a flourishing musical life. The area's first Latin dance was held in 1930, when a Puerto Rican civic association rented the Golden Casino on 110th Street and Fifth Avenue for the night. By the early 1930s, El Barrio also had its own radio music show, run by Julio Roque, an East Harlem dentist and musician who broadcast over Radio WABC (later part of CBS, but then independent), presenting local artists in Puerto Rican plenas, boleros, and some Mexican material. Even more important, in an area where most people could not afford nightclubs, the Jewish theaters were turning Latin. The Photoplay Theater became the San José, and the Mount Morris at 116th and Fifth Avenue, the Campoamor.

These theaters and others like them provided steady and varied work for many musicians playing in many different styles. In the pit of the Campoamor, Alberto Socarrás had a big band whose sound drew partly from black swing. One veteran recalls that "in one show I saw, Maestro Socarrás took an American tune—I believe it was "I Can't Give You Anything but Love"—and transcribed it in a Latin way, though of course it had the jazz idiom to it." At the Teatro San José, a band run by pianist José Escarpenter played for more traditional tastes with a book featuring many danzas and plenas.

As this suggests, a definite diversity was beginning to develop even "uptown," some bands playing more strictly Cuban-derived music, and others beginning to blend Latin and American elements. But the division was never very clear cut. Though Cuban musicians tended to preserve strong traditional elements and Puerto Ricans (less wedded to Cuban orthodoxy) were strong in the hybridizing wing, Socarrás in the 1930s and Machito in the 1940s were among the more experimental musicians of their time, and both men were Cubans.

Among the key groups of the mid-1930s was that run by veteran Augusto Coen, which featured one of the most popular lead singers of the day, Davilita. Coen's band was one of those talent-incubators common in the history of Latin music. Among its musicians was pianist Noro Morales, who had recently arrived from Puerto Rico and began his El Barrio career in the pit at the Teatro Hispano on 116th and Fifth Avenue.

In 1936, Coen's band-boy, Federico Pagani, who was to become an important promoter in later years, formed Los Happy Boys, another swing-oriented group which a contemporary describes as "not a great orchestra but the people liked them because they played the music of the time." It is hard to form a clear picture of the music played by these bands, though it is clear that El Barrio musicians were developing the crossover between black and Latin music that was so natural, given the strong Afro-Cuban element in the dance music.

According to a number of observers, the bands of those days tended to play very loudly. But Cuban violinist Alberto Iznaga had an orchestra with a violin and sax front line that was

both smooth and authentic, playing boleros, rumbas, the occasional paso doble (still popular with older dancers) and danzónes. "There were always danzónes, which were very big in
those days, and danzas, because most of the people attending
those dances were Puerto Rican." This repertoire suggests an
older group than might have danced to Los Happy Boys—a
reminder that Latin audiences varied by age and taste as much
as American ones.

Dance-bands were not the only groups in New York that
catered specifically to Puerto Rican tastes. The most famous of
all composers of the topical plena was Manuel Jiménez, nicknamed "Canario" (The Canary), who is credited with having
introduced the plena to New York. During the 1930s, Canario
ran a very popular group in El Barrio, and many of his plenas
from that period deal specifically with "Newyorican" subjects.

Other styles bridged big city and more rurally derived
sounds. Trios and quartets performing the older Cuban sones
and boleros were popular, and some—Cuarteto Caney, Cuarteto
Victoria, and Cuarteto Machin, started by Azpiazú's former
lead singer—were strictly local.

Some of these groups were authentic enough to make use
of the marimbula, a bass instrument derived from the African
finger-piano. In El Barrio they were made of orange crates and
bedsprings. But for all that, the quartets were not folk artists.
Some stuck to a Cuban *guajiro* country style. Others, like the
one led by Johnny Rodriguez—a well-known singer whose
younger brother, Tito, was to become even more famous—sang
boleros in an internationalized though still purely Latin romantic style.

The quartets mostly played the bars, but they also performed in clubs like the Cubanacán, and sometimes moved
downtown, usually altering their style in the process. The
Cuarteto Caney, which had recorded many pure Cuban sones,
switched to piano-based "continental" Latin music when it
moved down to the Cuban Casino on 45th Street and Eighth
Avenue at the end of the decade.

Just as the uptown bands played in a number of styles, from

típico to heavily fusion-oriented, so the divisions between uptown and downtown bands were not watertight. One of Azpiazú's two trumpeters, Pedro Via, ran several groups both
uptown and downtown. By 1932, he was broadcasting over
Radio WJZ on Sunday afternoons with a band that included
Argentine, Mexican, Puerto Rican, and Cuban musicians, playing popular Latin numbers. If he had not run afoul of the
American Federation of Musicians, some believe that Via might
in the end have rivaled Cugat. Many other bands found their
way downtown on occasion, including Alberto Iznaga's Orquesta Siboney, which played the Half Moon on 79th Street in
1939.

The distinction between uptown and downtown bands was
even less clear-cut on recordings than live dates. Perhaps because there were relatively few outstanding Latin musicians at
that period, perhaps because of a form of mutual back-scratch-
ing, a bandleader would call in other major stars like Nilo Melendez for a recording session, rather than using his regular
band (a habit which explains a certain similarity in recorded solo
work.)

Both uptown and downtown groups also worked frequently
with American musicians, and even more frequently with American singers. A notable instance came in 1939 when the young
Dinah Shore had three separate recording sessions with Xavier
Cugat, during which she sang "The Thrill of a New Romance,"
"Quiereme Mucho," "San Domingo," "Jungle Drums," and "Cuban Episode."

As Latin music became more popular, Anglos began also to
lead Latin bands. Many of these were very short-lived, like the
recording group under Eddie Le Baron that in 1939 issued a set of
well-known Cuban numbers ("Amor Sincero" and "La Negra
Quirina" among them) in an imitation of Cugat with more gusto
than flair. But others are remembered as having contributed a
good deal to the music of the time. Daniel Santos, who was to
become a popular heart-throb throughout Latin America, began
his career singing on WBNX with the sweet bolero orchestra of
Alfredo Mendez, whose real name was Mendelsohn. Each suc-

cessive decade was to produce its examples of Jewish Latin bandleaders, many of them outstanding.

More significant in the long run was the crossover between black and Latin bands. Though a few blacks played with Latinos, and even ran their own Latin groups, like Wilbert Griffith, who played with José Budet and headed a band playing rumbas and tangos for a while, in the 1930s this mostly took the form of Latin musicians playing with black groups. Throughout the 1930s, Alberto Socarrás commuted between black and Latin music. Aside from leading his own band at the Cubanacán nightclub (which was opened specially for him) and at the Teatro Campoamor, he played with a large number of well-known jazz musicians. In 1933, he spent some months with the Benny Carter Orchestra (where he was not alone: when Teddy Wilson left the group, Puerto Rican pianist Nicolas Rodriguez took over). In 1934, Socarrás played along New Orleans clarinetist Albert Nicholas and saxist Gene Sedric in the Sam Wooding Orchestra. He took his own band up to the Apollo Theater several times, once appearing on the same bill as blues singer Bessie Smith. And in 1937 his band began three years as resident dance group at the Cotton Club, playing opposite Duke Ellington, Louis Armstrong, and Cab Calloway.

Other Latins played in the black groups of the period, including trombonist Fernando Arbela, and at least one well-known jazzman had a Latin background—Luis Russell, who came of the English-speaking community of Panama. (Socarrás decisively won a battle of the bands with Russell at the Apollo one night.) But most of these men did not influence the music they played. By far the most influential, in the long term, was Mario Bauza.

Bauza, who played bass-clarinet with the Havana Philharmonic and clarinet and success in various nightclub groups, came to the U.S. in 1930 and soon recorded with Antonio Machin's Cuarteto Machin—not on reeds but on trumpet, which he learned in two weeks! In 1931–32, he got a job as a saxist with Noble Sissle's Orchestra, then playing the Park Central Hotel. But he continued to play trumpet and began to appear at Harlem's Savoy Ballroom as a trumpeter with a band called Hi Clark and His Missourians, before moving to Chick Webb as lead trumpeter in 1933. A year later he became the band's orchestral director.

Bauza stayed with Webb until 1938, during which time he was partly responsible for the discovery of Ella Fitzgerald. Then, after short stints with Don Redman and Fletcher Henderson, he joined Cab Calloway in 1939.

Just as had happened with the habanera and tango, the popularity of Latin music and the interchange of musicians provided an occasional Latin undertow to 1930s jazz. The most famous example was Puerto Rican trombonist Juan Tizol's work with Duke Ellington, with whom he played for many years, composing the well-known "Caravan," an effective piece of exotica, as well as other Latin-tinged pieces.

Whether or not there is any truth in the theory put forward by the *Music-World Almanack* for April 1931, that the black dance called the "shimmy" borrowed some of its movements, "especially those of the shoulder and the body," from the rumba, its popularity provoked a quick response from Cab Calloway. His huge hit, "Minnie the Moocher," was issued by Brunswick in May 1931. Backing it was a piece called "Doin' the Rhumba," of which *Metronome's* record review commented that it was "just as hot [as "Minnie the Moocher"]—mean work on the trumpet and novelty vocal chorus." Calloway returned to Latin-jazz in the late 1930s and 1940s, recording "The Congo-Conga" in 1938 and "Vuelva" and "Chili Con Conga" the following year.

On the fringes of jazz and classical music, Harlem stride pianist and composer Luckey Roberts wrote, in 1939, an unpublished *Spanish Suite* for piano and orchestra, in three movements: "Spanish Venus" (based on the ragtime tango he had written twenty years earlier), "Spanish Fandango," and "Porto Rican Maid."

Not all the Latin-jazz numbers of the 1930s were Cuban. At the very end of the decade, Artie Shaw made two recordings of "Carioca," from *Flying Down to Rio,* and one of the Mexican ranchera, "El Rancho Grande," before turning his band over to another leader and taking a long vacation in Mexico.

On the whole, however, 1930s jazz had relatively few Latin

elements, it was, rather, a period in which the groundwork for the Latin-jazz of the 1940s was laid. The one exception was an extremely isolated case. Chicago boogie woogie pianist Jimmy Yancey showed an extremely strong habanera and tango influence in both his bass patterns, some of which were pure habaneras, and the phrasings of his right hand.

Yancey's strong Latin tinge was probably a simple archaism. He had been a vaudeville player until 1913, when he quit professional music to become a groundsman for the Chicago White Sox. This meant that he was playing professionally during the period when the habanera was at its peak in black music—the period of "Memphis Blues" and "Panama"—and the beginning of the tango era.

It seems clear that Yancey simply continued to play in the style that he had used professionally; although the major boogie woogie pianists of the next generation—Albert Ammons, Meade "Lux" Lewis, and the like—regarded Yancey as a mentor, they only used his habanera bass when they were playing numbers named after or dedicated to him, and in the 1930s it seems to have been a purely personal idiosyncracy.

It was not only in the interlinked areas of show business, dance-bands, and jazz that the 1930s were a period of great creative development for Latin music in the United States. The Chicano music of the Southwest was going through an equal flowering, partly brought about by the record companies' discovery that it was not necessary to restrict themselves to middle-class versions of Mexican music, since ordinary Chicanos, poor as most of them were, were as ready to buy their own music as were blacks or hillbillies.

A large number of regional corridos were issued by Vocalion, Okeh, Columbia, Bluebird, and Decca, recorded on two sides of a 78 rpm record to accommodate their length, and with lyrics reflecting a wide range of specifically Mexican-American concerns. Many were about crimes, some of them involving celebrated court cases. One dealt with a case in which one Juan Reyna killed a policeman while allegedly being beaten up in a squad car. Reyna was convicted of manslaughter despite a jury that was hung until the last moment, and was sentenced to one to ten years. The "Corrido de Juan Reyna" recounted all this in faithful detail, and a sequel told of Reyna's apparent suicide in jail five months before his release.

The corridos had always mirrored social concerns, but it is legitimate to see in this song, and in "La Tragedia de Oklahoma," both a reflection of rising political consciousness and a stimulus to it. "La Tragedia de Oklahoma" dealt with an even more famous case, in which two students from Mexico, one of whom was related to the president, were shot by deputies near Ardmore, Oklahoma.

Other corridos told of more general experiences. "El Lava-platos" (The Dishwasher) recounted humorously the woes of migrant labor, in couplets like

> Ay que tormento (X2)
> Es el mentado cemento

(What a torment is that damned cement!)

The "Corrido de Texas" told a straight-forward story of travelling workers, and of

> Esos trenes del TP que cruzan por la Louisiana
> Se llevan los mexicanos para el estado de Indiana

(Those TP trains passing through Louisiana, taking the Mexicans to the state of Indiana.)

More direct—and typical of a strain of overt protest songs—were corridos like "El Deportado," which observed bluntly,

> Los güeros son muy maloras (X2)
> Se valen de la ocasion
> Y a todos los mexicanos (X2)
> Los tratan sin compasion.

(The whites are very evil, they take advantage of the situation and treat all Mexicans without pity.)

The 1930s were a time not only of rising social significance for Chicano music, but of considerable musical change. The accordion first appeared on record around 1930, though Texas-

Mexicans had been using it for dance numbers since at least the turn of the century. Though vocal duets with guitar backing remained the most popular form in Chicano music during the decade, a generation of creative musicians whose work was spread widely on record, began to give the accordion a growing dominance.

One of the most important was Narciso Martinez, known as "El Huracan del Valle," who recorded a large number of instrumental polkas, mazurkas, schottisches, waltzes, and even blues. Martinez, who was born in 1911 in Reynosa, began to record for Bluebird in 1936. Though he was not the first accordionist to record, he was the first to appeal to a wide audience, which included local Bohemians, Czechs, and Germans; in fact it is not clear how many of his numbers were Mexican, and how many he adapted from Bohemian material.

Martinez was a pivotal figure in Chicano accordion playing. In the words of one writer, he "accomplished for the accordion something like what B.B. King did for the electric guitar in blues. By dropping the bass end of the accordion and concentrating on the upper scales, Martinez forged a personal style that became an integral part of all norteño accordion styles."

Another well-known accordionist of the time was Santiago Jiménez, who began recording from Decca in the late 1930s and is the father of Flaco Jiménez, whose style has influenced Texan rock players.

Nor were the accordionists the only artists to bring fresh life to Chicano music in the 1930s. Singer Lydia Mendoza, "La Alondra de la Frontera," was typical of vocalists who bridged the purely amateur popular music of earlier years and the increasing professionalism that was to come. Mendoza began playing mandolin with her mother and father in San Antonio in the late 1920s, and in 1934 began to record solo, accompanying herself on the 12-string bajo sexto. Like Narciso Martinez, she greatly widened the Chicano repertoire. Though she sang many numbers learned from her mother, she also learned many more, from corridos to Spanish art songs.

Just how much influence 1930s Chicano music had on contemporary Anglo-Texan styles isn't clear. Pianist Knocky Parker, who played with the Light Crust Doughboys, once described the style called "Western swing" as a "mixture of Mexican mariachi music from the south with jazz and country strains coming in from the east." Given how vague most American musicians have always been about Latin influences, and the fact that the Dough-boys featured an accordion along with fiddle, guitar, banjo, steel guitar, and drums, it is quite possible that their music also took in a Texas-Mexican strain.

Certainly the country music of the Southwest took both guitar techniques and songs from Mexican sources. The "Spanish Two-Step" has been suggested as the origin of "San Antonio Rose," and "El Rancho Grande" was played by almost all western-swing bands and has become a "standard" in country music. Bill C. Malone has also suggested, in his *Country Music U.S.A.*, that the "blue yodel" of singers like Jimmy Rodgers may have been influenced by Mexican song, "characterized by shouts and wails which were similar to the hillbilly yodel." Protest singer Woody Guthrie's corrido-like singing and guitar on a number of his Texan ballads has already been mentioned, and it is perhaps significant that Guthrie began playing with his uncle in Pampa, Texas, in the late 1920s and early 1930s.

Another area is even more obscure. The possibility of Chicano influence on Texan bluesmen has never been examined; but it is noticeable that the 12-string guitar work of Huddie Led-better (Leadbelly) contained many runs like those used by Chicano bajo sexto players (the similarity is particularly striking in Lydia Mendoza's accompaniment to her "Pero Ay Que Triste," recorded in San Antonio in 1934 and re-issued on a Folklyric album).

There is a sad tailpiece to the great Latin wave of the 1930s. Don Azpiazú—the man who had, in a sense, started it all—never really benefited from what he had done. In 1932 he went home to Cuba after a successful tour of Europe. In the late 1930s he returned to New York and played the Rainbow Room with the Casa Loma Orchestra, before going on to the Seville Biltmore Hotel, and came back again in the early 1940s, recording a version of "Amapola." But the Latin scene had changed too much for him. When he died in Cuba of a heart attack in 1943, his role in introducing Cuban music to the U.S. had been virtually forgotten.

Azpiazú may in part have been hampered by his temperament. According to people who knew him, he was a notably stubborn man who insisted on what he considered right. He was possibly the first Cuban bandleader to mix black and white musicians, and he also broke the color bar in the U.S. in 1931. In St. Louis, according to his son, the band was told to use the service elevator. "My father said, 'That band will go in the front elevator or I don't play here tonight.'" In 1931, Azpiazú was at the crest of the wave. In the late 1930s, however, he is said to have lost his job at the Rainbow Room for refusing to stick to Cuban music and leave American numbers to the Casa Loma Orchestra.

If it is true, that incident underlines a more general problem faced by many Latin musicians in the States. Not unreasonably, American impresarios regarded them as Latin experts; but they were often at least as interested in creative fusions. Sammy Kiamie believes that "Don Azpiazú was 25 to 30 years ahead of his time in his styling." Raul Azpiazú adds that his father always liked to play American music, and "always had it in mind that Cuban music would intermarry with American music, as it happened later with the mambo. . . . He would translate the old songs that people sang in the cotton fields in the South into Spanish and have the singer perform them with his band."

In sum, the 1930s was a period of extremely important consolidation for Latin styles in the United States. By its close, they had become overwhelmingly the most important non–U.S. element in U.S. popular music. Argentinian, Cuban, Mexican, and to a growing degree, Brazilian rhythms were permanencies on radio, bandstand, screen, and stage. Meanwhile in East Harlem a separate circuit of clubs, bars, and theaters had produced the first generation of indigenous Latin bandleaders playing for Latins, among them many who were to be major stars of U.S. Latin music's Golden Age.

Alejo Carpentier has argued that Cuban music was greatly harmed by its popularity in the U.S. and Europe, because foreign publishers demanded simpler pieces and a more commercial style. It certainly changed; but, since the Cuban music of the 1940s included the rise of the great trumpet conjuntos, of the blending of Afro-Cuban music with the string-and-flute charangas, Carpentier's gloom seems ill-founded. As so often, what was perceived as decay was in fact revitalization.

The same was largely true of the specifically U.S. Latin forms. They necessarily developed by taking in American elements, and were at first liable to do so relatively gracelessly. But there is nothing in that any different from the universal process of musical development, in which hybridization has always played an important—often the most important—role.

Besides, if evidence were needed that the events of the 1930s were healthy, the developments of the 1940s amply provided it.

FIVE

The 1940s:
The Watershed

In several respects, the 1940s were a crucial decade for Latin music in the United States. The last major Latin-American arrival, the Brazilian, put down roots. Both a truly American-Latin idiom, the mambo, and a true hybrid, Latin-jazz, began to develop. Another surge of popularity and massive infiltration of Tin Pan Alley, though rich in trivia, helped make Latin rhythms an almost subliminal part of U.S. popular music.

The developments of the 1940s fall naturally into two halves, with 1946 as a pivotal year. The early part of the decade marked time of barrier-breaking. In 1940, Alberto Socarrás played opposite Glenn Miller at the Glen Island Casino in New Rochelle—the "first sepia orchestra of its history," as it was put at the time. He also toured Boston and several midwestern cities. A review in *Boston Life* accurately reflected the reactions of most Americans to their first encounter with good Latin music: "If two weeks ago anyone had told us that Boston would go strongly for a flute player with rhumba rhythms we might have been polite, but not impressed. Yet after one session at the Beachcomber with Socarrás and his magic flute, even our jaundiced expression changed to one resembling joy everlasting . . ."

At last, Latin musicians were getting some publicity, after years as the Invisible Men of American music. *Time* magazine, in January 1944, ran a Music section piece on the flute. Though it focused mostly on the classically oriented Flute Club and conservatoire music in general, it went out of its way to name Socarrás among the "master exponents."

The single most important event of the decade, for Latin music's development as an autonomous U.S. substyle, was the formation of Machito's Afro-Cubans. Latin record producer Al Santiago once wrote that "Machito's Afro-Cubans were the greatest Latin band ever, no ifs, ands or buts." They were certainly the most influential, both in the New York Latin style and the growth of Latin jazz.

Singer–maracca player Frank Grillo, nicknamed Machito, had come to New York in 1937, singing with a string-and-percussion group, Las Estrellas Habaneras, and violinist Alberto Iznaga's Orquesta Siboney, besides recording eight sides with Xavier Cugat. In 1940, Machito formed his own band with a front line of three saxes and one or two trumpets. Shortly thereafter, Mario Bauza joined the group as musical director, and began to develop the sound that was to set standards for almost twenty years.

"Our idea was to bring Latin music up to the standard of the American orchestras," Bauza has said. "So I brought a couple of the guys that arranged for Calloway and Chick Webb to write for me. I wanted them to give me the sound—to orchestrate it." Calloway arranger John Bartee and Bauza spent many nights after work writing for the proposed group, and the band was in rehearsal several months before its first appearance.

According to Bauza, its blend of Cuban rhythm section and repertoire with a trumpet and sax frontline that played the most powerful of black swing voicings took time to be accepted. Once it was, however, the band essentially redefined New York Latin music, whose leading practitioners had all been white and society-club oriented, as a hot, progressive, black music. Yet from the beginning the Afro-Cubans moved between uptown and downtown audiences. The revamped group opened at the Park Plaza, on 110th and Fifth Avenue, opposite Pagani's Happy Boys. They next worked at the Beachcomber, on Broadway in the 50s. After another stint of several months uptown, the band moved down to La Conga, on 53rd Street between Seventh Avenue and

Broadway, replacing pianist Anselmo Sacassas's orchestra, and stayed there for almost four years as house band.

The early Afro-Cubans consisted of three saxes, two trumpets, piano, bass, bongó, and timbales. From the start, Bauza included non-Latins in his wind sections, partly because he wanted jazz-oriented players, and also because there were relatively few top rank Latin hornmen in New York. Bauza hired musicians rather than "names," and few of his sidemen—American or Latin—became particularly well known, with the exception of the young Tito Puente, who spent a while with the band in the early 1940s, and pianist Joe Loco. But René Hernandez, who replaced Loco, was perhaps the finest Latin arranger who has ever worked in New York, and players like Carlos Vidal and José Mangual inaugurated a U.S. percussion revolution. Only during the later Afro-Cuban jazz era did "name" American musicians play with the Machito band, which was originally a strictly Latin—thus vocal and ensemble oriented—group.

The Americanisms used by the Afro-Cubans did not water down their Cuban elements: they augmented them. Machito himself was one of the finest soneros in New York at the time of his arrival (indeed Bauza claims he was the first), and the Afro-Cuban's arrangements always kept the (Cuban) two-or three-part structure. This consisted of a "head" that presented the basic theme; a montuno section during which the *coro* (chorus) began its unvarying refrain and the singer or an instrumentalist improvised; and—a novelty inherent in the big-band format—a section of contrasting riffs for brass and reeds, which was to come to be called the "mambo" section. The Afro-Cubans are also said to have been the first New York group to add a conga to its rhythm section on a regular basis, bringing in Carlos Vidal in 1943.

Though the great days of the Machito band were from the mid-1940s onward, they made their mark early with a 1940 recording of "Sopa de Pichon." Such was the power of Bauza's new concept, with its balance of Cuban and American elements, that it even survived the temporary loss of Machito to the American army early in the band's career. Bauza and Graciela, Machito's sister and lead singer, kept it going until his return in 1943, with Polito Galindez singing lead vocals.

Machito's was not the only band that played both up and downtown at that period. Alberto Socarrás moved from the Cotton Club to play opposite Ella Fitzgerald's Orchestra (the former Chick Webb band) at the Tropicana in 1940, and later played with French jazz guitarist Django Reinhardt and violinist Eddie South at the Café Society. Johnny Rodriguez did a stint at La Conga (where his featured number was "La Conga del Año Nuevo").

Nevertheless certain bands still tended to work the American market, while others played more for Latins. Cugat, Madriguera, and even Pancho's tango orchestra remained permanent fixtures in the hotels. In 1943, Pupi Campo formed a new orchestra to play hotels like Caesar's Palace and the Fontainebleau, as well as the Chateau Madrid. Among the people working for him were two who were to make a name in the next Latin generation—Tito Puente, and pianist Charlie Palmieri, who conducted the band during a brief stint with the Jack Paar Show.

Another newcomer to become a major figure later in the decade, pianist José Curbelo, arrived in the U.S. in May 1939, and played for a while with Xavier Cugat. In 1942, Curbelo put together a group consisting of two trumpets, three saxes, piano timbales, and bass, with Polito Galindez as lead singer. Curbelo mostly stuck to the "American" circuit, playing opposite Machito at La Conga in 1942, and (like Socarrás before him) working the big Catskills resort hotel, Grossingers, in 1944.

A less recent arrival who became an important figure during the early 1940s, pianist Noro Morales, came to the U.S. in the mid-1930s and belonged to several East Harlem groups before organizing a sextet to play at El Morocco and the Stork Club. During the 1940s, Morales became one of the major names of downtown Latin music. He formed a big band early in the decade, among whose members were Pupi Campo, singer Tito Rodriguez, and a well-known dancer of the period, Diosa Costello.

Despite his popularity with Latins as well as non-Latins (in 1947 he won a "La Prensa" readers poll), Morales did not have any particular influence, but he excelled in a style that peaked during the 1940s, and has totally vanished since then, the quintet for piano and percussion. British critic Ernest Bornemann once wrote that Morales's late 1940s group was "an unsteady unit. At its best it is the equal of any . . . especially when led by Esy Morales on flute. But at times the band can sound like a tired Cugat." It is true that Morales's music often suffered from the commercial demands of a downtown career; but he was a convincing, exhilarating, and sometimes exciting pianist with a very strong sense of musical logic and structure. His sextet performances of "Linda Mujer" and "Begin the Beguine," recorded in the middle of the decade, opened in an "international Latin vein" dangerously close to cocktail piano, but gained strength with some effective chord changes when he began to improvise. Band versions of two uptempo *guarachas*, "Bim Bam Bum" and "Vamo' a Jugar La Rueda," with Machito singing lead vocal, showed him off as a forceful but not domineering band pianist. A late recording for MGM Records on two sides of a 78 rpm record, *Puerto de Tierra*, opened as an effectively brooding Latin jazz piece, but soon degenerated into wide-horizons mood music with Hollywood strings and brass.

A reissue album of Morales's work on the small Tropical label shows him at his best and worst. Some tracks are essentially skilled cocktail piano. But many of the sextet numbers show highly effective contrasts between busy Afro-Cuban percussion and a sometimes florid but always interesting piano style that occupies a very personal space between "international" Latin and more traditional Cuban playing. Two in particular still stand out. These are "Stop-21," a fast samba with bop tinges, and "Serenata Ritmica," which is full of breathtaking improvised runs cutting clear across the percussion patterns.

The band numbers are equally variable, but they also include some outstanding pieces, notably "Dame Un Cacho" and "Ya Empezo," both powerful pieces with fine singing and excellent piano work.

By its nature, the piano-quintet style was a crossover, fusion idiom. Especially early in the decade, it was often very close to the cocktail style of piano. Such players as the popular Jan August and even more popular Carmen Cavallero played a music that contributed nothing. But many Latin pianists worked in the style during the 1940s. Among them were Rafael Audinot, whose

1940 Cuarteto Caney recording of "Rumba Rhapsody" and "Los Hijos de Buda" (Mexican Jumping Bean) was typical in its mixture of cocktail-piano floridity and Cuban cross-rhythms. A forgotten Cuban pianist with a classical background, Jose Melis, was fond of medleys—called potpourris—one of which blended *Peer Gynt* and a bolero! Typically, one side of his records would be a lush medley in romantic vein, and the other a samba or other Latin rhythm opening in cocktail-Latin style, but developing into a more interesting Cuban-American blend.

The piano-and-rhythm Latin style tended to produce ephemeral work, played as background music to indifferent audiences. But though it has totally vanished as an idiom, it was not without its effects. As the decade went on, it tended increasingly to fuse with jazz piano, and finally merged into the 1950s Latin-jazz quintet style of which George Shearing was the best-known proponent.

Latin music's mass popularity was developing from the beginning of the decade. An extremely important part was played by Hollywood, with a large number of musicals built around specifically Latin-oriented plots (often tied to a country or city title), and many others that included a Latin number or two in a non-Latin script. Though few aspects of Hollywood have been so thoroughly ignored by its historians, these musicals greatly advanced the spread of Latin rhythms and melodies into American culture, and were in particular largely responsible for the introduction of the samba to the canon.

The process began well before the U.S. entered the Second World War. Desi Arnaz, one of the earlier arrivals, made a film version of *Too Many Girls* opposite Lucille Ball, and sang and played in various other unmemorable films, of which the best known was *Father Takes a Wife,* starring Gloria Swanson and Adolphe Menjou. In connection with this Arnaz tells an anecdote revealing of Hollywood's approach. According to Arnaz, Charles Koerner, then president of RKO, heard him perform "Perfidia" at a benefit in San Francisco, and bought the rights for him to sing it in *Father Takes a Wife.* Unfortunately, Arnaz was playing the role of an operatic tenor. As a result, this romantic "international-Latin" composition by a Mexican marimba player was sung on screen as an operatic aria backed by a symphony orchestra. There was a final absurdity: since Arnaz was not an operatic singer, the song Koerner had bought especially for him was dubbed by an unnamed tenor!

One of the most famous of 1940s Latin musical stars, still remembered with derisive affection for her energy and her headdresses, was already in Hollywood when Arnaz arrived. This was Carmen Miranda, whose first U.S. film was the 1940 *Down Argentine Way*, starring Don Ameche and Betty Grable. In 1941 she went to Broadway to appear in Olsen and Johnson's *Sons of Fun*, then returned to Hollywood for *That Night in Rio*. This unusually realistic piece of ethnic casting also starred Don Ameche and Alice Faye, and included the massively popular and long-lasting song "I Yi Yi Yi Yi," besides "Chica Chica Boom Chic," "They Met in Rio" and "Boa Noite" (all of which, characteristically, were untouched by Brazilian hands, being written by Harry Warren and Mack Gordon). The same year, Miranda continued the travelog with *Weekend in Havana*, with the same female star and songwriters.

Of Carmen Miranda's many other musicals during the early 1940s, one of the more important was *The Gang's All Here*, which gave Ary Barroso's "Brazil" one of its several lives as a U.S. hit. She also filmed *Four Jills in a Jeep*, with a remarkable cast that included Alice Faye, Betty Grable, Jimmy Dorsey, Dick Haymes, George Jessel, Carole Landis, Martha Raye, and Phil Silvers.

Carmen Miranda's U.S. films contained a good deal of self-parody. Her absurd costume with its banana headdress made that clear enough. Essentially, they were in the tradition of the Busby Berkley production numbers, with lavish sets ("tropical" in Miranda's case), and Miranda herself massively winsome or strutting in front of complexly choreographed dancers. They made no statements about Latin music, and to object to their stereotyping is about as valid as objecting that *Oklahoma* gave a false impression of American farmers.

Hollywood's most successful Latin was without doubt Xavier Cugat. In many of the musicals in which he appeared, Cugat played quite substantial supporting roles. His return came in the 1942 *You Were Never Lovelier*, in which he played second fiddle to Fred Astaire and Rita Hayworth. He also had a fairly prominent part in the 1944 MGM Esther Williams vehicle, *Bathing Beauty*, whose contribution to the spread of Latin music was Maria Grever's "Te Quiero Dijiste" (Magic Is the Moonlight)—originally published in 1932, as a Spanish canción! Among other Latin artists who did well during this period, Mexican singer Tito Guizar was already well established in Hollywood. Guizar made several minor films during the early 1940s including *Blondie Goes Latin, Brazil* (in 1944), and *Mexicana* (1945). This starred Constance Moore, who had also been featured in an obscure B picture named after a well-known Latin club, *La Conga Nights*.

Many of the Latinisms in the Hollywood musicals were at best marginal. *Argentine Nights* (1940) included a piece of supposedly fusion music that became a hit for the Andrews Sisters, "Rhumboogie." Woody Herman also made a successful version—which, typically, was straight swing until the final bars. *Argentine Nights* contained no Latins in significant roles but featured a close harmony group, La Verne, best known for "Beer Barrel Polka" and "Don't Fence Me In": this combination was typical of Hollywood's common mix and mis-match procedures.

The amount of at least notionally Latin music in films of the era varied widely. Many used one or more feature numbers. The 1941 *Six Lessons from Madame La Zonga*, starring Lupe Velez, included one song called "Jitterrhumba" which was an obvious emulation of "Rhumboogie." Many movies without Latin-American themes included one Latin-tinged number, like the "Kindergarten Conga" in the 1941 *Miami*, the bolero-ballad "Dolores" in *Las Vegas Nights*, or "Acapulco," from Betty Grable's 1945 *Diamond Horseshoe*.

Other films went much further. The 1941 *Blondie Goes Latin*, an archetypal B movie starring Tito Guizar, contained an oddity called "Brazilian Cotillion," "Querida," and a number whose title summed up American ignorance about the realities of Latin music, "You Don't Play a Drum (You Just Beat It)!"

Just as "Jitterrhumba" emulated "Rhumboogie," whole movies often fed off an earlier success, as did the title of Rodgers and Hart's 1941 *They Met in Argentina, Two Latins from*

Manhattan or the 1942 remake of the 1929 film *Rio Rita* with John
Carroll and Kathryn Grayson.

Walt Disney made an important contribution to the spread
of the samba in two films: the experimental 1943 *Saludos Amigos*,
mixing live and animated footage, in which Carmen Miranda's
sister Aurora sang "Brazil" (yet again!) and "Tico Tico"; and *The
Three Caballeros* (1944) in which Bing Crosby sang "Bahia" and
"Adios Muchachos" (I Get Ideas), backed by the Xavier Cugat
orchestra.

Hollywood's sudden interest in Latin music did not result
solely from the style's general popularity. The Second World
War had closed the usual European markets to exports, and the
film-makers were looking to the south for new ones. This
economic motive fitted neatly with the government's official
"Good Neighbor" policy toward Latin-America, and the film
industry capitalized on it in 1941, sending three DC3s full of
stars to Mexico City on a public relations goodwill mission.
Among them were Mickey Rooney, Norma Shearer, James Cag-
ney, Clark Gable, Robert Taylor, Bing Crosby, and Desi Arnaz—
the only Latin aboard. According to Arnaz, the mission was a
less than total success, the Mexicans being suspicious of this
sudden neighborliness.

However mixed the film industry's motives in turning to
Latin material, the 1940s film musicals both reflected and augmented Latin music's popularity in hybrid forms that made it
more acceptable to American audiences and more quickly absorbed into American styles. They were, in fact, part of the
process whereby Latin-originated rhythms were becoming a
part of the structure of U.S. music.

Latin successes in Hollywood naturally also created Tin Pin
Alley hits. Among the earliest was "Rhumboogie," from *Argentine
Nights*. One of the greatest was "Babalú," which has ironically
come to be associated with Desi Arnaz rather than with Miguelito Valdez and Xavier Cugat, who recorded it in 1941—five
years before Arnaz. Walt Disney not only helped the spread of
the Brazilian samba in general, but made national successes of
"Tico Tico" and "Bahia."

The influential role of film musicals was not echoed on 1940s Broadway, whose approach to Latin music differed little in the early 1940s from what it had been in the previous decade. Musicals tended to have their "Latin number"—often comic, like "Latins Know How" from the 1940 *Louisiana Purchase,* or Eddie Cantor's song, "Who Started the Rhumba?" in Vernon Duke's 1941 *Banjo Eyes.* Cole Porter in particular continued to show his liking for Latin rhythms in the 1940 *Panama Hattie* ("Visit Panama"), the 1941 *Let's Face It* ("A Little Rumba Numba") and *Mexican Hayride* ("Sing to Me Guitar"). But none of this reflected anything very innovative.

Though films, and to a lesser degree the stage, were important to the spread of Latin music, most major national hits, of course, had no connection with either. In 1940 came "El Cumbanchero" by Rafael Hernandez, a long-term member of the East Harlem musical community, and in 1941 another enormous permanent success, Mexican Alberto Dominguez's "Perfidia."

Ernesto Lecuona and Marion Sunshine both produced relatively lightweight works the following year: Lecuona publishing "Dame de Tus Rosas," whose English title was "Two Hearts that Pass in the Night," and Marion Sunshine a so-called "War Conga," "El Presidente." "Besame Mucho" and "Amor" in 1943, Agustin Lara's "Solamente Una Vez," Cuban Osvaldo Farres's "Acercate Mas" (Come Closer to Me), and Mexican Gabriel Ruiz's "Stars in Your Eyes," all 1945, were among the best known of a large number of successful songs by Latins during the period.

The immense success of Latin music inevitably led to a good deal of trivialization, exemplified by short-lived novelty numbers like "The Rhumba-Cardi," recorded by Dinah Shore and Xavier Cugat in 1940, or "Do the Dubonnet," which Enric Madriguera recorded two years later. But there were two sides to the more lighthearted manifestations of pop-Latin. Humor was an important part of the style. Some of it was throwaway, like the splendid 1941 title "I Came, I Saw, I Conga'd." But during the mid-decade, a vein of mild satire surfaced, which included two amusing plaints from the non-dancer: "South America, Take It Away" ("There's a great big crack in the back of my sacroiliac"), and "Caramba, It's the Samba." The 1946 "Chiquita Banana" was a mild spoof of Latin songs and styles. Stan Kenton's "Tampico" sniped quite effectively at the tourist trade. And Carmen Miranda's "The Matador Song" was far better than its famous A-side, "Cuanto le Gusta."

Another vein of humor was much more offensive. Too many lyrics relied on, spread, and reinforced the stereotype of the lazy and shiftless Latin. Prime examples, among songs very popular in their day, were "Managua-Nicaragua," and the thoroughly offensive Peggy Lee song, "Mañana (Is Good Enough for Me)."

A number of older songs, too, came—or in many cases returned—to popularity. The first major revival in 1940 was Lecuona's "The Breeze and I," an English language version of his 1930 "Andalucia." "Green Eyes," (Aquellos Ojos Verdes), which had first been recorded in the late 1920s; LaCalle's "Amapola," resurrected from 1924; "Frenesí" (published a couple of years earlier); "Quiereme Mucho" (1932) and "Maria Elena" (1933) all gained or regained mass popularity in 1941 alone. In 1944, a song so Americanized that almost nobody is aware of its Latin origin surfaced again: Maria Grever's 1934 "Cuando Vuelva a Tu Lado" (What a Difference a Day Made).

These songs were, of course, spread by records, and important changes in the record industry had a long-term effect in the popularization of more authentic styles. In the first years of the decade, when Latin music began reaching a truly mass public, it was usually non-Latin performers who scored the major successes—often at the expense of Latin versions.

Typical was Nilo Melendez's "Green Eyes." In Jimmy Dorsey's 1940 version, with vocalist Bob Eberly and Helen O'Connell, its Latin origin was totally undetectable. Dorsey scored another success the following year with "Amapola," which Cugat had recorded before him and which was also to be covered by such varied figures as Connie Boswell, Deanna Durbin, and Gene Autry! "Perfidia"—recorded by Glenn Miller, Harry James, and Ozzie Nelson—was another example. And "Frenesí," recorded by both Artie Shaw and Benny Goodman as well as Cugat, moved into that grey area between popular music and jazz occupied by a number of Latin and non-Latin ballads.

Just as the Hollywood musicals were given a great impetus by the World War and the hunt for new markets, so two apparently irrelevant events helped Latin music's spread in the crucial areas of recording and radio.

In 1941, the American Society of Composers and Performers (ASCAP) refused to issue new licenses to radio stations. Deprived of most popular stage and film music, the stations turned to recordings licensed by Broadcast Music Inc. (BMI), founded by the major radio stations in 1940. Because ASCAP was so powerful in the traditional sources of naturally popular music, BMI acquired much of its catalog from less traditional sources, including black and Latin music.

A second event further helped Latin musicians. In 1942, and again in 1947, the American Federation of Musicians prohibited its members from recording with the major companies over the issue of company contributions to the union pension fund. The result was the birth of a large number of small companies prepared to meet union demands. Unlike Columbia, Decca, and RCA-Victor, which had previously more or less monopolized the field, these new companies were prepared to take risks with newer styles and musicians—notable among them, bebop and Latin music.

The success of Latin music in New York and an increase in Latin immigration after World War Two also laid the groundwork for Latin entrepreneurs to move into the field. The rise of the jukebox industry, which was one of the causes of the second AFM strike, also helped the small companies by opening up a whole new market. All these events paved the way for the late-1940s interlinks between the jazz market and an independent Latin recording market, giving jazz-Latin crossover the economic basis it needed.

As far as mass-popular Latin music was concerned, the pivotal year of 1946 showed no particularly new trends. Tin Pan Alley successes in 1946 spanned all the categories of Latin music in the U.S., including "Chiquita Banana," Osvaldo Farres's

"Without You" and Noro Morales's "Rumba Rhapsody." Perhaps the most interesting happening was Nat "King" Cole's first Latin-influenced album, *Rumba à la King*, which he recorded in Cuba with—among others—one of the island's greatest trumpeters, "Chocolate" Armenteros.

Broadway, as usual, noted and commented on the continuing triumph of Latin music, in Harold Rome's highly successful musical, *Call Me Mister*, in which Betty Garrett's performance of "South America, Take It Away" made her a star.

In Hollywood, Xavier Cugat made *Holiday in Mexico*, with vocalist Carlos Ramirez, light-classical pianist Jose Iturbi, Jane Powell, and Ilona Massey—and music by Noro Morales. The samba was kept going in *Thrill of Brazil*, with Ann Miller and Evelyn Keyes; and Desi Arnaz appeared in what he himself calls a B Minus picture, *Cuban Pete*, wrapped around his new act at Ciro's nightclub.

This act was typical of the lusher strata of contemporary nightclub-Latin music. Arnaz has described his aim to "combine the Latin rhythms of Machito with the lushness of [André] Kostelanetz." He commented to a backer, about bands of Machito's type, "The rhythm is great but the sound is not melodically good enough—it's tinny." (!)

Arnaz's orchestra maintained the old 1930s balance of brass, woodwinds, and strings, and featured an American singer, Amanda Lane. Arnaz himself continued his conga act, closing his first show with "Babalú," which—despite its earlier association with Cugat—became the single tune by which he is most remembered. His Copacabana show, however, contained a new song that was to become a light-Latin standard: "The Coffee Song" ("They've Got an Awful Lot of Coffee in Brazil").

Though 1946 was superficially not much different from the years that preceded it, several events hinted at important changes under the surface. First, a more authentic music was beginning to move downtown. During 1946, Gabriel Oller—a long-term record producer in El Barrio—organized a dance at the Manhattan Center. The five groups playing included Machito's Afro-Cubans, but also bands catering mostly to Latins, including Alberto Iznaga and José Budet.

This dance provided a significant statistic for any promoters who might have been watching. Oller's Latin bands drew a public of 5,000, and many more had to be turned away. The night before, the popular Harry James Orchestra had drawn 500 people.

A still more significant event for the long run occurred when former bandleader Federico Pagani, who had been working as a promoter since 1940, persuaded the owner of the Alma Dance Studios on 53rd and Broadway to let him run Latin nights. Those Latin nights were to turn the Alma Studios—eventually renamed the Palladium—into the center of the New York big band mambo.

Put briefly, the first half of the 1940s saw Latin music become an established style and influence within mass popular music. During the second half of the decade, two major creative movements developed that were to reach maturity during the 1950s. One—the mambo—belonged to the central core of U.S. Latin music, the other—Afro-Cuban jazz, or Cubop—was a fusion style; but both were extremely tightly intertwined, especially during the 1940s.

Though its impact was sudden and dramatic, Cubop did not spring fully armed from anybody's head. It was one flowering of a fusion process that had been going on ever since the days of the habanera, and has continued ever since. Many of the swing bands of the early 1940s had dabbled in jazz-Latin fusions. Though most of these were fairly superficial, they were also increasingly Latin. Glenn Miller's 1940 "The Rumba Jumps" and Cab Calloway's "Conchita," recorded the following year, used rumba rhythms; but most of the examples from that period were no more Latin than Jimmy Dorsey's "Green Eyes." Harry James's "La Paloma" and "Estrellita" were essentially popular-oriented ballads, and Artie Shaw's famous 1940 "Frenesí" was a foxtrot.

By 1945, things were changing. In August that year, Woody Herman recorded "Bijou," subtitled "Rhumba à la Jazz," with a Latin rhythmic base throughout (except for a few contrasting 4/4 passages) and fairly progressive writing for the saxophone section. Though the effect was rather jerky, this was a clear, if clumsy, attempt at Latin-jazz. Nor was Herman alone in his "jazz rumbas." The following year, the Charlie Barnet band recorded "The New Redskin Rumba," and Harry James's orchestra (of which Juan Tizol was a member at the time), a piece called "Keb-Lah," which was—aside from some good trumpet from James—essentially a rerun of "Caravan."

At this time, more jazzmen were beginning to play regularly with Latins. In 1946, Cuban pianist René Touzet, who was leading a group at the Avedon Ballroom in Los Angeles, hired drummer Jackie Mills. Mills persuaded Touzet to hire trumpeter Pete Candoli and altoist Art Pepper. He also took on arranger Johnny Mandel, who, according to Marshall Stearns's *The Story of Jazz,* first developed the Latin-jazz blues, "Barbados," later recorded by—and credited to—Charlie Parker.

Though Cubop was, seen from one perspective, simply part of an ongoing fusion process, it differed in many respects from what came before. Not only did it spring from the new bebop movement, which at the time seemed a total break from the jazz past with its emphasis on harmonic improvisation and apparent abandonment of melody, but its Latin and jazz elements were more equally balanced than was the case with most of its predecessors. More basically still, it was a serious undertaking by men convinced of the importance of what they were doing.

Cubop had three creative leaders: Stan Kenton, Dizzy Gillespie, and Machito. Kenton, a white bandleader based on the West Coast, was the first to experiment seriously and at length with Latin-jazz crossover as a regular part of his activities.

At first the level of Kenton's Latinism was no greater than that of his contemporaries. A September 1941 recording session with his first band included Margarita Lecuona's "Taboo" and Enric Madriguera's "Adios," and in February 1942 he recorded the old tango, "El Choclo," all with a straight 4/4 beat.

By mid-1946, Kenton was attempting much more experimental works. In July of that year, he recorded a piece called "Ecuador" that was reported in "Downbeat" as part of a suite being written by Pete Rugolo. Though this suite never materialized, by early 1947 Kenton was firmly committed to Latin music as part of the developing style that he called "progressive" jazz. In mid-January 1947, he recorded a number called "Machito," which represented a transition between light-Latin jazz and Cubop itself. The rhythm, sustained by a conventional section without Latin percussion, was like many other Latin-swing patterns. But the writing for the wind instruments was very far from pop-swing.

A couple of weeks after recording "Machito," Kenton appeared on a double bill at New York's Town Hall theater with Machito and His Afro-Cubans. In April he disbanded for a while, before forming a new group in September. This included Brazilian guitarist Laurindo Almeida as a regular member of the lineup, as well as his longtime bongó player, non-Latin Jack Costanza. The new band's repertoire included a large number of Latin compositions, among them "Journey to Brazil," "Bongo Riff," and "Introduction to a Latin Theme." But Kenton was also a front-runner in the use of Latin instruments in non-Latin compositions like "Fugue for Rhythm Section."

With this group, on December 6, 1947, Kenton made one of his most popular Latin-jazz recordings: a new arrangement of "The Peanut Vendor" that combined the charm of Azpiazú's original recording with ensemble writing that was both startling and exciting, including a hair-raising four-trumpet passage full of then-revolutionary discords.

What made "The Peanut Vendor" such an important recording was that—for the first time on record—it combined serious and experimental jazz writing with an authentic Latin rhythm-section: three percussionists from Machito's band, including Machito himself on maraccas. Not only was it a totally successful fusion, with no grating whatsoever between its various parts, but it even managed to combine experimentalism with popular appeal.

Dizzy Gillespie's interest in Latin music goes back at least to the days when he and Mario Bauza were partners in the trumpet section of Cab Calloway's band. According to Bauza, Gillespie sat in with the Machito band a couple of times in 1942 or 1943, when it was playing the Park Plaza (he was also hired by Alberto Socarrás for a week in 1943), and Bauza remembers that Gillespie was already considering Latin jazz at the time the two men were with Calloway.

When Dizzy and myself got to bulling, we always said that jazz was a great thing but the rhythm was very monotonous. So we were always thinking, trying to see if we could innovate something else.

On September 29, 1947, Gillespie took his new big band into Carnegie Hall, New York, for a concert that gave Cubop overnight status as part of avant-garde jazz. Once again, Machito's group was involved: for it was Mario Bauza to whom Gillespie turned for advice when he decided to include Cuban percussionists, and present a number called "Afro-Cubano Drums Suite."

Chano Pozo just got in town, so I sent a guy called Chiquitico with the bongó, and Chano with the conga. After that concert Chiquitico didn't want to remain with the orchestra, but Chano did.

Gillespie succeeded in blending the bebop that was then the creative cutting edge of jazz with the purest Afro-Cuban percussion and singing yet. His work was also significant in that— to a greater extent even than Kenton, at least up to that time— he moved right away from the prevailing concept of Latin fusions as "fun." Like Kenton, Gillespie took Latin-jazz seriously. Well before Kenton did so, he began to develop extended forms. Many of these belong to the 1950s, but by February 1948 an "Afro-Cuban Suite," composed by Pozo and Gillespie, was a regular part of the band's repertoire. Equally important, Gillespie—like Kenton—remained committed to Latin-jazz as a style, and during the late 1940s he consistently commissioned Cubop works like George Russell's "Cubana Be" and "Cubana Bop." This commitment and continuing interest was far more important in the development of Cubop than the actual quality of the early Gillespie bigband Latin-fusion numbers, which were as awkward as any new departure. Above all, Gillespie's position as a leader of the bebop movement ensured that a generation of musicians took up Cubop as a significant movement.

Gillespie's association with Pozo was not a long one, because the conga player was killed in 1948. But Pozo's effect on jazzmen's attitudes to Cuban music was permanent. Born Luciano Pozo y Gonzales, he was a member of the *abakwá* secret society, whose roots trace back to eastern Nigeria, and his singing and playing was strongly Afro-Cuban. Though his reputation as a conga player has been assailed by some Latin musicians, it has been well said that, whereas most conga players are bottom-heavy or top-heavy, Pozo supplied both rhythmic support and melodic improvisation. But he was more than a conga-player. As a composer he gave Latin-jazz several standards, notably "Tin Tin Deo" and "Manteca." Perhaps most important of all, his work was a major factor in breaking down the old stereotype of Latin music as something agreeable but essentially light. Whatever else Pozo's music was, it was certainly deep.

The third—and pivotal—group in the coming-of-age of Latin-jazz was, of course, Machito's Afro-Cubans. Their work with Kenton and Gillespie was only a start. In 1948, producer Norman Granz approached Machito about recording for him. It was Granz who first paired the Afro-Cubans with Charlie Parker, after taking him to a rehearsal at the Palladium dance hall to hear them.

Parker's first recordings with Machito were perhaps the best. An example is "Mango Mangüe," which Marshall Stearns called the "most successful Latin jazz," though since it preserves the Cuban three-part structure it is really more akin to salsa. It opens with magnificently tight and cohesive playing from Machito's reed section. Parker makes absolutely no attempt to phrase according to Latin patterns in his solo, but the frame of the full band is strong enough to contain him: interestingly, his soloing works best over the vocal coro, perhaps because their refrains act as a formal bridge between the alto and the rhythm section.

Interestingly, Latino Latin-jazz aficionados tend to prefer another Machito recording, the 1949 "Tanga" (which Machito was playing in concert as early as 1947), on which Parker does not play. The jazz-minded can appreciate the mambo section riffs, in which brass doo-doo-wahs are set against a sax theme reminiscent of "Fascinating Rhythm," and the soloing from Flip Phillips. Machito's singing in *Tanga's* opening is a model of the sonero's art, and Luis Miranda's conga patterns hark almost directly back to the Congo-Angola roots.

Machito's involvement with Parker and other jazzmen made him a hero to New York bopsters, and the band played and recorded at various times with tenor sax players Dexter Gordon, Zoot Sims, Stan Getz, Johnny Griffin, and Brew Moore, altoist Lee Konitz, and trumpeter Howard McGhee. Bauza himself says that the dates with Dexter Gordon (who never recorded with the band) were by far the most exciting and successful in sheer swing and jazz joie de vivre.

Members of Machito's band were not, of course, the only Latins to be involved in Latin jazz from its inception. At one time Puerto Rican bongó player Sabu Martinez recorded alongside Chano Pozo in Gillespie's band. *Congacero* Carlos Vidal played with Parker and Charlie Barnet among others. Another *bongosero*, Chino Pozo, joined trumpeter Fats Navarro for a 1948 session with tenorists Wardell Grey and Allen Eager, pianist Tadd Dameron, and Kenny Clarke on drums. Though there is only one Latin percussionist on the recording, "Lady Bird," "Jahbero," and "Symphonette" are remarkably successful, perhaps because Fats Navarro was himself part-Cuban and was raised in Key West in Florida, and therefore came naturally by the fusion.

Among the more thoroughgoing Cubop experiments was a band formed by drummer Cozy Cole called the Cuboppers. This was a seven-piece group with, according to a *Downbeat* report for March 1949, "a front line of drummers," including Bill Alvarez on bongo and Diego Iborra on conga, both of whom had also played with Gillespie's big band. It also had Billy Taylor on bass. The Cuboppers made four sides for Decca and four for Candy Records including a number called "La Danza" and two Chico O'Farrill arrangements, "Botao" and "Mosquito Brain," before vanishing.

By 1949, the Cubop style was a movement, not merely a

cooperation between a couple of bands and a handful of soloists. It gave its name to a club, Cubop City, where one of bop's early disc jockeys, Symphony Sid Torin, was master of ceremonies and Machito played regularly. Torin, after whom the number "Jumping with Symphony Sid" was named, eventually concentrated entirely on Latin music in his radio shows. The Cubop movement also stimulated changes in the styles of established Latin artists. Noro Morales, whose playing had blended American pop with Cuban techniques, was one who took in a good deal more jazz at this time. In 1949, he recorded a version of "The Peanut Vendor," which a review in the British *Melody Maker* gave the quaint title of "rhumbop."

The Cubop of the 1940s was a new fusion with a new jazz style, and as such its first steps were, in retrospect, often faltering. Though jazz and Cuban music share the same roots, their European ingredients—largely English on one hand and largely Spanish on the other—are almost as far from each other as any two western European traditions can be, and though their common African ingredients come from roughly the same areas, those areas are so large and varied, and the subsequent "American experience" was so different, that for practical purposes the diversities are as great as the similarities. As a result, attitudes to phrasing, and basic ways of producing and using rhythm, were so different that it was almost impossible for jazzmen and Latin musicians simply to come together and play without either the jazzman or the Latin feeling constricted.

During the rumba era this problem was irrelevant both because the "rumba," as the U.S. knew it, was heavily Americanized and simplified, and because so many American groups simply ignored it. In Cubop, Latins and Americans were trying to work together without losing any crucial elements of either style.

It is hardly surprising that the results were at first spotty. Dizzy Gillespie's "Woody'n You" with his big band and conga player Chano Pozo, recorded in December 1947, moves between sections in which Pozo is prominent, and passages with jazz rhythms to which Pozo contributes a rather uncomfortable bumping. Similar problems occurred in a concert that the Gillespie big band played in Paris in February 1948, preserved in a live album on French Vogue. Two numbers featured Chano Pozo: a Gillespie composition called "Algo Bueno" and the six-minute "Afro-Cuban Suite." Pozo sounded uncomfortable on "Algo Bueno," and after a couple of choruses the band reverted to a straight 4/4 with conga trimmings, to accommodate soloists who presumably could not handle clave-band rhythms. "Afro-Cuban Suite" showed a similar fragmentation. The root of the problem seems to have been that Pozo's lead conga playing and Afro-Cuban singing needed a frame of other percussion parts.

Yet "Afro-Cuban Suite" did show hints of what was to come. Gillespie himself was already far more at ease with Cuban rhythms than Charlie Parker ever became. Without apparently altering his own phrasing in any way, he flows above the Cubanisms so that he and they complement and enrich each other. He and Pozo played a magnificent duet passage, and Pozo closed with an extended Afro-Cuban vocal-and-conga passage, that almost transcended the lack of other percussion.

There were, in fact, two approaches to early Latin-jazz, only one of which produced a real fusion. When a group added a conga—or conga and bongo—without considering the need for absorbing them, they functioned as a fifth wheel in what was really jazz with Latin fringes. The results might be pleasant, but the percussionists' contribution was not essential to the basic fabric of the piece.

As a true fusion, Latin jazz almost always involved a full Latin rhythm section: not merely a set of percussionists, but a bass-player able to play the bass patterns called *tumbaos* that peg the percussionists. For Latin percussionists to relate to a jazz group without the bassist providing this link is a little like water-skiing without a rope.

During the late 1940s, various media developments helped the spread and diversity of both Latin music and Latin-jazz. In New York, a number of small or specialist recording companies sprang up. Gabriel Oller, who had run a record store and acetate-cutting studio in East Harlem during the 1930s, moved to midtown and formed Coda Records in 1945 and the SMC label—named after his Spanish Music Center and a source of recordings by the Cuban founder of the contemporary conjunto style, Arsenio Rodriguez—in 1948.

SMC, and companies like it, documented the more típico aspects of Latin music, where the American-oriented companies tended to be interested in its pop and fusion aspects. Chano Pozo, for instance, recorded a series of percussion 78s for Oller at around the time he was recording with the Gillespie band.

Just as was happening with bebop (and Latin-jazz), small Latin recording companies also provided an outlet for young musicians who had no way of selling substantially enough to interest the majors. Typical was Tico Records, formed in 1948. Tico's first recording was by the newly formed conjunto of Tito Rodriguez, who had recently left Curbelo's band to form the Mambo Devils. Characteristically of the period, one side—"Hay Craneo" was in Spanish, the other, "Ardent Night," in English.

Tito Puente left Curbelo's band around the same time as Rodriguez, formed a conjunto called the Picadilly Boys, and also signed with Tico. Puente's second recording—"Abaniquito"— was one of the first mambos to become a major hit among non-Latins. It was greatly helped by another new phenomenon— English-language radio programs run by disc jockeys who were also taste-makers. Dick "Ricardo" Sugar's broadcasts on WEBD introduced and popularized "Abaniquito": Sugar, Pedro Harris, Symphony Sid Torin, were important in the formation of a permanent and knowledgeable non-Latin public for authentic Latin music.

A similar diversification was helping to spread Chicano music on the West Coast. Before the Second World War, the big companies' ethnic divisions had pretty much monopolized recording of norteño music. During the war, regional recording of all sorts lagged. But when peace returned, a large number of local companies sprang up, mostly centered on Texas and California, though there were others in New Mexico, Arizona, and even Chicago.

Ideal, Falcon, and Del Valle in Texas, Imperial of Los Angeles, and the rest, had an important effect on recorded Chicano music. The big companies before the war had often avoided highly controversial corridos like those that documented clashes between Anglo police forces or the Texas Rangers ("Los Rinches") and Chicanos. Many owners of the backstreet studios were businessmen with little interest in controversial material that might cause problems. But they were near to the music and its public, and some of them took risks. Moreover, the mere existence of a large number of companies allowed for a great range of recording from highly traditional to more experimental.

Stylistically, the most important development in 1940s norteño music was the triumph of the accordion sound. Whereas the instrument had been used almost exclusively for instrumentals in the 1930s, now Narciso Martinez and his colleagues recorded behind many vocal duets. By the late 1940s, in fact, a record without an accordion would hardly sell.

Among pioneers in the reverse process—adding vocals to accordion groups—were the most popular of all 1940s norteño bands: Los Alegres de Teran, who more than any other developed the contemporary norteño style by blending their voices with the accordion work of Eugenio Abrego.

Though the most important developments of the late 1940s were elsewhere, Latin music's mass popularity also continued. In Hollywood, the Latin "Golden Age" included some postwar classics. In 1947, Bing Crosby and Bob Hope made *Road to Rio,* which included the Andrews Sisters as well as Dorothy Lamour, and the same year Groucho Marx and Carmen Miranda were paired in *Copacabana.* Among the lesser movies, fairly typical was *Carnival in Costa Rica,* in which Dick Haymes sang a couple of boleros, "Mi Vida" and "Another Night Like This." But one of the better pieces of Latin music on film was not in a musical. This was "Jungle Fantasy," played by the band of flutist Esy Morales, a brother of pianist Noro, in *Criss Cross.*

Hollywood also continued to feed songs back into Tin Pan Alley. A notable example was the 1948 film *A Date with Judy*— one of many that united Cugat and Carmen Miranda—in which Miranda sang a song called "Cuanto le Gusta," which promptly became a samba hit, even though its composer was Mexican. (A similar versatility was shown by the 1947 "Wedding Samba," which had started life as the "Wedding Rhumba" in 1940, and was to return yet again in 1950.)

The samba's growing popularity brought about a number of other resurrections. Typical was "Come to the Mardi Gras," (Não Tenho Lagrimas), which had originally been published in 1937 without making much stir. But the record for longevity was set by "The Loveliest Night of the Year"—a late 1940s pop version, with English lyrics, of Mexican Juventino Rosas's 19th-century waltz, "Sobre las Olas".

By the late 1940s, the Latin thrust in popular music was flagging. Most of the mass hits were "international Latin" in style, like the 1947 Bing Crosby vehicle, "Quizás, Quizás, Quizás." One exception was "La Raspa," whose folk qualities stemmed from measures of the traditional "Mexican Hat Dance." (Like Maria Grever, its composer, Gus Moreno, spent most of his life in Spain.) Significantly, most successes of the time were written by very familiar names: Lecuona's "Another Night Like This," René Touzet's "Made for Each Other," and Enric Madriguera's "Take It Away."

But the Latin flavor in mainstream pop music was about to be renewed and strengthened by developments in the now self-propelling hardcore U.S. Latin scene. This time, the vehicle was the mambo.

The mambo had originally developed in the Afro-Cuban religions. Its name is probably of Congo-Angolan origin, and it is variously said to have been brought into the Cuban conjunto's repertoire by Arsenio Rodriguez or bassist Cachao Lopez. In New York, it came together with the burgeoning big-band Latin sound to become perhaps the first Latin idiom largely developed in the United States.

Though Machito continued to be the chief creative force in late 1940s Latin New York, several other big bands were of major artistic importance. In 1945, Marcelino Guerra, who had been brought to the U.S. as an arranger by Robbins Music, formed a group said by some to have been better than Machito's. Based on a band called Luis Varona's Second Afro-Cubans, which Guerra took over, the recordings that it made on the obscure Verne label are collectors' items. The best of the up-town groups, it featured jazz trumpeter Doc Cheatham until it broke up in 1947, when Guerra joined the Merchant Marine.

An important downtown band was run by Cuban pianist José Curbelo, who had worked for a while with Cugat before forming his own group in 1941. Curbelo played the Broadway nightclub circuit using the combination of American popular elements and strong Cuban music that was the foundation of Machito's success.

Curbelo's band came to its peak in 1946, when he hired two future leaders of the New York mambo school, sonero Tito Rodriguez, and *timbalero* Tito Puente, along with a rhythm sec-tion that included Chino Pozo on bongó and Machito sideman Carlos Vidal on conga, both of whom were also recording ex-tensively with jazzmen.

A reissue album of several of Curbelo's 1946–47 recordings clearly shows the genesis of the New York mambo in the mid-40s. It includes several rumbas; one guaracha whose third section was to become the basis of the instrumental mambo's charac-teristic riff-and-counter-riff. (One of them was even called "El Rey del Mambo.") Since like many of the jazz groups of the time, Curbelo's band played what was popular, it also includes a so-called calypso-rumba, "Mary Ann," and two Brazilian-in-spired pieces, "Ed Sullivan Samba" and "Boogie Woogie na Favela."

The best track is perhaps a fast rumba with some fine flamenco-inflected piano from Curbelo, "Rhumba Gallega." But equally interesting are the guarachas, which—especially "El Rey del Mambo"—prefigure the classic stabbing mambo trumpets and rolling sax riffs, and "Boogie Woogie na Favela," a New York Latin cross of samba and boogie woogie that is a reminder that commercial considerations need not stifle the panache typi-cal of the 1940s U.S. Latin scene.

Indeed, though the immediate results were sometimes dire, the hybridization process was fundamental to the development of the U.S. Latin style. The big band mambo itself was one of its major products. Bandleader Orlando Marin once remarked that Cuban music is voices and drums, and the rest is a luxury. It was fitting that the two members of Curbelo's band who were to be the leaders of the mambo generation in New York were a lead singer, Tito Rodriguez, and a timbalero, Tito Puente. Both, however, were far more than that.

As a public relations gimmick, Tito Puente's title of "King of the Mambo" was more valid than most. Puente, who was born in New York of Puerto Rican parents, brought the hot 1940s big band mambo style to a pinnacle during the 1950s and 1960s, giving it an intense and nervous quality that was pure New York. A virtuoso arranger and timbales player who also plays several other instruments, Puente formed his own conjunto, the Piccadilly Boys, in 1947, signing with the new Tico Record Company soon after. Since then he has recorded some 120 albums, of which the 1958 *Dance Mania*, for RCA Victor, is generally considered one of the finest. Though he has worked in many veins, his fame has rested solidly on his driving big-band mambo style.

Pablo "Tito" Rodriguez was born in San Juan, Puerto Rico, in 1923. Besides being equally talented as an up-tempo improvising sonero and a romantic ballad singer, he was a percussionist who ran an extremely tight, professional, and creative big band. After stints with the guitar groups, Cuarteto Mayari in Puerto Rico, and Cuarteto Caney in pre-war New York, Rodriguez spent brief periods with Enric Madriguera and Xavier Cugat (as bongosero-vocalist). Then he sang five years with Noro Morales, before switching to José Curbelo in 1946. In 1947 he formed one of the first conjuntos in New York, the Mambo Devils, soon expanding it to a big band. Rodriguez became one of the main features at the Palladium Dance Hall on Broadway, besides touring and playing Las Vegas, Miami, and other major show business centers. During the 1960s he moved to Puerto Rico for a while, still recording and playing intensively. He died of leukemia in New York in February 1973.

Though the 1950s were the high days of the U.S. mambo, its formative date is 1947, when Puente and Rodriguez organized their own conjuntos. From then on they—along with Machito—were at the center of the New York style.

Though the mambo reached its musical peak in New York,

one of its greatest popularizers never gained much following there. This was Perez Prado.

Prado played piano with the famous Cuban orchestra, Casino de la Playa, in the early 1940s. In 1948 he moved to Mexico and that year began recording a series of mambos, mostly instrumental, in the RCA Mexico City studio. These were originally released in the Latin market in the U.S., but several—notably "Mambo No. 5" "Mambo No. 8," Mambo No. 10," and "Caballo Negro" (Black Horse)—also picked up crossover sales, partly because the U.S. was at the time in the middle of the second A.F.M. recording ban, but also because bandleader Sonny Burke, vacationing in Mexico, heard Prado's "Que Rico El Mambo" and covered it with "More Mambo." When several other groups recorded Prado-styled mambos, RCA moved some of the Prado best-sellers from the Spanish to the popular listings. There they attained true hit status, even though Prado did not play the West Coast in person until 1951.

Though much of the Latin music of the 1940s was frankly silly, it was also a decade of enormous creativity. Above all, it was the first decade in which Latin elements began to move below the surface of U.S. music, so to speak, and establish themselves as an integral part of it. The process took long and worked two ways, with the central U.S. Latin styles themselves becoming more fundamentally Americanized and distinct from their Brazilian, Cuban, and Mexican models.

SIX

The 1950s:
Mambo Time

During the 1950s, Latin music made a major change of course. It achieved its greatest popular outreach during the early part of the decade, but at the cost of a dilution (not of the best examples, but of the average) which contributed to its decline as a nationally popular style. In the latter years there was both a retrenchment and a return to the Latin roots for refreshment.

Latin music's decline in national popularity did not reflect a loss of creativity in the hard-core styles. The big-band mambo continued strong in New York throughout the decade, and Latin jazz came to maturity. The mambo's period of major success spanned the first half of the 1950s. Perez Prado was perhaps the first to reach large non-Latin audiences. In 1951, he made a West Coast U.S. tour with a big band heavy on brass and featuring Kenton trumpeter Pete Candoli. At his opening date in September, a crowd of 2,500 jammed into the Zenda Ballroom in Los Angeles. Two weeks later, a Sunday afternoon concert in San Francisco drew 3,500 Mexican- and Anglo-Americans.

Prado proved to be less successful in New York, where his heavy brass sound and his over-simplification did not sit well with Waldorf-Astoria clientele used to Xavier Cugat, nor with a hard-core Latin public accustomed to the greater sophistication of Machito and Curbelo, Tito Puente and Tito Rodriguez. But to a greater extent than any of these, Prado symbolized the mambo to the American public—and its commercialization to most Latins.

There were, in fact, three Perez Prados. Many of his early recordings were effective, individual, if somewhat simple, approaches to the mambo style. Though some of his most financially successful records were of almost no musical interest, he developed a bright octave sound with an ingenious and fairly simple use of contrasts between brass and reeds, and punchy rhythm sections based on such fine percussionists as Mongo Santamaria, though even the best of Prado's work lacks the richness of the New York school. Because it abolishes the Cuban three-part structure, and has virtually no instrumental solos, it lacks both formal and internal complexity.

An early vocal mambo, "Maria Christina," uses Prado's trademark of bright brass voicings and clarity of sound to admirable effect. "Que Rico el Mambo"—the basis of the mambo's mass popularity—and "Mambo No. 9" are almost archetypal, with their simple group-chanted vocals, the grunting "Unh!" in the breaks that became Prado's trademark, and their rolling sax riffs and stabbing brass phrasings. Another early work, "Mambo No. 8," uses similar ingredients to even greater effect, partly because the percussion is tighter and the brass writing more subtle.

Some of Prado's mass-popular works—notably "Moliendo Café"—rank as among the most awful works of their time; some, like "Cerazo Rosa," were extremely, if misplacedly, ingenious, others, like his piano version of "The Peanut Vendor," were essentially cocktail-lounge playing.

But Prado also frequently showed leanings toward a progressive mambo that lay somewhere in between Tito Puente and Stan Kenton (whom he greatly admired). By the mid-1950s, there were many signs of this: a little modal piano doodle at the end of "La Faraona," moments of subtle ensemble writing in many of his arrangements. Occasionally Prado would attempt a more large-scale approach. His "Concierto para Bongó" was an attempt at the kind of Latin-jazz suite that Kenton, Gillespie, and Johnny Richards were writing. A smaller-scale but more subtle example was his 1956 "Mosaico Cubano," which used percussion to separate its different sections, and contained some effective and even moving moments.

Yet ultimately Prado rarely transcended the problems

caused by his great popularity. The tension between the show-man and the creative artist has frequently been fruitful, as the work of both Machito and Puente illustrates. Even at his best, Prado's work almost always suffered from it; perhaps because he lacked a clearly defined constituency, capable of relating to both elements at once, so that he succumbed to the temptation to overmuch dilution posed by his considerable success during the early 1950s.

Puente and Rodriguez were largely protected from this temptation by their sizeable and knowledgeable Latin and non-Latin public—and perhaps by the security of a working life centered on the newly named Palladium Dance Hall, the center of the New York mambo in the 1950s. Yet while Prado could often be banal, and worse than banal, at his best he balanced authenticity and outreach as successfully as most Latin popu-larizers.

If Prado symbolized the mambo's impact on the American public at large, Tito Puente and Tito Rodriguez symbolized its creative achievement. The great era of the New York mambo can be said to date from 1952, when the Palladium Dance Hall switched to an all-mambo policy featuring the big bands of Puente, Rodriguez, and Machito.

Both Puente and Rodriguez's bands continued the Machito formula of swing orchestrations heavy on the brass, braced by a structure that preserved the Cuban coro and montunos, and a complete Afro-Cuban rhythm section. Rodriguez's band was a trifle smoother, its arrangements slightly simpler (perhaps be-cause Puente was as much of an arranger as he was a per-former). But though he was a masterful singer as strong as in the fast improvised *sonerismo* as in romantic boleros—his band was far from being secondary to his vocals.

At its peak, the Rodriguez band's blend of Cuban-oriented numbers and tight, solo-filled instrumentals equalled any of his rivals'. Among his vocal classics was his "Mama Guela": in a live version still available on record, this moves from slow brass fanfares straight into a brief montuno, then an extended passage of brass riffs, another montuno in which Rodriguez improvises from the start, a tight bop-tinged alto solo, more vocal, then a choppy, almost nervous mambo section.

Among Puente's recorded output, his *Dance Mania* album of 1958, which introduced singer Santos Colon, is perhaps the finest. Among his most influential early compositions was "Pa' los Rumberos," which was among the vehicles by which Santana was to create his fusion of rock and Latin music some ten years later.

Puente's sound was always busier and more nervous than Rodriguez's, based on heavier brass writing. His arranging, like his timbales playing, was fast, tight, jumpy, bravura. They stood almost in the same relation to their Cuban predecessors as Chicago jazz did to New Orleans.

Both in New York and on the West Coast, the top bands had many rivals. In 1952, Merced Gallego, playing tea dances in San Francisco's Sweets Ballroom, found himself dubbed the "king of the mambo" in California. In New York, in 1953, Curbelo played two highly successful weeks at the Apollo Theater opposite Ella Fitzgerald. Another very popular, often jazz-tinged, band was run by Alfredito—Brooklyn-born singer-vibraphonist Al Levy.

Alfredito, whose popularity in the 1950s almost matched that of the "big three," was not the first or the last Jewish Latin bandleader. In the 1930s Alfred Mendelsohn, known as Alfredo Mendez, had been instrumental in the early success of Bobby Capo, and in the 1960s and 1970s Larry Harlow was a leading *salsero*. Like the links between Latin and black musicians, the Jewish connection in New York Latin music is a strong one. Aside from bandleaders a large number of sidemen (and disc jockeys like Symphony Sid and Dick "Ricardo" Sugar) Latin music in New York always had a strong Jewish public. From Curbelo in the 1940s onward, almost every Latin musician of any note sooner or later played the Catskill resort hotels in the summer. In New York, in fact, Latin music's hard-core non-Latin audience was almost entirely "ethnic"—largely Jewish and Italian—and black.

In 1954, the mambo's year of maximum outreach, however, the mambo's audience was the entire country. The beginnings of the national buildup had been noted by *Variety*, in a 1953 story headlined, "New Vistas open for Latino bands; Hinterland Yens Mambo, Rhumba beat." By the following year, the hinterland was receiving them. An outfit called Mambo USA, which included Noro Morales, Miguelito Valdes, and Mongo Santamaria, toured widely. According to a spokesman of the largest agency then booking Latin groups, Tito Rodriguez, Ralph (Rafael) Font, La Playa Sextet, and Cesar Concepcion were particularly popular among Anglos, and got 25 percent more of the take than American bands because demand so far outran supply. In Harlem, the Savoy Ballroom and Apollo Theater had mambo nights on Mondays. The Palladium offered mambo lessons, an amateur contest, a show and dancing to two bands, all for $1.75. Most significantly of all, the jazz-based Music Box club changed its name to La Bamba and its music to Latin.

Like so many other aspects of Latin music, the mambo's origins are a subject of argument. As we have seen, the music was originally Cuban, but New York musicians so built on the root form as to create a New York style. The same is true of the dance. Though it has been claimed with almost certain truth that the basic steps of what became the mambo were danced in Cuba years before the dance got its name, New York Latinos, and notably the young Latino Palladium crowd, built a dance out of the neat, flowing yet bustling basic paterns and a thousand lindy-based variations. A contemporary definition in *Down Beat*, "rumba with jitterbug," put it as well as any.

Two distinct factors were involved in the gradual decline of Latin music from the national scene during the late 1950s. One, ironically enough, was the phenomenal success of the chachachá. In its original form, this was a product of the Cuban charangas. An adaptation of the second theme of the older danzón, it was made famous by one of the greatest of all charangas, the Orquesta Aragón. The chachachá, which swept Cuba in 1953, maintained a remarkable balance of fire and grace. In its original form (and as the charangas still play it in New York), it combined a clarity and crispness to which the flowing flute, the legato swing of the fiddle *guajeos*, and the sharp tone of the timbales—prominent in charanga rhythm sections—all contributed. The rhythm itself, with the triple fourth beat (the chachachá pattern from which the dance got its name and its characteristic double step ending each measure) was catchy, and compared with the Afro-Cuban mambo, simple.

When the new dance arrived in the U.S. in 1954, this

simplicity was without doubt one reason for its immediate success with dancers for whom the contemporary mambo was
overly demanding. But the chachachá that swept the U.S. was
not as the charangas played it. When New York bands played
Cuban compositions, they transcribed them for brass and reeds,
as Tito Puente did with the Orquesta Aragón's "Pare Cochero"
and the Orquesta America's "Rico Vacilon." Sometimes (Puente's
"Happy Cha Cha Cha" and "Cha Cha Cha de Pollos" are examples) a flute lead preserved something of the original flavor; but
when a violin was used, it usually only provided a bland flavoring
in the big-band style. The best of the New York chachachás—
numbers like Machito's "El Campesino" or José Curbelo's magnificent "El Pescador"—were in fact treated pretty much like
mambos.

The mid-tempo chachachá rhythm of "El Campesino" was
unmistakable, and the relatively ornate piano and unison vocal
both provided links with the charangas; but the tone as a whole
was set by the characteristic mambo-oriented stabbing brass and
rolling saxes. Curbelo opened "El Pescador" with brass chords,
before a magnificently precise duet vocal; again the New York
big-band sound dominated, this time with contrasting and inter-
linking trombone and trumpet riffs, both ensemble and solo, that
built tension unhurriedly over taut and subtle percussion.

Unfortunately, the chachachá's characteristic melody lines
and simple rhythms lent themselves to a dilution that was all the
more tempting because of its colossal success. The flood of
attempts to capitalize on its popularity swamped the elegant
original form. While the New York bands used its crispness and
clarity to form an effective contrast to the mambo's greater
density of sound and rhythm, the chachachá became corrupted
into something so simplistic as to be almost unrecognizable. Even
Stan Kenton, for all his experience in Latin-jazz, had problems
with it. Three chachachás featured in the 1959 album *Viva Kenton*
had effective ensemble writing and soloing, but the rhythm
pattern comes over as all too idiosyncratic.

As played by most American bands, in fact, the chachachá's
features were so exaggerated that it was almost a novelty number, and—like all novelty numbers—it burned out as fast as it
flared up. A few years of lumpy rhythm sections, mooing sax

sections, and musicians raggedly chanting CHAH! CHAH! CHAH! were enough.

Not all the mass-popular chachachás were without merit. Perez Prado's enormous hit, "Cerazo Rosa" (Cherry Pink and Apple Blossom White) was an effective piece of arranging, in which almost parodically languorous solo trumpet work, screaming ensemble brass, exaggerated contrasts between saxes, trumpets and trombones, and springy simplistic syncopation contributed to a witty whole. But none of its commercial rivals approached "Cerazo Rosa" in craftsmanship or originality. Even Prado himself never repeated it, though he tried.

The chachachá represented to some extent a case of self-destruction, but lowest-common-denominator commercialism was not the only factor in Latin music's disappearance from the national scene. Equally important was the rise of rock and roll. The roots of the new style—black rhythm-and-blues on the one hand and black-influenced white country music on the other—seemed far removed from anything Latin. True, Mexican music supposedly had an impact on white rock and roll singers in the late 1950s, when Buddy Holly played a style sometimes labelled "Tex Mex." Wherever the label comes from, however, virtually no Mexican influence is discernible in Holly's music.

Holly played what has been called a "dense yet open" guitar, described by British critic Dave Laing as "a unique metallic sound where each chord echoes into the next," and it is true that this sound was also associated with Ritchie Valens, another southwestern rock singer who did use occasional Mexicanisms and was himself part Chicano. But there is little to link Holly's music with any Chicago or Mexican sounds, and a great deal of similarity with the guitar work of black musicians Chuck Berry and Bo Diddley. Though rock was later to take in Mexican and Chicano influences, Buddy Holly seems to have had little to do with the process.

The decline of Latin music's popularity was really noticeable only in retrospect. At the beginning of the 1950s, it still formed an important and remarkably varied element in Tin Pan Alley. The mambo and the chachachá did not totally displace older styles. The samba had become part of the standard social-dance repertoire, and even the rumba was still sufficiently popular that the Dance Guild could put out a booklet called "Rumba Made Easy" as late as 1956. More remarkable still, the tango was still very much alive after almost forty years: a Decca recording of Leroy Anderson's "Blue Tango" sold more than a million copies in 1952. Frankie Laine's "Jealousy"—a version of "Jalousie" that preserved the tango rhythm—was another success. The bolero meanwhile was gradually becoming naturalized as a basis for sentimental ballads like Patti Page's "All My Love."

One of the most peculiar phenomena of early 1950s popular music was a singer with a four-octave range, Yma Sumac. Said to have been born Zoila Imperatriz Chararri Sumac del Castillo in the Peruvian Andes, Yma Sumac came to the U.S. in 1947 and sang at Carnegie Hall and with the Montreal and Toronto symphony orchestras. After an appearance with the Hollywood Bowl Orchestra, she recorded an album in 1950 called *Voice of the Xtabay*, which sold over half a million copies.

Yma Sumac's success was based on novelty. But the more conventional Latin and semi-Latin styles were regarded by the music business as a sure standby in hard times even before the success of the mambo and chachachá. In July, 1952, *Variety* ran a headline, "Music Execs Again Look to Latin Music To Bail Them Out of Music Slump." The story beneath reported that "such Latino-flavored tunes as *Kiss of Fire, Delicado, Mi Capital, Poinciana* and *More than Love* have been getting a big push on both pub and disker levels."

Variety also documented an unsuccessful attempt to promote the northeast Brazilian baião, "a new Brazilian rhythm with a syncopated quality that fits easily into current pop tastes." This had appeared in the U.S. in August the previous year, when the Antobal Music Co. announced publication of a baião called "The Happy Bird."

Unlike the samba before it and the bossa nova after, the baião never really caught on. But it did produce an interesting pre-figuration of the bossa nova. Saxist-flutist Bud Shank and guitarist Laurindo Almeida were members of a Hollywood-based quartet which played jazz-baião in a local club, and in 1953 recorded a 10-inch jazz-baião album for Pacific Jazz, *Brazilliance*. Its flute-led sound rested heavily on Almeida's classical-oriented acoustic guitar playing, in an almost eerie prefiguring of the gentle almost chamber-music quality of the early 1960s jazz-bossa recordings of Charlie Byrd, Almeida, Stan Getz, and others, as well as of their Rio originals.

The slippage of Latin music throughout the 1950s was particularly noticeable on Broadway. Several musicals contained the by now almost traditional Latin number or two. Among them were the 1952 "Don José of Far Rockaway" from *Wish You Were Here*, and two enormously successful songs: "Hernando's Hideaway," from the 1954 *Pajama Game*, a monument both to the tango's durability and Broadway's continued talent for squeezing juice out of apparently long empty fruit, and (in the following year) "Whatever Lola Wants, Lola Gets," an Americanized bolero from *Damn Yankees*, both by the same songwriting team, Richard Adler and Jerry Bach.

But the Latin impulse in stage musicals was dying fast. *West Side Story*, which was first staged in 1957, and filmed in 1961, used Manhattan's growing Latin population and ethnic tensions as its themes. Latin actresses—Chita Rivera and Rita Moreno respectively—had notable successes in the stage and film versions. Musically, the ensemble number "America" caught a little of the New York Latin flair, and "Maria" was in the standard international-bolero rhythm. But *West Side Story* totally failed to recapture the fiery mambos that were the music of Bernstein's real-life prototypes.

The era of the Latin film musical was also drawing to a close. The 1950 *Nancy Goes to Rio* was essentially the *Down Argentine Way* formula of ten years earlier, and even starred Carmen Miranda herself, along with Jane Powell and Ann Sothern, both by now old hands at the genre. Though the 1952 *The Fabulous Señorita* featured a newcomer, Rita Moreno, Latin musicals had become set into an overly familiar pattern, using overly familiar stars, and neither new directors nor new artists were interested in what was by now a hackneyed genre. Nor, as Latin music's popularity began to decline, did non-musical films often contain a featured Latin number. One of the last to do so was *Port Afrique*, in which "Una Aventura Mas" was sung—badly—by Pier Angeli.

Latin music's weakening position on Tin Pan Alley was much less obvious. First it reached perhaps its greatest overt influence in 1954, with the impact of the chachachá and the mambo. Nat "King" Cole recorded an album called *Papa Loves Mambo*, and there was a rash of pieces like saxist Earl Bostic's "Mambostic," Rosemary Clooney's successful "Mambo Italiano," and Sophie Tucker's "Middle Aged Mambo" and "St. Louis Blues Mambo."

Dancers who might have been confused by the new fashion were reassured by Mrs. Arthur Murray that the mambo was "the rhumba—with a jitterbug accent." Though quaint, that was quite a penetrating description. The mambo owed a great deal to jazz, from which it borrowed instrumental solos (and often soloists) and ensemble writing techniques, as well as a general big-band brashness that was distinctively American.

The mambo was also hugely influential on black popular music, which was going through very important changes as jazz and the blues (in the form of the popular 1940s "jump" blues) grew slowly apart. Infusions of mainstream popular music fed into the formation of the new style called rhythm-and-blues— and rhythm-and-blues (which was, like all black styles, an important source for Tin Pan Alley) was eventually the vehicle for the return of the Latin tinge to mass-popular music.

While rock-and-roll appeared to turn away from Latin inflections, in fact, rhythm-and-blues was increasingly affected by them. One line of influence came from New Orleans, and entered mass-popular rhythm-and-blues via the piano playing of Antoine "Fats" Domino, which had a markedly Latin cast. Domino acquired much of his style from an older New Orleans pianist, "Professor Longhair," whose real name is Roy Byrd. Byrd, who recorded an album called *Mardi Gras in New Orleans* for Atlantic in 1950, has described his own playing variously as a "combination of offbeat Spanish beats and calypso downbeats," and "a mixture of rumba, mambo and calypso." Given that the Latin component in earlier New Orleans music seems to have been a good deal stronger than has been generally recognized, Byrd's style probably represented a refocusing of more widespread elements. In any event, his Latinized New Orleans piano rhythms became part of mainstream rock-and-roll during the 1950s.

Another source of rhythm-and-blues' Latin tinge was more immediate. Arnold Shaw, in his history of rhythm and blues, *Honkers and Shouters*, credits Atlantic Records with introducing

Latin meters and instruments during the late 1960s, citing a remark by Atlantic record producer Ahmet Ertegun that "the samba beat, guaracha, baião and other Afro-Cuban [sic] rhythms added color and excitement to the basic drive of r&b." In fact, the process began earlier than that, and the catalyst was the immense popularity of the mambo. In 1954, the year of the mambo's greatest popular outreach, Ruth Brown's "Mambo Baby" reached first place on the r&b record charts, and—surely by no coincidence—Lavern Baker's major hit, "Tweedle Dee," got much of its flair from a Latin-inflected riff that was essentially a simple onbeat clave pattern.

The examples of Latin-tinged 1950s rhythm-and-blues are many. Lloyd Glenn's "Old Time Shuffle Blues" set a conga-like pattern against the basic boogie beat. The Coasters, whose 1955 "Down in Mexico" used its Latinisms to humorous effect, also recorded a "Loop the Loop Mambo." More fundamentally, the powerful and idiosyncratic beat of Bo Diddley, which was to be enormously influential on later British rock, had Latin ingredients, and the maraccas (part of his sound since he formed a street trio in 1949) were integral to his major 1955 hits, "Bo Diddley" and "I'm a Man."

Bo Diddley's Latinisms may have been picked up in the air, or "on the street." But 1950s rhythm-and-blues developed an even more direct black-Latin link. Not only did small record company producers like George Goldner and Teddy Reig record both black and Latin music, and musicians like conga-player Ray Barretto play on many r&b dates, but in Harlem and the Bronx young blacks and Latins were making common musical cause. Several mid-1950s New York rhythm-and-blues groups combined black and Latin members, among them the Harptones and the Vocaleers, both locally successful at the time. More important was a quintet called the Teenagers which suddenly came into the limelight in 1956. Its home base was West 164th Street, and its five black and Latin singers were all in their early teens—except the lead singer, Frankie Lymon, who was only twelve.

Lymon's song, "Why Do Fools Fall In Love?," was a sudden immense hit, selling two million copies. The Teenagers appeared on the Ed Sullivan Show, toured with Bill Haley and the Comets, had a record-breaking engagement at the London Palladium. The

Teenagers collapsed and Lymon never repeated that early success, but he and singers like him were major influences on the
bugalú generation of young New York Latin singers.

The consolidation of rhythm-and-blues' rather eclectic Latin
tinge continued in 1957 with two sizeable successes. One was
Clyde McPhatter's lugubrious "Long Lone Nights," which uses a
marimba and a shuffle rhythm clearly influenced by the bolero.
More significant was Chuck Willis's "C. C. Rider," which was
based on much the rumba-inflected patterns that Fats Domino
had made popular.

The same rhythm was brought back into the mass-popular
mainstream in 1959 by Ray Charles's enormously successful,
"What'd I Say," which clearly portended the growing Latinization
of black music that was to take place throughout the 1960s.

Meanwhile, a similar, equally long-term, Latinization was
taking place in jazz. The problems that had plagued early Cubop
were gradually being overcome. Jazz historian Marshall Stearns
has remarked that as late as 1950 musicians at home in both
idioms were rare and in demand. But they were learning very
fast. The decade opened with a rarely surpassed jam, "Cubop
City," in which trumpeter Howard McGhee and tenorist Brew
Moore fronted the Machito Orchestra. The following year, the
Afro-Cubans recorded a more major work, an *Afro-Cuban Jazz
Suite,* with altoist Charlie Parker, tenorist Flip Phillips, and drummer Buddy Rich. (This was also to have included trumpeter
Harry Edison, but Edison was one jazzman who could not cope
with the contrasts between Latin and jazz rhythms.)

The *Afro-Cuban Jazz Suite* was an early example of that 1950s
Latin-jazz specialty, the multi-movement extended work. Its
composer, Chico O'Farrill, a Cuban trumpeter, moved to the U.S.
in 1948 as a result of hearing the first Gillespie-Pozo recordings.
After writing a few arrangements for Noro Morales, O'Farrill
joined Benny Goodman briefly. Taken as a whole, the *Afro-
Cuban Jazz Suite* shows definite formal advance on earlier extended
works. Comparing it with other Latin-oriented recordings by
Charlie Parker the same year sheds light on Parker's problems
with Latin fusions, as well as on the distinction between fully
developed Latin-jazz and jazz with a Latin tinge.

In March 1951, Parker recorded several numbers for which

José Mangual on bongó and Luis Miranda on conga were added to his regular musicians—pianist Walter Bishop, bassist Teddy Kotick, and drummer Roy Haynes. The results were, on the whole, lamentable. "My Little Suede Shoes" limps along on a semi-tango rhythm whose lack of clave hamstrings the percussionists and which all the others simply ignore. In "Un Poquito de Amor"—a Latin composition—Bishop plays a calypso vamp, and Parker is so ill at ease as to sound like a high school bandsman until the straight bop 4/4 rhythm takes over. The only adequately cohesive performance is the samba "Tico Tico," which Parker plays authoritatively while the Cuban rhythm section turns the beat into something between a calypso and a biguine. Like many later examples, this one suggests that the largely clave-less Brazilian rhythms adapt more easily to Latin-jazz than Cuban patterns.

Like many similar sessions, the results show that for Cuban drummers working within the truncated 4/4 jazz patterns rather than clave is like running one-legged. They also suggest that whether or not Parker liked playing with Latin groups, he either could not or would not do it effectively unless he was virtually forced to.

Significantly, when—as in the *Afro-Cuban Jazz Suite*—Parker was set off by a complete brass section and a full rhythm section, the results were far more successful. Though he remained intransigent as ever in the *Afro-Cuban Jazz Suite*, the setting was strong enough to contain him. In "Mambo," he takes off hard, fast, and lyrical from a dense mass of interweaving sax and trumpet riffs, while the percussion, in clave, smokes under him in a way far removed from the polite knocking to which jazz settings often reduced them.

Many jazzmen proved more attuned to Latin-jazz than Parker, but of them all, Dizzy Gillespie has always most thoroughly understood the style. In 1953, Gillespie recorded Ernesto Lecuona's "Siboney" as part of a quartet with tenorist Stan Getz. The format was the common one of Latin-rhythmed choruses interspersed with straight jazz time, yet the result was far more integrated than most similar work because Getz showed much of the understanding that was to flower during the bossa nova era ten years later, while Gillespie's melding of Latin rhythmic approaches and his own was totally seamless.

In 1954 Gillespie recorded a new, extended version of the 1947 *Manteca*, a four-movement work arranged by O'Farrill. The personnel blended Gillespie's current small group, several jazz-oriented studio musicians, including Lucky Thompson, and the Machito rhythm section plus conga-player Candido Camero. Gillespie's solo work throughout is totally appropriate to its setting, and his solo in the 6/8 "Jungla" is brilliant from the moment when he merges waist deep in inspiraciones through passages of passionately restrained lyricism to a close over spare supporting chords.

Gillespie's ease with Cuban rhythmic structures allowed him to go beyond merely playing with Latins into a Latinization of jazz itself. His "Siboney" was a true "Latin jazz" weighted on the jazz side, and it was achieved without any Latin musicians.

In October 1956, Getz and Gillespie returned to the studio with Sonny Stitt, pianist John Lewis, and guitarist Herb Ellis. One of the numbers they recorded was a version of "Otchi Tchernaya" (Dark Eyes). In the 1920s, this had been published as a "Russian Tango," and Gillespie's version used a curter and less languorous semi-tango rhythm behind the theme statement. Straight 4/4 backed the sax solos, but the Latin feel returned with Herb Ellis's bongó playing, the mambo-like sax riffs behind Gillespie's solo, and the bassist's brisk held-note patterns, like the first part of the habanera rhythm, under Lewis's piano solo.

Gillespie was not the only bandleader who was still working seriously with Latin-jazz. The same year, Stan Kenton recorded a long work by composer/arranger Johnny Richards, the suite *Cuban Fire*, each of whose movements is based on a different Cuban rhythm. "People like Willie Rodriguez (bongocero on the recording) . . . took me to dances, weddings, festivals and quite literally introduced me to every aspect of Latin American musical life available in New York," Richards has said.

At the time, Kenton made considerable claims for *Cuban Fire.*

The United States has never really had this kind of combination before. The people either like the rhythmic complexities and didn't mind the melody and harmony being slight, or they forgot the whole thing. If you wanted to be dramatic you should say that this album, besides being interesting in itself, really points the way toward a new use of Afro-Cuban rhythms.

In retrospect, *Cuban Fire* pointed the way nowhere. Like much of Kenton's "progressive jazz," Richards's writing augmented standard big-band writing with techniques brought in from conservatory music. Despite pompous moments, a real cohesion and musical logic held together what might have been three very disparate elements. But the jazz current was flowing away from the third-stream direction that Kenton had taken, and until the mid-1970s, *Cuban Fire* remained a solitary example of a style soon relegated to soundtracks. Then Chico O'Farrill returned with two compositions for Gillespie and the Machito orchestra, recorded under the title, *Afro-Cuban Jazz Moods*. Unlike the 1950s suites, these do not have sections based on different rhythms, but move from rhythm to rhythm within each movement. The classic brass-and-sax sound is enriched by O'Farrill's liking for lush harmonic writing and a singularly bravura display from Gillespie.

Besides *Cuban Fire*, Kenton also recorded a large number of small-scale works using a wide range of Latin rhythms, including the 1951 "Artistry in Tango"—a work whose overall effect is of a rather sinister parody—and the 1956 "Sophisticated Samba," as well as the tribute, "Viva Prado." Among the best of these short pieces were "Jam-Bo," with piano by Nat "King" Cole, and the magnificent "23°N-82°W" (named after Havana's map coordinates), with a rich clave opening for trombones and memorable solos by trombonist Frank Rosolino and altoist Lee Konitz.

During the late 1950s, the Cubop style gradually lost steam. In 1957 trombonist Jimmy Knepper recorded an attractive piece called "Idol of the Flies," notable for fine trombone playing and the traditional mix of jazz and Latin rhythms. But on the whole, the Latin element in jazz appeared to be becoming more marginal again. Fairly typical were the 1958 Riverside sessions pairing Red Garland and New York conga-player Ray Barretto. Garland played Ponce's "Estrellita" in almost as Americanized a style as Harry James had done in the early 1940s; though something of the habanera pulse can still be felt, Garland's piano phrasing tilted the rhythmic emphasis too far toward jazz. Barretto's work was perfectly adequate, but in musical terms it is essentially tacked on. The uptempo "Blues in Mambo" is more effective—but again, Barretto was basically there to justify the use of the word "mambo" in the title of what was essentially straight blues. The session was not the result of a commitment to Latin-jazz— Garland has said that "the mambo was popular then, and we were trying to . . . reach the Latin American audience"—and the result was lame.

Though the jazzmen's interest in Latin-jazz was waning by the late 1950s, the Latins' was not. The finest recorded example of the area where Latin-jazz and jazz-oriented mambo mingled was recorded in 1958. This was Machito's album, *Kenya* (later reissued as *Latin Soul Plus Jazz*). The soloists included Herbie Mann on flute, Joe Newman and Doc Cheatham on trumpet, Cannonball Adderley on alto sax, Johnny Griffin on tenor, and Patato Valdez and Candido Camero on congas. The fire and cohesion of the result surpasses almost every other example of the genre. The frontline writing combined mambo and bop runs, jazz soloists were perfectly adapted to the clave-based rhythms, the rhythm section stretched out in percussion improvisations as sophisticated as the wind soloing, and the previous gap between jazzmen and Latin musicians had totally vanished.

In reality, Latin jazz was not so much declining as changing its focus. New York jazz musicians might be losing interest, but California was not. The piano-and-rhythm style of the 1940s, which had often degenerated into superficial cocktail music, had been strengthened by an increasing infusion of jazz style, and during the late 1940s and early 1950s was transmuted into the Latin jazz quintet genre.

It is always dangerous to ascribe any fusion music primarily to one or other side of its equation, since—as in the case of Machito and the jazzmen with whom he played—developments mostly take place simultaneously in jazz and in Latin music. But the quintet style owes a great deal to two jazzmen. The first was Nat "King" Cole, whose efforts at popular outreach had, as we have seen, involved Latin music since the late 1940s. Even more important was British pianist George Shearing.

In 1949, Shearing had formed a successful bop-oriented quintet with a distinctive piano-and-vibes sound. In 1953, he reorganized his California-based group to reflect a definite Latin jazz orientation, hiring Willie Bobo on timbales, Cal Tjader on vibraphones, Mongo Santamaria on conga, and Armando Peraza on bongó. Peraza and Santamaria were both Cubans who had arrived in the U.S. together in 1950. Peraza had played for a while with Slim Gaillard, and Santamaria with Perez Prado. Tjader, a Swedish-American, had begun his professional career with pianist Dave Brubeck. East Harlemite Willie Bobo had early become involved with jazz, was Machito's band-boy for a while, then played with Tito Puente before joining Shearing.

The quintet's music was an odd hybrid of cocktail piano, small group bop, and a full Cuban percussion section. Though it was enormously popular at the time, it has been critically somewhat underrated for several reasons. The tight piano-vibraphone work had a dulcet quality that *sounded* a little trivial, and the band's repertoire included a lot of boleros and other slow numbers that fitted right into the background music image. But a still available album, *Latin Escapade*, shows that there was more to Shearing's quintet than that. Even relatively banal standards like "Perfidia" and "Old Devil Moon," though they open in cocktail vein, usually move into a montuno with a brisker rhythm and interesting improvisations, and in uptempo pieces like his own "Poodle Mambo" and Puente's "Mambo with Me," Shearing combines Cuban and bop piano techniques with results that, though often subdued, were always interesting.

Shearing's large popular success was another example of the fact that jazz has frequently reached its widest audiences in Latin fusions. It also gave impetus to the whole jazz quintet movement, for it had the economic advantages of a small group at a time when most big bands were in financial trouble.

All four of Shearing's own musicians were to be important in 1960s and 1970s fusion music, and the work they did then was begun in the 1950s. Tjader began recording under his own name in 1954. Santamaria also recorded a number of important albums toward the end of the 1950s, most of which reflected a combination of jazz and pure Afro-Cuban styles.

Meanwhile various Latin musicians were adopting the quintet (or sextet) style. José Curbelo formed a quintet that at one time featured jazz tenorist Al Cohn; and in 1954 Gilberto Calderón organized the extremely popular Joe Cuba Sextet. Other Latins contributed to the small-group Latin-jazz style in a more free-lance capacity. Notable among them was the brilliant Cuban saxist-violinist José "Chombo" Silva, who toured Europe with James Moody in 1950, participated in a series of epochal jam sessions in Havana in 1956, and recorded on four of Tjader's best early albums, besides playing with Machito, Cesar Concepción, and René Touzet.

While the developments of the 1960s were to be much more significant, the 1950s were also a time of flux for Chicano music. In particular, the influence of Mexican ranchera music showed up in longer, more decorated instrumental runs, and a more impassioned—often exaggerated—and less typically folk style of singing. Typically, the style of the popular Trio San Antonio, a norteño group with traditional instrumentation, showed a new crispness. The rancheras themselves began to rival the older corridos in importance in the work of bands like Los Donneños. At the same time new instruments were introduced, as in Los Hermanos Prado's fine performance of the ranchera "A Puña-ladas," which used a saxophone playing what was essentially a mariachi trumpet part, as well as playing in unison with the accordion.

The Cuban bolero also began to be popular at the end of the decade, a development that was to affect Anglo-American country music to an increasing extent. This was a later development, however, for very little Mexican influence showed up in the country music of the 1950s, though Marty Robbins wrote a saga ballad called "El Paso" that showed strong corrido influences.

For most of the 1950s, the overall tendency in Latin music was a continuation and consolidation of the various syncretizing movements. Not only was the big-band mambo the first clearly North-American Latin style, but for the first time Latin inflections were beginning to be part and parcel of American music.

At the end of the decade, however, a contrary movement got underway: the reaffirmation of Latin elements. On one level this was nothing new. While the most influential of the new big bands in the 1940s, such as Machito's Afro-Cubans, made great use of Americanisms, they also—as we have seen—reinforced the Cuban side of the equation both rhythmically and structurally. Despite its negative aspects, the chachachá was part of a similar movement: one of its effects was to reintroduce the flute as an important Latin instrument. Herbie Mann made a number of excellent recordings with Machito—before forming his own Latin-oriented group in 1959. A veteran charanga flutist, José Lozardo, played with Cal Tjader in California, and a number of young musicians became interested in the instrument. But Cuban-style flute playing really came into its own at the end of the decade, when the charanga format suddenly caught on in New York. Though Gilberto Valdez had led a New York-based charanga in the early 1950s and the great Cuban flutist Fajardo played with his All-Stars at the Waldorf Astoria and the Palladium in 1959, the major vehicle for the craze was a group started by New York pianist Charlie Palmieri.

Palmieri, who had led various small groups after working with Pupi Campo and other major New York midtown bands, was typical of many influential Puerto Rican and Newyorican musicians who have been almost as enthusiastic about jazz as about Cuban music. This dual enthusiasm has been crucial to the growth of U.S. salsa.

During the late 1950s, Palmieri's group was playing a number of compositions by the great Cuban charanga, the Orquesta Aragón, adapted to a trumpet-led format. In late 1959, Palmieri heard a young percussionist called Johnny Pacheco practicing the flute in the kitchen of a club where he was playing, and hired him. Shortly afterward he moved to a full charanga format by adding violins. On New Year's Eve of 1959–60, Charlie Palmieri's Charanga Duboney, with Pacheco on flute, played its first dance and set what was to be a revolution in motion.

The charanga fad of the early 1950s was only part of a revitalization that also involved several non-Cuban styles. The first was the Dominican merengue. Merengues had been played in 1940s New York: Aside from the Americanized work of Damiron and Chapuseau, a merengue group—Josecito Roman— played the first Latin date at what was later to become the Palladium. But it was in the early 1950s that the authentic típico merengue sound was introduced, when Angel Viloria organized a group with accordion and sax lead, playing the rural style associated with the northern Dominican province of Cibao.

Viloria's band contained a number of musicians who were to become a part of the general New York Latin scene, among them his vocalist, Dioris Valladares, and the tambora drummer. Luis

Quintero, who joined Viloria in 1952 and formed his own merenge group in 1954.

While the merengue never had the runaway success of the major Cuban rhythms on the American market, it did become a permanent part of social dance, its brisk, sideways-stepping two-step swing being relatively easy to master. Meanwhile, merengue groups soon began the blending process. Dioris Valladares was to record with one of the hottest of jazz-influenced recording groups, the Alegre All-Stars, and Luis Quintero's merengue group featured at least one Puerto Rican singer, Mon Rivera, who himself ran a popular group featuring the Puerto Rican plena.

The plena had been reintroduced into the big band format in the 1940s by Cesar Concepcion. In 1957 it was brought back into fashion by Rafael Cortijo, an Afro-Rican percussionist and bandleader with a sensational lead singer, Ismael Rivera.

Cortijo, who came from the village of Loiza Aldea, a center of Afro-Rican music, had a considerable knowledge of its folk forms. Aside from scoring successes with plenas by Canario and others, he also introduced the three-drum Afro-Rican bomba to the dance format in 1957. Though their instrumental sound was that of the prevailing brass-and-sax frontline, recordings such as "El Bombón de Elena" and the ravishing "Caballero que Bomba" depended partly on the sure improvisations, brilliant timing, and husky voice of Ismael Rivera, but they were also strongly Puerto Rican in their use of female voices in the coro and their ability to tinge the fastest numbers with melancholy. Like the big merengue bands, Cortijo y Su Combo brought professionalism to a sound that preserved much of the small-town típico quality and provided an important balance to the big-city ethos of the 1940s and the mambo era.

Cortijo's music was rich in a quality that confuses non-Latins and perhaps contributes to misunderstanding of Latin music. On the one hand, his attachment to tradition goes far beyond lip service. In the 1970s he was to produce the most avant-garde recording in the entire field. Yet he also regards himself as an entertainer who "plays for the people." That mix, long gone from most jazz, is still strong in Latin music, and the tension implicit in it ran through the whole of the 1960s.

As far as the greater American public was concerned, the mambo meant only one person: Cuban pianist Perez Prado.
BMI Archives

The young Tito Rodriguez, one of the "big three" in the high days of the Palladium Dance Hall.
BMI Archives

Tito Puente, bandleader, timbalero, vibraphonist, composer, arranger—and New York's contender for the title, "King of the Mambo."
Jay Photography

Brazilian guitarist Laurindo Almeida and reedman Bud Shank teamed for a 1950s preview of the bossa nova in an album of jazz-baião.
Bill Claxton, courtesy Pacific Jazz Records

The new style called rhythm-and-blues was influenced by Latin music almost from the start. An early example was the 1954 "Mambo Baby," by Ruth Brown.
BMI Archives

Dizzy Gillespie, a pioneer of Cubop, was also a pioneer of extended Latin-jazz suites during the 1950s.
Prestige Records

Major figures of the Cubop movement: Stan Getz, Machito, Mario Bauza, Charlie Parker.
Mario Bauza

Among the most notable of Latin-r&b fusions was the idiosyncratic and highly influential rhythmic approach of Bo Diddley.
BMI Archives

The 1950s were a peak period for southwestern Chicano music, and among the leading norteño groups was Los Alegres de Teran.
Courtesy Chris Strachwitz, Arhoolie Records

The true father of U.S. jazz-bossa, guitarist Charlie Byrd, missed the fame it brought others.
Steve Zweig

The bossa nova's huge popularity was a triumph of jazz-Latin fusions. Left to right, Stan Getz, Antonio Carlos Jobim, and singer Astrud Gilberto.
W. H. Schneider

The Cuban influence continued in the quintet style of California vibraphonist Cal Tjader.
Fantasy Records

Conga player Mongo Santamaria's 1960s groups laid the foundation of the threeway jazz–Latin–r&b fusions of the following decade.
BMI Archives

Chicano and Mexican music came back to national attention in the early 1960s through the recordings of Trini Lopez.
BMI Archives

During the 1960s Chicano music took on a tough, flashing quality owing much to black idioms. Accordionist Flaco Jimenez (left) was a leader of the new style.
Courtesy Chris Strachwitz, Arhoolie Records

In 1960, a totally new fusion was created by the rock-salsa blendings of a young San Francisco group led by Carlos Santana (left).
BMI Archives

Johnny Pacheco, a leader of New York salsa on charisma and a boundless enthusiasm for a pure Cuban sound.
David Haas

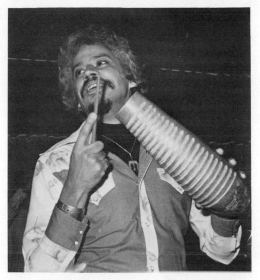

Conga-player Ray Barretto has maintained a career-long involvement with crossover styles as well as with pure salsa.
David Haas

Percussionist Ralph MacDonald spread black-Latin fusions very wide as a major studio musician.
TK Records

Willie Colon, veteran of the bugalu era and among the most creative of 1970s salsa talents.
David Haas

Brazilian percussionist Airto, here playing a berimbau, helped make his country's rhythms an enduring part of jazz.
David Haas

Eddie Palmieri extended the boundaries of 1970s salsa with electronic experiments and modal piano playing.
David Haas

Argentinian tenorist Gato Barbieri's fusions covered far wider Latin-American ground than any before them.
David Haas

Freddy Fender, Chicano recruit into the
ranks of country music.
ABC Records

*In California, Latin-jazz remained healthy in the hands of men like Joe Henderson (left),
and Luis Gasca (right), seen here with producer Orrin Keepnews.*
Fantasy Records

Though Latin rhythms have had an enormous influence worldwide, almost the only Latin bandleader to build a career in Europe was Britain's Edmundo Ros.
BMI Archives

Most famous of all Chicano-influenced artists of the 1970s was soft-rock singer Linda Ronstadt.
'Jim Shea, courtesy Asylum Records

SEVEN

The 1960s:
Going Underground

The apparent retrenchment of Latin music continued during the 1960s. The Cuban-based core style returned to its island roots. Hollywood lost interest. Popular music had a last fling with Brazilian music early in the decade and then passed on. Cubop was hardly a memory as the creative cutting edge of jazz became involved in the New Thing, with its emphasis on polytonality, free rhythm, and other elements borrowed from the European avant-garde.

Yet many respects, the 1960s were a particularly crucial decade in the Latinization of American popular music. In earlier eras, its Latin ingredients had been persistent but fairly marginal, and the most popular versions of Latin compositions were often de-Latinized beyond recognition. Throughout the 1960s, however, in the words of salsa bandleader Ray Barretto, "The whole basis of American rhythm . . . changed from the old dotted-note jazz shuffle rhythm to a straightahead straight-eighth approach, which is Latin."

As far as popular music was concerned, this process was far from obvious at the time. On the contrary, the era of Latin influence appeared to be over. On Broadway, the 1960 musical *Wildcat* included a song called "El Sombrero," but that was pretty much the last of the Latin feature numbers in stage musicals;

Hollywood was abandoning the musical as a genre, and the only Latin-American theme was a rock-and-roll vehicle, Elvis Presley's 1963 *Fun in Acapulco.* In mass-popular music—from the 1961 "Mexico" to the 1969 "Lo Mucho Que Te Quiero"—Latin titles continued to surface. But with the exception of the 1962–64 bossa nova rage, most were individual exceptions to a general rule, momentary novelties like "Twist, Twist Señora," and very occasional crossovers via rhythm-and-blues—notably Ray Barretto's 1962 million-selling "El Watusi" and Joe Cuba's 1966 "Bang Bang."

In the New York Latin heartland, the beginning of the decade was taken up with a major craze for the charanga. Charlie Palmieri's Duboney, with Johnny Pacheco on flute, became so popular during 1960 that the band was working several dances each night. Palmieri used four violins to catch the full, but never sticky sound of his Cuban idols, the Orquesta Aragón; Pacheco's crisp but lyrical flute provided an almost perfect foil. The Duboney swung mightily, and it ranged over a wide repertoire of both Cuban and what Palmieri calls "continental Latin" cocktail pieces.

The Duboney brought about a sonic revolution. For more than twenty years, the dominant sound in hot New York Latin music had been brass and saxes. Now it was flute and violins. But there was much more to the charanga style than that—a distinctive duet singing style, a rhythm section in which the crisp timbales sound dominated, and quite as important, a classicism of sound and form that gave the charangas a grace and tension quite new to the New York scene.

Within a year, New York was full of new bands. The charanga introduced or reintroduced several major Cuban flutists, notably the great Fajardo, Pupi Legarreta, and Belisario Lopez, besides Alberto Socarrás, who returned to record a couple of albums. Among the younger musicians, Pacheco split off from Palmieri to form a group with a somewhat brasher, younger sound. Cuban singer Roberto Torres founded what was to prove one of the longest-lived of New York charangas, the cooperative Orquesta Broadway.

In 1961, conga-player Ray Barretto formed a charanga to

record for Riverside Records, and went on to make a number of "crossover" recordings, including a surprisingly elegant version of "Greensleeves," and his novelty piece, "El Watusi." That same year, percussionists Mongo Santamaria and Willie Bobo formed a charanga called La Sabrosa, which was to be extremely influential outside the traditional Latin market.

Most of the new groups lasted the three years or so that it took for the charanga to lost its novelty. But several—notably Broadway, Legarreta's group, and the Orquesta Tipica Novel—remained to provide a permanent alternative sound, always present though never dominating until another rise in interest during the late 1970s.

Two factors consolidated the U.S. charangas. One was a new dance associated with them, the fast and syncopated *pachanga*, which became almost as much of a rage in Latin New York as the chachachá had been nationally. The other was the U.S.'s break in diplomatic relations with Cuba in 1960–61.

For twenty years, American-Latin musicians—many of them Puerto Ricans to whom Cuban music was at least slightly alien—had been an important part of the Americanizing tendencies that had established a recognizable U.S. Latin substyle. Meanwhile, the still substantial market for típico Cuban music had been met by visiting bands. This was no longer possible. Yet a growing Cuban refugee population added to the demand for the downhome sound, and gave the Cubanizing trend that was already setting in by the turn of the decade a powerful impetus on which a new generation of New York Latin musicians came to prominence.

The U.S. charanga movement was by no means purely imitative of its Cuban models. Mongo Santamaria's Sabrosa in particular combined the classic charanga sound of flute and violins, with jazz-oriented soloing from brass and saxophone soloists, varying the formula from track to track. The results were not really Latin-jazz—the balance was too heavily tipped toward the Latin side of the equation—but included some singularly fine jazz playing, notably from the brilliant Cuban tenorist, José "Chombo" Silva. La Sabrosa, out of which came "Afro-Blue"—virtually a jazz standard of the 1960s—was in fact an early example of the fusion approach that was to make Mongo Santamaria such an important figure in the gradual Latinization of black music.

Around 1965 the charangas vanished almost as suddenly as they had come, perhaps because they were simply too opposed to the general sonic drift of 1960s music, perhaps—as has been suggested—because the pachanga was too energetic a dance to be more than a fad, and they had become too closely associated with it.

Even at their height, the charangas had never ousted all other formats. In 1960, one of the new generation of band-leaders, Orlando Marin, formed a flute-led Latin-jazz sextet featuring the jazz-oriented scat singing of Francisco Fellove, and in 1962 he expanded to a big band. The long-established Machito, Tito Puente, and Tito Rodriguez big bands continued to flour-ish—Rodriguez indeed had two notable hits in 1962, "Vuela la Paloma" and "Cuando Cuando."

Big bands were becoming less and less possible economically, however, and most of the younger bandleaders turned to a pure Cuban trumpet conjunto sound (as did Johnny Pacheco), to a variant adding one trombone, or to a modified orquesta with a frontline consisting of two trumpets, flute, and trombone.

Notable among this new crop of bandleaders were Ray Barretto, Johnny Pacheco, and Eddie Palmieri, whose careers illustrate clearly the diversity of the típico current in New York Latin music. All three belonged to the first large generation of New York-born Latinos, and their music reflects this fact.

Barretto—born in Brooklyn but raised in El Barrio—grew up listening to his mother's Machito albums by day and jazz radio programs by night. After early experience playing with black servicemen in Germany, he found his way to Minton's and the Apollo Bar in bop-era Harlem, where he jammed with musicians like Roy Haynes, Max Roach, Sonny Stitt, and Charlie Parker. In the mid-1950s he joined José Curbelo's band, then moved to Tito Puente and Herbie Mann. He also began to record with jazzmen like Red Garland, Lou Donaldson, Gene Ammons, and Cannon-ball Adderley.

In 1961 Barretto turned bandleader, forming a charanga for

a Riverside date, and recording subsequent charanga albums for Roulette and United Artists. In 1967, he switched to Fania Records for a conjunto album with rhythm and blues touches called *Acid.* In succeeding albums, he moved between strongly Cuban material and salsa with black elements. Typical were the clarity and passion of the title track, with its clean opening for bass and percussion under bop-inflected muted trumpet leading to extended percussion improvisations, and the somewhat similar blend of jazz, Afro-Cuban, and New York salsa elements in "Abidjan," from the 1968 *Hard Hands* album.

Pacheco, who came to prominence as flutist with Charlie Palmieri's groundbreaking charanga in 1960, had worked as a percussionist with various well-known groups, including Puente's, and had also recorded with jazz guitarist George Benson. Pacheco was one of the first to move to the pure conjunto form. His music showed little or none of the big-city drive of most New York bands, but reflected the Caribbean joy of its Cuban origins very closely—some said too closely, especially in the early days. Pacheco, in fact, was a little like the young jazz revivalists of the 1940s, whose relationship to their models was, according to your point of view, imitation or preservation. But Pacheco's bands always conveyed the music's original verve, and as much as on his playing or creative innovation, his long-term success has rested on personal charisma and an instantly communicated enthusiasm for Latin music.

After a period in the 1950s playing with other bands— notably Tito Rodriguez's—Eddie Palmieri founded his own first group, La Perfecta, in 1961, at the height of the charanga craze. La Perfecta had a flute-and-trombone frontline that his brother Charlie nicknamed a trombanga. (There is dispute as to whether he or Puerto Rican bandleader Mon Rivera originated the trombone frontline.)

Writer-broadcaster Pablo "Yoruba" Guzman has rightly called La Perfecta "one of those seminal units in musical history." Palmieri's first major success—"Muñeca," from his third album—showed the beginnings of the almost agonized swing that was to ensure a wide audience for his developing experimentalism. Palmieri's sound, which rested partly on trombonist

Barry Rogers's admiration for J. J. Johnson and Kai Winding, was the progenitor of a wave of trombone conjuntos in the mid-1960s.

"Muñeca" itself foreshadowed many of Palmieri's 1970s trademarks. Lead singer Ismael Quintana's purity of tone and improvisation; Palmieri's modal opening, reminiscent of McCoy Tyner, to a piano solo that developed in classically Cuban patterns; above all the strangely ambiguous brass sound, at once driving and despairing, were all hints of what was to come.

La Perfecta disbanded in 1968, and Palmieri began a period of struggle with personal and professional problems, out of which came some of the most important music of the 1970s. Its essence was an experimentalism combining a strong sense of Cuban tradition with a modal piano style that was the result of his admiration for McCoy Tyner. The 1969 *Justicia* album contains the germ of Palmieri's ever-lengthening free-form piano introductions in an inspired doodle on "My Spiritual Indian" and a breathtaking solo in "Verdict on Judge Street," besides a fine example of Palmieri's instinct for the past in a revival of the magnificent Rafael Hernandez bolero, "Amor Ciego."

The variety in these men's approaches reflects the fact that two streams developed in mid-1960s Latin music. Though the "return to the roots" continued in an emphasis on classic Cuban numbers and forms, American ingredients also remained strong.

Jazz continued to be a powerful force in New York Latin music—paradoxically, in a form introduced via Cuba. In 1956, the Havana recording company of Panart had organized a series of night-long jam sessions featuring many of Cuba's best musicians in long *descargas* mixing classic Cuban idioms with extended jazz solos in a far looser format than any of its predecessors. These recordings—the *Cuban Jam Sessions*—had a considerable impact on 1960s New York. While the charanga's popularity was at its height, Charlie Palmieri—whose enthusiasm for jazz was as strong as his love for classic Cuban music—became musical director of a series of descargas (the word, "discharge," is used by Latin musicians to mean a jam session) for Alegre Records, whose owner and producer, Al Santiago, was another jazz buff.

Though the Latin jam sessions involved Cuban, Puerto

Rican, and Newyorican musicians of several generations, they were essentially a product of the jazz-oriented tastes of the first generation of New York-born musicians. They were not Latin-jazz in the same sense as Cubop or other styles involving non-Latin jazzmen, though some of Machito's vocal pieces—"Mango Mangüe" and the like—came near it. Palmieri's Alegre All-Stars preserved the three-part Cuban form, but extended the mambo section into a solo vehicle far looser than anything attempted by Machito and the other big bands. The results, with their head (spontaneous) arrangements and sense of freedom and flow, were true jam sessions.

At their best the Alegre All-Stars' jazz-Latin fusions remain among the peaks of the style. Though none of the musicians involved were of the solo caliber of Charlie Parker or Dizzy Gillespie, several—notably saxist "Chombo" Silva—could out-blow most lesser jazzmen. In addition, since they were at ease with both jazz and Latin music, their work meshed the two elements better than almost any of its predecessors. The Alegre All Star sessions were studio-recorded, but in jam-session conditions, and the musicians were allowed to stretch out at will. The music's framework was strongly Latin, with the three-part head-*coro*-mambo form, and the traditional vocal *sonerismo:* but the solos were lengthy, jazz-based and searingly hot. The result was an almost perfect balance of jazz and Latin elements.

The Alegre All-Stars produced a half dozen or so albums, and a hundred imitations. Pacheco recorded an excellent "Flute and Latin Jam" that brought young New Yorkers and older Cubans together in a hybrid of jazz and charanga very like Mongo Santamaria and Ray Barretto's earlier examples. For a while, regular descarga nights were held at the Village Gate and the Red Garter in Greenwich Village. (The Red Garter sessions were the birth of the Fania All-Stars.) But one of the tightest Latin-jazz recordings ever made was by a small group of Latins and non-Latins who played in Latin bands. *Sabu's Jazz-Espagnole* was led by conga-player Sabu Martinez, who had played with Dizzy Gillespie, Art Blakey, and Charlie Parker, as well as Noro Morales and Miguelito Valdes.

The other really significant development in 1960s New York

Latin music was also a result of the Newyoricans' twin culture; but it sprang from a generation largely uninterested in jazz. This was the Latin bugalú, which blended the mambo with early black rock-and-roll, and was the first, and only, uptown Latin form to use largely English lyrics. Bandleader Willie Rosario—who did not approve of it—called it "American music played with Latin percussion."

The bugalú threw up a new generation of musicians, many of them very young, and—like the rock-and-rollers who inspired them—often musically very inexperienced. Their music was brash, and ignored many of the sacred cows of Cuban-derived orthodoxy. It was also exhilarating, and a genuine reflection of the impact of 1960s black music on young Latins.

The first recorded bugalús appeared on Brooklyn pianist Ricardo Ray's initial album, *Se Soltó*. The most important early singles, all issued in 1966, were Pete Rodriguez's "I Like It Like That," Johnny Colon's "Boogaloo Blues," and Joe Cuba's "Bang Bang." This last recording, the first bugalú to sell a million copies, reached considerable numbers of black teenagers, as did Hector Rivera's 1967 "At The Party," even though Cuba and Rivera were older than the "bugalú generation," and essentially co-opted a style that they did not create.

The bugalú generation did not simply imitate black music, but incorporated it in a sound that fused Latin rhythms and piano montunos with rhythm-and-blues and even jazz (Ricardo Ray recorded with Doc Cheatham, as Machito had done before him). Though the lyrics were English, the singing style was New-yorican, a slightly zany, good-humored, no-nonsense sound with as much Cuban as black gospel flavor. The bugalú groups also favored a modified conjunto sound with two trombones, developed from Eddie Palmieri's flute-and-trombone frontline, which was an important part of the style. But the rhythm work was far more strongly Latin than rhythm-and-blues, making use of the complete range of percussion instruments.

The bugalú was a fairly flexible style, and many bugalús were very close to mambos. Johnny Colon's lengthy "Boogaloo Blues" was one of the richest examples, with its slow *choong*-chicka son-montuno-like rhythm, its free-rhythm chanted English vocals, and repetitive trombone phrases building a brooding tension that was peculiar to New York, and was to be echoed in much of Willie Colon's best work of the next decade. By contrast, Joe Cuba's "Bang Bang" was an amiably rowdy piece whose main selling point was its double-entendre lyrics.

For two or three years the bugalú seemed to be the coming thing, and the acme of the young Latin New Yorker. Yet by 1969 it was dead, and another wave of purist Cubanism was under way. Many musicians of the bugalú generation are still convinced that they were sabotaged by agents and promoters, all older and—they said—tied into the more established musicians. Opponents retort that the bugalú was a fad, and that most bugalú musicians could not play well enough to survive beyond its fading.

Many of them did survive, though mostly as sidemen. Joe Bataan—a part Filipino, part-black singer who specialized in an offshoot of bugalú called Latin soul—went on to make a minor disco hit in the 1970s. Another, Willie Colon, was to be among the most creative and innovative bandleaders of the 1970s. Born in New York in April 1950, Colon began playing trumpet at the age of twelve. He switched to trombone when he was fourteen and formed a twelve-piece group, the Latin Jazz All-Stars. His graduation to professional musicianship came when he was refused a place in the high school band and dropped out of school. Soon afterward, he adopted the two-trombone frontline made popular among his contemporaries by Eddie Palmieri.

Colon scored an almost immediate and major success, helped by an ingenious and amusing "bad man" publicity joke (all his ablums have played with variations on the theme). Though he was theoretically almost unknown, his first album, *El Malo*— recorded in 1967, when he was only 17—sold some 30,000 copies, as much as many established salsa artists' albums. *El Malo* was distinguished from most other bugalú material by an unusually high proportion of instrumentals and solos, lyrics with a strongly realist New York flavor, and a jaunty rhythm section with a liking for the relatively four-square rhythms of Puerto Rican music.

The bugalú also affected the music of musicians not formally associated with it. Larry Harlow's Orquesta Harlow, formed in 1966, mixed bugalú and rhythm-and-blues inspired compositions with more classically Cuban pieces, before becoming an important part of the next tipico revival. And when he switched to the Fania label in 1967, after several years of failing to repeat the popular success of "El Watusi," Ray Barretto gained major popularity among Latin audiences for the first time with his album, *Acid,* which ingeniously blended Latin, jazz and rhythm-and-blues ingredients, besides including a couple of highly experimental tracks, "Espíritu Libre" and "Drum Poem." *Acid* was a logical outgrowth of Barretto's long jazz-related experience and his work as one of the busiest studio conga players in New York, recording with an enormous number of rhythm-and-blues and jazz groups. It was not strictly bugalú, but its success was made possible by the bugalú's popularity at the time.

The bugalú had an important influence on black music. Rhythm-and-blues groups soon picked it up, and though the black boogaloo never became the fad that the twist had been, it was probably one of the single most important factors in moving black rhythm sections from a basic four-to-the-bar concept to tumbao-like bass lines and increasingly Latin percussive patterns.

Even more important was the work of Ramon "Mongo" Santamaria. Santamaria, one of the best Afro-Cuban conga-players in the U.S., came to the States with fellow-conga player Armando Peraza in 1950, and worked with Perez Prado and Tito Puente during the 1950s before joining Cal Tjader in California. While with Tjader he made two albums, *Mongo* and *Yambú,* that combined heavily Afro-Cuban percussion and vocals with Latin jazz.

Throughout the 1960s, Santamaria led several groups containing both Latinos and jazzmen, and made a long series of recordings with Atlantic and Columbia that combined rhythm-and-blues and soul pieces with Latin music and jazz. He also had a remarkable eye for both coming trends and coming musicians. In the late 1950s he had included reed player Paul Horn on one of his earliest albums. His first pianist, in 1961, was a Brazilian, João Donato, and he also hired pianist Chick Corea in the early 1960s.

Flutist Hubert Laws joined Santamaria in 1963, and in the late 1960s he hired Luis Gasca, a San Francisco trumpeter who was to be part of the Californian Latin-rock movement in the early 1970s.

Santamaria was not the only musician to record mixes of rhythm-and-blues, jazz, and Latin during the 1960s (even excepting the bugalú bands, whose development was entirely different). In 1966, Machito recorded an album of Latinized soul hits called *Machito Goes to Memphis,* and veteran conga-player Candido Camero recorded another, *Thousand Finger Man.* Santamaria's old colleague Wille Bobo worked with Miles Davis, Stan Getz, and Cannonball Adderley among others, and made a popular rhythm-and-blues hit in "Spanish Grease." But none of these men had such a permanent and profound influence as Santamaria. Aside from the considerable intrinsic merit of his best recordings, he has been cited as a major influence by many black percussionists of the 1970s, and it seems clear that his work has been one of the largest single factors in the increasing Latin influence in 1970s rhythm-and-blues.

This influence was mostly to be felt in the 1970s, especially on a new generation of black percussionists. But rhythm-and-blues continued to reflect a Latin tinge throughout the 1960s. Among many other examples, three former members of the Impressions—one of them Curtis Mayfield—made a recording with a Latin-influenced rhythm called "He Will Break Your Heart," which spent some time at the top of the rhythm-and-blues charts in 1960–61. The same year, Chris Kenner recorded a song called "I Like It Like That," which made number two nationally, and was covered by Joe Cuba. Ray Barretto's "El Watusi" was matched on the rhythm-and-blues side by the Orlons' "The Wah Watusi."

More generally, Latin overtones seeped into some of the work of r&b oriented blues singer Bobby Bland, and producers Leiber and Stoller introduced a Latin-influenced shuffle beat into a number of Drifters records. One of these reflected a much wider scale preoccupation of the early 1960s: a version of the hugely popular bossa nova, "Desafinado." The Brazilian bossa nova's accession, just as Cuban-derived styles seemed to be falling completely out of public favor, was further confirmation that by this period the Latin tinge was a permanent and apparently necessary aspect of American music.

The bossa nova's commercial success in the U.S. was quite equal to the chachachá's ten years earlier. Since even in Brazil it was a fusion of samba and jazz, it had a natural potential for further fusion with jazz.

The most influential recording in the development of bossa nova in the U.S. was also the first. Its moving spirit was guitarist Charlie Byrd, who had heard the music while on a tour of Brazil in spring 1961. Byrd's group was playing what he called jazz samba in Washington by late 1961. In February 1962 he and saxist Stan Getz made the recording that was to be issued in June as *Jazz Samba*. The album, issued in June, sold several hundred thousand copies, and a single of "Desafinado"—a composition by Antonio Carlos Jobim and João Gilberto—went to the top of the popular music charts and won Stan Getz a Grammy for best solo performance of the year on records. It also re-established Getz's career, which had been flagging since his return from overseas.

Getz's success had an ironical edge to it. By his own statement, he knew nothing about the bossa nova until Byrd gave him Gilberto's second album (and first U.S. release), *Brazil's Brilliant João Gilberto*. Yet because Byrd's guitar solo was cut from the single version of "Desafinado," the track seemed to be entirely Getz's work, and Byrd has never really got the credit due to him as the single main source of "jazz-bossa."

Nevertheless, Getz's earlier work with Gillespie had shown considerable ability to work with Latin rhythms, and his delicate style was ideally suited to the gentle, rippling melodies and glancing, oblique rhythms of the bossa nova (80 percent of "Desafinado" is played on offbeats). The result was one of the rare instances in which really musicianly performances achieved huge and almost instant popular success.

Jazz Samba was issued in June. By mid-July, the bossa nova was already becoming extremely popular, helped by the record companies' quick reaction to its initial success (a Mercury Re-

cords executive told *Down Beat* that the industry had been caught
by the sudden vogue for the twist and were not going to get
caught again).

A new and artistically successful Latin-jazz movement, the
bossa nova was also for a while a popular fad complete with
buttons, t-shirts, and so forth. In November, Audio-Fidelity
Records sponsored a concert at Carnegie Hall which presented
leading Brazilian bossa nova artists, Jobim, Gilberto, and Sergio
Mendes—as well as Charlie Byrd, Stan Getz, and Dizzy Gillespie.

The next year or so produced some of the finest recordings
of the 1960s, as well as a good deal of flummery and potboiling.
Getz recorded an album with João Gilberto that included "Girl
from Ipanema," sung by Gilberto's then wife, Astrud. *Life* magazine (in its first record review ever) called the album as a whole
"the best Bossa Nova ever made," but Getz equaled it in the same
year with a recording with guitarist Laurindo Almeida. Meanwhile popular artists jumped on the bandwagon with a flood of
ephemeral recordings, among them a "Soul Bossa Nova," "Boogie
Woogie Bossa Nova," and one of those mild cultural protest
songs that themselves tended to become part of Tin Pan Alley's
Latin thrust—"Blame It on the Bossa Nova."

Several other jazzmen made important contributions to
jazz-bossa. Flutist Herbie Mann, who had left Machito to form
his own Latin-oriented group in 1959, cut an album called *Right
Now* for Atlantic Records with a rhythm section that included
Patato Valdez on congas, Willie Bobo, and Johnny Pacheco. He
also traveled to Brazil to record *Do the Bossa Nova with Herbie Mann*
with Brazilian guitarist Baden Powell and Jobim. Bud Shank and
Almeida's jazz-baião, "Brazilliance," was reissued. Along with a
host of popular artists, Ella Fitzgerald, Al Hirt, and Coleman
Hawkins all recorded "Desafinado," which had become a new
American standard.

By February 1963, the bossa nova's huge popular success
was provoking critical hostility, notably in *Down Beat,* where Gene
Lees wrote a piece called "Anatomy of a Travesty." In reality,
some of the best was to come, including Getz's recordings with
Gilberto and Almeida and a tour by black bossa nova guitarist
Djalma de Andrade (nicknamed "Bola Sete"). Bola Sete, who had

appeared at the Sheraton-Palace Hotel in San Francisco in 1962, and played with Dizzy Gillespie at the Monterey Jazz Festival during a West Coast tour, besides recording for Fantasy, returned for a second successful appearance at Monterey with pianist Vince Guaraldi. Nor was the critics' concern with the bossa nova's purity necessarily appropriate, since its major proponents—especially Antonio Carlos Jobim—used string sections even on his earliest recordings with Gilberto, and always wrote in the ambit of mass-popular music.

Both in Brazil and the United States, in fact, the bossa nova bridged "mass" popular music and "art" popular music. In the U.S., it provided several new standards to the popular repertoire and also had some significant effects on jazz.

As Leonard Feather has pointed out in *The Book of Jazz*, most of the bossa nova jazz guitarists were not particularly jazz-oriented, despite the style's origins in Brazilian admiration for cool jazz. There was, however, one exception—the black guitarist Bola Sete, who, Feather remarks, "showed equal facility in every medium—electric and unamplified, Brazilian and modern jazz, and every stop along the way." Bola Sete's appearances with Dizzy Gillespie and pianist Vince Guaraldi were examples of how compatible jazz and Brazilian music could be.

Feather has also commented that the bossa nova gave a "badly needed impetus" to jazz guitar and helped revive the acoustic instrument; and in the long run, Brazilian rhythms became a part of both the jazz avant garde and its popular wing.

The early effects of the bossa nova on jazz were not particularly innovative. In albums like Kenny Dorham's *Una Mas*, a skeletal bossa nova rhythm was used rather as Cuban-derived rhythms were being used, as a change of pace. The bossa nova—and occasional contemporary samba rhythms—stood up better to this kind of marginal use than their Cuban cousins, probably because they originated in guitar patterns and could be played by a rhythm section of piano, bass, and drums without losing virtually all of their quality, like Latin-Caribbean patterns based on an interplay between the bass and several percussion instruments.

This relatively superficial bossa nova presence in jazz might well have disappeared gradually, except for the presence in the U.S. of a number of Brazilian musicians, among them a young husband and wife, percussionist Airto Moreira and singer Flora Purim. Moreira, known professionally as Airto, was a dance-band musician in his early teens. He spent two years absorbing the Afro-Brazilian music of the Brazilian Northeast at its source, before becoming the best known jazz drummer in southern Brazil. Then he formed a group to play pure "Brazilian" music in contemporary vein. Purim, born of a prosperous family in Rio, absorbed Afro-Brazilian street music as well as classical music and jazz, and became a singer of bossa nova and American compositions with a Rio big band.

The fact that Airto and Purim were at ease with both jazz and Brazilian music—far more so than Gilberto and the other slightly older bossa nova musicians—made it easier for them, when they moved to the U.S. in 1967, to adapt to the jazz-bossa and jazz scenes. Purim fairly soon went on a two-month European tour singing bossa nova with Stan Getz, which led to a job with Gil Evans, and then a place in avant-garde pianist Chick Corea's original Return to Forever group, where she began developing a style mixing Brazilian phrasings with jazz and "non-verbal" cries, squeaks, and glissandi, closer to contemporary conservatory experiments with non-traditional vocal music than to earlier jazz scatting.

Airto's percussion was as unorthodox as Purim's vocals. He had never seen his role in the traditional light of a rhythm-maker, and used a wide range of traditional and self-invented devices to achieve color as well as sound patterns. This experimental approach earned him—on the recommendation of keyboardist Joe Zawinul—a place on two cuts of Miles Davis's seminal *Bitches' Brew* album, an important document in the developing "electric jazz" or "jazz-rock" movement. His use of bells, rattles, and shakers to decorate and accentuate the group *sound,* rather than carry it forward rhythmically, became a cliché of 1970s jazz.

Airto moved on to Corea's highly influential Return to Forever, where his percussive experiments laid the groundwork for the success of other Brazilian percussionists—such as Dom Um Romão, and Guilherme Franco, whose first American recording was Archie Shepp's *Cry of My People* album.

Airto was not the only influential Brazilian musician to settle in the United States, nor the first. Trap drummer Edison Machado arrived in 1963, at the height of the bossa nova's success, and remained to record with Getz, Herbie Mann, Sergio Mendes, and many others. Another important musician, though not well-known to the public, was Severino D'Oliveira, "Sivuca," a multi-instrumentalist who came to the U.S. and spent four years with South African singer Miriam Makeba, besides working with Oscar Brown and Harry Belafonte. A third was keyboardist Eumir Deodato, who made his mark in popular music in the 1970s with his recording of the theme to the film *2001: A Space Odyssey.*

The most commercially successful of all was Sergio Mendes, a pianist from Rio who played in the 1962 Carnegie Hall bossa-nova concert and recorded with Cannonball Adderley. Mendes settled in San Francisco in early 1965, and soon had a popular hit with a version of "Mas Que Nada."

Mendes's sound, based on English lyrics and the use of female voices as instruments, brought him wide success in mass-popular music. He consistently produced light and elegant recordings out of mixtures of American and Brazilian elements, characteristically teaming one Brazilian and one American number. His "Festa," for instance, opened with piano that seemed influenced by Ray Charles, with typically Brazilian female voices behind, over a rhythm like a cross between soul and a Brazilian carnival march. Similar formulae gave Mendes a long succession of moderate hits.

The 1960s also established Brazilian music as a powerful factor in both popular and avant-garde jazz. Like earlier Latin-jazz, it was to pave the way for the return of jazz, which had become even more intellectual elitist, to popularity. It did so amid general critical indifference, and sometimes hostility.

A similar hostility bedeviled another remarkable Latin-jazz experiment that was to achieve some popular success, the work of Argentinian tenor saxist, Leandro "Gato" Barbieri. Barbieri, brought up in the Argentinian city of Rosario, early fell under the spell of Charlie Parker and John Coltrane, and totally rejected the tango and other local forms. In the mid-1960s he settled in Rome, and then Paris, where he met trumpeter Don Cherry, who called him "one of the leading jazz musicians emerging from the European scene because of the originality of his conception." During the late 1960s, Barbieri became established as a free-jazz musician playing with Cherry, Carla Bley, and others. But towards the end of the decade he made the first of several recordings that were to make him a kind of one-man Latin-jazz avant garde—a series of experiments with a range of Latin-American music far wider than had ever been attempted.

Over nearly a dozen albums, Barbieri locked horns with several Brazilian styles, as well as with the tango, the folk-and-politics oriented cabaret songs of Atahualpa Yupanqui, Andean Indian, and Cuban and Newyorican music. Most of this recording took place in the 1970s; but Barbieri's course was set before his first American album, *Third World*. Though he reacted against local music in his youth, he was unable to ignore it, since an Argentinian law of the early 1950s obliged local groups to play 50 percent local music. He also played with visiting Latins like Perez Prado, who toured with a rhythm section and hired his frontline locally; and in 1959 he spent six months in Brazil.

Third World reflected Barbieri's brush with Brazilian music in several ways, among them the use of the Afro-Brazilian agogó bell and the inclusion of a version of Heitor Villa-Lobos's "Bachianas Brasileiros," which applied Bach's contrapuntal techniques to Brazilian folk music. Barbieri's next album, *Pampero*, contained Barbieri's first tango, an improvisation on one of Carlos Gardel's most famous numbers, "Mi Buenos Aires Querido." Barbieri revived this number and the equally famous "El Dia Que Tu Me Quieras" because, he said, "they're very big, rich themes." This remark reflects an important aspect of his style. At his best, his lush and gutty soloing is a remarkable recreation in post-Coltrane jazz terms of a *macho* romanticism that is peculiarly Latin-American. But Barbieri's musical concepts stem from his own musical development. Jazz formed his personal musical roots, but though he was emotionally alienated from Latin tradition to which he came fresh as a developed musician, it had been part of his environment from childhood.

As a result, Barbieri occupies a unique position in Latin-jazz. While he has more gut empathy with Latin music in all its varieties than almost any non-Latino, he lacks the strong sense of tradition of most Latin musicians, and was musically formed by involvement with a very experimental jazz school.

The critical hostility to Barbieri may have had something to do with the fact that he was turning his back on free jazz. Like most advocates of new artistic movements, many free jazz enthusiasts overly depreciated other contemporary trends. Reading the critics of the time, one would gain the impression that—with the possible exception of the Brazilian element already discussed—Latin jazz was extinct.

The reality was somewhat different, even in the polymorphous jazz avant garde. Pianist Chick Corea's 1967 album, *Inner Space,* his first as leader, was a mix of Latin (mostly Cuban) elements and jazz. Rahsaan Roland Kirk also recorded a fusion album, *Slightly Latin,* with Montego Joe on congas and Manuel Ramos on percussion, and a clave-based beat in "Raouf." Trumpeter Freddy Hubbard included Ray Barretto on several tracks of his *Backlash* album, though without using him to very great effect except on the track "Little Sunshine."

There was also a great deal of interaction between Latin and jazz musicians. Chico O'Farrill, for example, arranged several albums for Count Basie in the late 1960s. Particularly important was the contribution of several Latin musicians with a real understanding of jazz, who played regularly with both jazzmen and Latin groups. "Chombo" Silva has already been mentioned. An equally excellent saxist was Mario Rivera, from the Dominican Republic, who came to the U.S. in 1961 and played with Sonny Stitt and Roy Haynes, as well as Tito Puente and Tito Rodriguez. Another was keyboardist Eddie Martinez, from Colombia, who came to the U.S. in 1964, and played with Ray Barretto, Mongo Santamaria, and—during the 1970s—Gato

Barbieri. During the 1960s, Cal Tjader continued to be one of the most consistent non-Latin exponents of small-group Latin-jazz. His best-selling 1964 "Soul Sauce" was based on Dizzy Gillespie's "Guachi Guara," but one of his most interesting recordings was the album *Bamboleate,* with Eddie Palmieri's band. The almost tortured yet intensely swinging sound of La Perfecta set off Tjader's mellifluous vibraphone perfectly and provided a bite lacking in some of his other recordings.

The 1960s were also a time of significant change in Chicano music. The accordion-based norteño style reached its peak during the decade with the huge success of the group called Los Relampagos del Norte, and its popularity had spread sufficiently that the Mexican record companies—which had totally ignored it—began leasing masters from the small Chicano companies for distribution south of the border.

This success was in part due to a continuing rise in Chicano ethnic and political consciousness that both affected the music and reinforced its role. While record-company owners often continued to be shy of overtly political material, and compositions such as those on the deaths of President Kennedy and Martin Luther King were part of a long-standing tradition, other corridos showed a new approach. One of these was "Los Rinches de Texas," which grew from an incident during a strike of melon-pickers in Star County, Texas, in June 1967. For the customary stand-up heroism of the lone Mexican against the *rinches cobardes,* the author of this corrido substituted a protest more characteristic of the 1960s:

> Esos rinches maldecidos
> Los mando el gobernador
> A proteger los melones
> De un rico conservador.
>
> Mr. Canalis, Señores
> Es el mal gobernador
> Que se aborrece al Mexicano
> Y se burla del dolor.

(Those hated rangers were sent by the Governor to protect the melons of a rich conservative. . . . Mr. Connolly, sirs, is the bad governor who hates Mexicans and mocks at suffering.)

Musically, meanwhile, the norteño groups were expanding their style in a manner traditional to Mexican music—by taking in Cuban elements. The bolero rhythm, which had begun to be popular at the end of the 1950s, greatly consolidated its hold in the 1960s, and with it the regular use of congas and bongós added a totally new rhythmic dimension to the music.

But far more radical changes got underway as younger musicians began reworking the norteño style under the influence of country music and rhythm-and-blues, in a development reminiscent of the New York bugalú.

The movement known as the Onda Nueva, or New Wave, is typified by two musicians, one of whom remained in the Chicano community while the other moved into the Anglo mainstream.

José María De León Hernandez, known professionally as "Little Joe," was born in Temple, Texas, in 1941. His family had produced musicians at least as far back as his great-grandfather, who came from Potosí, Mexico, and his grandfather and father played weddings and other local functions in Temple.

Little Joe began playing in 1955 with a group called David Coronado y Sus Latinaires, which he took over in 1959 and renamed Little Joe and the Latinaires. The Latinaires' early music included songs that had been in the family for a long time, including compositions by Little Joe's grandfather, and their first local success came with a song about cotton picking written by his father, called "Corrido del West." But their second major recording, in 1962, suggested the changes that were taking place: its title was "Echale al Piano"—loosely, Hit that Piano.

For some years, the Latinaires contended with the small local market and restricted recording possibilities. Then, in 1968, Hernandez formed his own recording company, Buena Suerte. The following year he issued a highly successful album with a strong political flavor, *Arriba,* which included a Vietnam protest song called "A La Guerra Ya Me Llevan."

The music of Little Joe and the Latinaires reflects both

regional roots and the ways in which these are modified by time and outside influence. As Hernandez himself put it:

> The way we arrived at our music was the way we grew up. I learned Mexican songs from the same radio that played country and western . . . and rhythm and blues were real heavy around here because of the blacks.

The Latinaires were one of the first Chicano groups to use brass and saxophones and to treat the electric guitar as a lead instrument. In 1964, they added an electric organ as a lead instrument, and—clearly under the influence of charanga and bugalú—began featuring flute and trombone.

The Latinaires' blending of styles, all of which were present on the local music scene, was a natural development. As Hernandez has remarked, each of his musicians "has played rock and roll and country—*real* hillbilly country—and has had to play that mariachi junk and has played [norteño] conjunto."

Little Joe Hernandez and musicians like him reshaped Chicano music by taking in other American styles. Other Chicanos simply moved into the mainstream of Anglo-American country music. The most famous of these was Johnny Rodriguez. But more interesting musically than Rodriguez, whose rapid success rested on love songs in a standard commercial pop-country style, was Freddy Fender. Fender was born Baldemar Huerta in San Benito, Texas, in 1936. His migrant parents spoke no English, and he grew up listening to Mexican radio stations across the border, "always Mexican music, *rancheras* and *boleros.*"

By the early 1950s, however, Fender was tuning in to Nashville radio stations, and also being exposed to the blues in black migrant workers' field camps. His musical horizons were further widened when, in the Marines, he heard both Fats Domino and Elvis Presley for the first time.

By 1957, Fender was singing in South Texas bars. Soon afterward he recorded a single symbolic of the New Wave's musical eclecticism: it consisted of an English-language song of his own, "Oh Holy One," and a Spanish version of Otis Blackwell's "Don't be Cruel," which had been popularized by Elvis Presley.

But Fender's real success began in 1960, with a slow rhythm-and-blues type number called "Wasted Days and Wasted Nights" which combined black musical elements with something of the ranchera's high-octane sentiment, an emotionalism whose power saves it from being ludicrous.

After a jail sentence on marijuana charges, from which he was released in 1963, Fender spent five years playing in New Orleans, an experience that reinforced his black influences. Then he returned to the San Benito Valley and continued to play on weekends while working as a mechanic, while recording blues, rock, country, rhythm-and-blues, and Mexican numbers (including "Alla en el Rancho Grande") for many small Texas labels and Mexican companies—before signing with ABC records' country-oriented Dot label.

Most of Fender's work is squarely in the U.S. country tradition, enriched by echoes of black singers like Fats Domino and Chubby Checker, and a certain Tex-Mex hang-loose rowdiness, or in a fairly pure ranchera style—accordion and all—as in his Dot recording of "I Love My Rancho Grande," sung in Spanish, whose main concession to fusion is a jaunty country electric-guitar solo. The point about his singing is that he is at ease in both styles, and that his acceptance by what was until recently a very ethnically chauvinist idiom has paralleled a progressive increase in Mexican musical elements.

During the 1970s, in fact, the rise in Tex-Mex fusion music was to be mirrored by a Mexican influence on mainstream country music. But that influence had not yet made itself felt; what Latin touches did occasionally emerge were in the folk revival movement, especially along its more popular fringes.

Perhaps the best known of the Mexican-folknik fusion singers was Trini Lopez. Born in the Dallas ghetto known as "Little Mexico," Lopez began playing guitar around the age of eleven, and his first musical experience was gained in family sing-a-longs of Mexican material. He played both Mexican and American material locally, before moving to Los Angeles in 1960. There he began appearing regularly at a club called PJ's, where he caught the attention of Frank Sinatra, who recorded him for his Reprise label.

Lopez's repertory squarely straddled Mexican and American folk-popular material. His first major success was "If I Had a Hammer," but he was also responsible for the widespread popularity of "La Bamba," and of a version of a song traditional in several Latin countries, "Hojita de Lemon," under the title of "Lemon Tree."

Trini Lopez's music was a genuine fusion of Mexican and Anglo-American elements. In his stage show at PJ's he gave Mexican-derived strummed guitar rhythms to such varied material as "America," "Cielito Lindo," "This Land Is Your Land" (to a near-habanera beat), "What'd I Say?," "Gotta Travel On," and "Volare" (in which he inserted excerpts from "Chiapanecas"), besides making a showpiece of "Granada" over several different rhythms.

Owing in large measure to Lopez's influence, there was a noticeable increase in Latin-derived rhythms used by American urban-folk singers during the 1960s. This continued into the 1970s, when it became part of the Latinization of soft- or California-rock and the fringes of country music. An early example was "Someday Soon," by Ian Tyson, one of the "urban folk" generation of 1960s singers. This love song about a rodeo rider made use of contemporary country-music themes and melodic procedures, but much of its effectiveness comes from its easy bolero rhythm.

"Someday Soon," which was recorded in the 1960s by Julie Felix among others, and revived in the mid-1970s by at least two pop-country singers, Tanya Tucker and Crystal Gayle, was an early example of how country and popular music overlapped with Mexican-flavored rhythms to achieve a romantic or beguiling effect.

Though Trini Lopez's music was one large factor in this trend, it was reinforced by a Cuban influence through the popularity of Pete Seeger's 1966 recording of "Guantanamera," a ballad in the Cuban country guajiro tradition,. previously a recording by the Cuban guajiro singer, El Indio de Nabori, on the Panart label. Its correct title is "Guajira Guantanamera," which translates inelegantly as "Guantanamese Farm-Girl," and, though it was originally a love song, it became something of an anthem for Fidel Castro's guerillas. Seeger's version was hugely popular during its heyday, and it is one of the Latin songs to have received more than one million live performances.

The folk fringe was by no means the only area in which Mexican music exerted influence in the 1960s. In 1963, a young Los Angeles trumpeter called Herb Alpert was launching a small recording company when a trip to Tijuana gave him the idea of rewriting one of his tunes as a bolero and giving the brass a strongly mariachi sound. The consequent single, "The Lonely Bull," by Herb Alpert's Tijuana Brass was issued in August 1964 and sold 700,000 copies. By the end of 1965, Tijuana Brass had recorded four albums, including *Whipped Cream and Other Delights,* which sold more than 600,000 copies and produced a number-one single, "A Taste of Honey," in summer 1965. The group reached the peak of its success in April 1966, when no fewer than five of its albums were listed in *Billboard* magazine's Top 20.

Tijuana Brass, which Alpert disbanded when it got in the way of his growing A & M record company, was in retrospect an outstanding group. Though it perpetuated the American-Latin stereotype of lightweight froth, many of its renditions had genuine charm. Also in the American-Latin tradition, it was highly eclectic. The enormous popularity of "A Taste of Honey"—a semi-mariachi version of a British film theme with a mishmash of marimbas and vaguely Mexican brass—obscured the real quality of much of the rest of *Whipped Cream and Other Delights.* "Green Peppers," an ingenious combination of mariachi brass, marimba, and bossa nova; "Lemon Tree," which perfectly caught the non-sentimental romanticism of the best Mexican and Cuban music; "Whipped Cream," a musical joke with much of the feel of New Orleans creole jazz; and the polka "El Garbanzo," were all genuinely distinguished.

The enormous popularity of Tijuana Brass, and the subsequent decline of its sound into supermarket Muzak, have obscured the fact that Alpert produced some of the most effective and delightful of all eclectic American-Latin music. Its huge success reintroduced a Mexican tinge into meainstream U.S. popular music after something of an absence, and the rediscovery of

Mexican rhythms by California songwriters of the 1970s may possibly stem in part from the popularity of Tijuana Brass when they were children.

The style least affected by Latin music during the 1960s was rock. Yet even rock was to be influenced by Latin music in the coming decade; early signs were noticeable by the end of the 1960s in developments that somewhat paralleled Puerto Rican musicians' effect on Cuban music in New York. From the base of a blues-rock band, a young Mexican-born San Francisco guitarist, Carlos Santana, began to develop a style that blended the acid-rock of the Haight-Ashbury era with blues and New York salsa.

Santana, who was born in Mexico, came to the U.S. when he was ten. Though his father was a mariachi violinist, he turned away from Mexican music, and in high school in San Francisco he was listening almost entirely to black music, and especially blues. When he did rediscover a Latin form, it was not the Mexican idiom of his background, but the big city New York sound.

Santana formed his first group, a blues band, around 1966, and was already locally popular when he was joined by conga player Mike Carrabello and timbalero Chepito Areas. His first album, *Santana,* was recorded in 1969. It included a piece by Nigerian drummer Olatunji, "Jingo," and Willie Bobo's "Evil Ways," both strongly Latin-influenced, as well as fine blues piano and good blues-influenced vocals by Santana himself. Though Santana's band was the inspiration of the so-called Latin-rock movement of the 1970s, its early ingredients were not totally different from those of other young Latin bands—including the New York bugalú groups. Their almost equal balance, however, was typically Californian.

One of the major developments of the 1960s, in fact, was the emergence of California as a most important crossover center. Herb Alpert was *sui generis,* but in jazz Cal Tjader and in rock Carlos Santana were only the best known of a floating group of musicians who were together to make San Francisco the focus of a further blending of rock, jazz, black, and Latin elements during the 1970s. Among these musicians were the Escovedo brothers, Coke and Pete. After some years running a Cuban-style conjunto, the Escovedos formed a Latin-jazz sextet, which Pete kept going when Coke joined Santana.

The inspiration for the Californian crossover movement was not Mexican, as might have been expected, but Cuban and New York. Cubans and Puerto Ricans living in the West, and increasingly also young Chicanos, joined the non-Latin enthusiasts from the rumba and mambo days to form a public large and enthusiastic enough to support a growing Latin school. Concerts such as the 1962 Hollywood Bowl "Latin Holiday Festival" featuring Joe Cuba, Tito Puente, and Tito Rodriguez helped to keep the West Coast in touch with current development in New York, while bands like Eddie Palmieri's regularly played the Club Las Virginias in Los Angeles, and several East Coast musicians, including Joe Loco, settled permanently in California during the 1960s.

The West Coast Latin public was less homogeneous than Eastern audiences, much less traditional-minded, and far more receptive to experiment and change. As a result, while New York Latinos turned increasingly to típico Cuban-derived forms at the beginning of the 1970s, and New York jazz appeared to abandon its Latin tinge, California became the center both of the continuing fusion and of a style—or perhaps more accurately a spirit—increasingly independent of the East.

EIGHT

The 1970s:
The Return to the Mainstream

In many respects, Latin music during the 1960s and 1970s mirrored the 1920s and 1930s. In each case, the first decade emphasized a growth that would take full effect in the second. The 1930s saw the introduction of Latin music as a substyle within U.S. popular music as a whole; the late 1970s saw its clear emergence as a major ingredient in the sound of almost all American popular idioms.

Yet, paradoxically, Latin music had not for a long time seemed so irrelevant to the mainstream as it did in the early 1970s, despite occasional Latin-influenced hits—Paul Simon's "El Condor Pasa" was one, Gato Barbieri's *Last Tango in Paris* film theme another. The level of awareness in the music industry itself was summed up by a remark made to me, about one of the most creative of Latin musicians, by a young record-company executive: "Willie Colon? Doesn't he play at those Latin get-togethers?"

New York Latin musicians themselves were depressed about the state of their music on two grounds. On the one hand, they were acutely conscious that it was generally ignored. On the other, many were perturbed by developments within the hard-core style. The return to Cuban orthodoxy continued unabated after the collapse of the bugalú movement. By 1970 and 1971, all the most successful bands were firmly committed, at least in theory, to the tipico Cuban sound. Though most were less purist than Pacheco's highly successful trumpet conjunto, the prevailing rhetoric was of roots, purity, and a concept (related to the growth of Latino political awareness) of "community music." By 1973, even Ray Barretto, whose whole career rested on forms of crossover and stylistic blending, was speaking of commitment to the grassroots.

The result was an orthodoxy that bothered many musicians. In mid-1974, Louie Ramirez, one of the period's most successful arrangers, commented,

Everybody who hires me wants two trumpets or two trumpets and one trombone. I say, why don't we use an oboe? But if it's not típico, it's no good. It's a thing like, "let's progress, but at the same time let's keep it típico!" But típico music is two chords. It's soul, but musically it's primitive! Aretha Franklin's drummer told me, "You know, in the fifties and sixties you guys were doing some heavy things. Now you're kind of like calypso bands!"

Aside from the possibility of two views on this equation of the simple with the primitive, the reality was less clear cut. Even while the típico rhetoric held sway, a renewal was taking place in Latin music. One significant factor was that the hot, creative New York style had at last found a name. Some time around the early 1970s, it began to be called "salsa."

The word—it means sauce—had long been used by Cuban musicians in the sense of "spice" or pep—something vaguely parallel to the original meaning of the word "swing," though a little looser. A well-known Septeto Nacional number was called "Echale Salsita," which means roughly, "Swing It!" and a piece might be said to have "salsa y sabor"—sauce and savor.

Like the word "jazz" in the teens of the century, the usage of "salsa" to denote a style of music seemed to appear from nowhere. It has been attributed to Izzy Sanabria, the publisher of *Latin New York* magazine, who is said to have coined it while emceeing a Fania All-Stars concert, but bandleader Willie Rosario has said he first heard the word used in its present sense in Venezuela in 1966.

Most musicians regard the word as essentially meaningless. Mario Bauza says "What they call salsa is nothing new. When Cuban music was really in demand the kids didn't go for it. Now they call it salsa and they think it belongs to them. It's good as a gimmick." And as a much younger musician—a Puerto Rican— once told me, "Salsa is Cuban music, that's all."

Even if this had really still held true of 1970s New York salsa, its new name would have been important in the music's spread because it provided a succinct label that had always been lacking. But in reality, though New York salsa still contains more Cuban elements than any other, by the early 1970s it was drawing from a wider range of Latin American idioms than ever before. Moreover, despite the general belief that the típico concept was strangling creativity in the early 1970s, musicians continued experiments to which the framework of the típico provided a creative tension and discipline. Larry Harlow's ardent espousal of Cubanism did not prevent him from writing new brass voicings, or using a violin and flute to add semi-charanga colorings rather as the big New York bands had done in the 1950s. Harlow and Jenaro "Heny" Alvarez also created a "salsa opera" called *Hommy,* a version of the Who's Tommy, which was presented at Carnegie Hall on March 29, 1973, with Celia Cruz and Cheo Feliciano singing the main parts.

One of the most avant-garde salsa albums ever produced appeared in 1974, at the height of the típico wave. Rafael Cortijo's *Maquina de Tiempo/Time Machine* blended Afro-Rican bombas and plenas with jibaro aguinaldos and Cuban guarachas in an extraordinary amalgam of Afro-Latin tradition, contemporary jazz soloing, and ensemble writing, and even the first use of the Brazilian cuica friction drum in salsa.

Maquina de Tiempo was one of the most brilliant Latin-jazz fusions ever recorded within the salsa tradition. It was also a commercial disaster. But two bandleaders were able to combine experimentalism with popular success throughout the early 1970s. These were Eddie Palmieri and Willie Colon.

In 1971, Palmieri continued the experimentalism signaled in his 1969 *Justicia* album by forming a unit which combined a black group (Harlem River Drive) and his salsa band. His aim of using them to play one salsa set, one rhythm-and-blues set, and a final fusion jam proved ahead of its time. But the potentialities are illustrated by a remarkable number, "Azucar/Sugar," preserved on a live album recorded at Sing Sing prison, which changes from r&b to salsa through almost imperceptible gradations.

Meanwhile, Palmieri was achieving remarkable commercial as well as artistic success with a highly personal mixture of savage swing, modal piano experiments that stemmed from an admiration for jazz pianist McCoy Tyner, and a passion for the Cuban past. The resulting style came to maturity in "Adoración," the major cut on his 1973 *Sentido* album, which opened with a long piano prelude, and in the 1974 recording *Sun of Latin Music*. Much of this latter album was straightforward though powerful salsa, for Palmieri never forgot that the dancers were the backbone of his public. But two tracks brought his experimentalism to its peak. "Un Dia Bonito" moved from a seven-minute piano-and-tape-sounds prelude via Afro-Cuban percussion into a constantly building piece of high-brass salsa. The enchanting "Una Rosa Española" opened as a danzón with violin and French horn *floreos*, moved through a Puerto Rican danza and ended with a searingly brassy son montuno, in a miniature history of Cuban music.

Palmieri's work raises various intriguing issues. First, it depends heavily on his arrangers, notably Machito's pianist, René Hernandez, and on his sideman. In addition, some of his effects are jackdaw memories of older bands. Yet the total effect is pure Palmieri, and (as is so often the case) when his sidemen have played without him they have never matched the flair of his own recordings.

Secondly, despite its clear avant-gardism during the típico era, Palmieri maintained stoutly that his music was típico. The key, he once told me, was "the rhythmic phrasings of the instruments. I can use the same phrasing as the old groups use, and I could extend it, and build master structures around it—make it with such high-tension chords that everybody would blow their minds—but the phrasing would not disrupt the rhythmic patterns. Rhythm is your foundation."

Palmieri's main creative rival among the bandleaders of the

early 1970s, Willie Colon, was a product of the bugalú generation and less wedded than Palmieri to Cuban orthodoxy. He brought to New York salsa a jaunty and original sound and an imaginative use of new ingredients, above all several new Latin-American influences. The most important of these was jibaro music, the country style of Puerto Rico. But he also used Panamanian, Colombian, and Brazilian elements.

Colon's first major single success, "Che Che Colé," from his second album, *Cosa Nuestra* (issued in 1972, but containing some material dating back to 1970), was a Ghanaian children's song learned from an African musician working in New York, under which he laid a sequence of some seven Caribbean rhythms. His next album, *The Big Break,* contained another West-African inspired piece, "Ghana'E"; a piece from the Colombian-Panama stylistic area (until then untouched by New York Latin musicians), "Pa' Colombia"; and a prophetic venture into Brazilian sounds in "Barrunto."

Colon's important involvement with Puerto Rican jibaro country music began with two Christmas albums in which he used the brilliant *cuatro* (ten-string) guitar picker, Yomo Toro for extensive *jibaro* folk oriented soli in several aguinaldos. His skill in putting a wide range of influences to strongly personal use was brought to a peak in the 1974 album *Lo Mato,* notably in a song about crime in the streets, "Calle Luna, Calle Sol," in which lyrics, melody, and arrangement worked together to brilliantly sinister effect; a markedly jazz-influenced piece, "Junio 73"; and three tracks making use of Brazilian rhythms, harmonic voicings and melodies.

In mid-1974, feeling locked in by the popularity of his two-trombone sound, Colon handed his group over to his lead singer, Hector LaVoe, and woodshedded, coming back after six months with an album, *The Good, the Bad, the Ugly,* that made even more flexible use of Brazilian, rock, salsa, Cuban and Puerto Rican country music, Panamanian and big-band mambo elements. "Toma" had Spanish-from-Spain overtones in its ensemble work; "Potpourri III" interwove a series of old plenas bound together with Colon's indefinable but instantly recognizable two-trombone voicings; "Doña Toña" used the rhythm, and some of the sound, of the 19th-century Puerto Rican danza. Most brilliant of all, perhaps, was "El Cazangero," which opened with strong samba elements, and moved into brash New York salsa enlivened by a throwback to the sax-and-brass mambo sound of the 1950s. The album also contained a track symbolic of a new era of feedback between salsa and "American" music, "EMC^2", which had strong rock elements, including electric guitar work by Elliot Randall of the group Sha Na Na.

Salsa, born of a cross between jazz and Cuban music, had been a fusion style from its inception, and it was almost inevitable that rock touches should become part of the New York style by the mid-1970s. Bandleader Larry Harlow is very conscious of the Cuban past, yet New York Latin-rock pioneer Randy Ortiz considers Harlow's use of electric instruments crucial to this process. "Adding the electric instruments gave a moving, vibrating, explosive feeling—the moving, electric feeling of New York."

An early example of rock guitar was contained in Cortijo's 1973 *Time Machine*. By the middle of the decade, some of the younger headlining bands, like Típica 73, were experimenting with reverb and other electronic gadgets on tres and bass to get a rock feel, and Eddie Palmieri's young Cuban violinist, Alfredo Delafe, was using a wawa pedal.

The rock tinge in salsa was a normal part of the process by which the music had always developed. It was distinct from the hybrid of rock and salsa called Latin-rock. This began as a Californian phenomenon, and overwhelmingly its most important force has been Carlos Santana. Santana's second album *Abraxas*, released in September 1970, turned the Tito Puente composition, "Oye Como Va," into a central Latin-rock statement, with a totally salsa-based vocals and rhythm section under powerful rock guitar and strongly jazz-oriented organ. Many of its other tracks maintained a similarly equal balance, and even in those that did not (which included a moody "Samba Pa Ti"), the Latin elements were always more than peripheral.

After a third album containing another Puente classic—"Para Los Rumberos"—along with several other salsa-inspired pieces, Santana, who had come under the influence of the Oriental mystic Sri Chinmoy, turned his mind to more experimental and jazz-rock oriented music for a while.

Aside from the group El Chicano, which came out of the East Los Angeles barrio and scored an early success with "Viva Tirado" in 1970, both the other leading Californian Latin-rock groups of the early 1970s had connections with Santana. One was Malo, founded by Santana's younger brother Jorge in 1971. This, like the Santana band itself, mixed Anglo and Latino musicians. Among the latter, the most notable was Cuban conga-player Francisco Aguabella, one of a handful of master-drummers working in the U.S.

Brass was an important part of Malo's sound, as it was of the third Santana-related group, Azteca, which was started by those of Carlos Santana's musicians who did not share his new musical interests. Both groups were somewhat more jazz-oriented than the original Santana band, thanks in part to two outstanding solo trumpeters, Luis Gasca and Tom Harrell, both of whom belong to a generation of musicians at home in both Latin and non-Latin music. Neither Malo nor Azteca were as commercially successful as Santana, though in many respects—notably their use of brass and their jazz soloing—their music was even more interesting.

None of the major Latin rock groups sprang from the salsa mainstream, and many of the Latins involved were musicians of Mexican-American background, who, unable to relate to the pop corridos and rancheras of northern Mexico and the Mexican U.S., borrowed from New York salsa. But almost all the Californian Latin-rock groups depended for their rhythmic underpinnings on an Antillean percussionist, usually a conga player: Cuban Armando Peraza or Newyorican Victor Pantoja with Santana, Pantoja again with Azteca, Francisco Aguabella with Malo.

Some early attempts at Latin rock did develop in New York. An excellent group called Toro, formed in 1972, made one album for Coco Records under the aegis of Larry Harlow; and a band by the name of Changó, from Woodstock, made a few recordings in a California-inspired style; but lacking both strong salsa roots and an audience with California's receptivity to fusion, Changó was little more successful than Toro.

A third Latin-rock group formed in 1972, Seguida, was little more successful, though more ambitious. Seguida sprang from the core New York salsa market, grouping up to eighteen salseros and rock-minded barrio musicians in an attempt at a more thoroughgoing fusion than the West Coast had achieved. Seguida's founder, Randy Ortiz, aimed at a true blend in the core of both rock and salsa: the rhythm section: "You take the bass of each, and work from there. The solos can be anything, but you have to find the trick of combining the rock bass and the Latin *tumbao* so that they're perfectly fused."

A total fusion of salsa and rock rhythms was not the only option.

Latin-rock is inevitably a somewhat vague concept, since the diverse elements of both its root styles allowed for a wide range of combinations. At its simplest and most balanced, it frequently consisted of an essentially Latin rhythm section, often with strong rock echoes in the bass-playing, over which were placed out-of-clave rock solos for guitars, keyboards, and sometimes brass.

The changes rung by the various early California and East Coast groups on this basic formula were many, but they did not alter the basic principle that there should be strong enough elements of both idioms to differentiate the music from both rock-tinged salsa and Latin-tinged rock. In practice, despite inevitable grey areas, Latin-rock was clearly recognizable as such. Ortiz's more rigorous definition has mostly held good for the East Coast Latin-rock groups—not only for Seguida but various Puerto Rican and Miami-based groups that have been only locally known and recorded on small labels if at all.

Puerto Rico was in fact something of a Latin-rock center in the mid-1970s. Pure rock was the musical choice of many of the islands' young bands, while others moved between salsa and Latin-rock: Tempo 70, both of whose albums on the Mericana label mixed Latin rock and straight salsa tracks, was fairly typical; and one, Raices, had strong Brazilian influences.

Miami's Latin-rock groups also followed Ortiz's formula. Wild Wind used rock-oriented guitar solos over rhythm section that mostly blended clave and rock. Opus moved more freely between its salsa and rock poles; all of these groups had a free approach to the frontline, with riffs and solos that might come from either rock or salsa.

For several reasons, Latin-rock—unlike Latin-jazz—never really got off the ground in New York. One was that young New York Latinos were more influenced by black music than rock. Another was the powerful New York disco scene, which was very receptive to Latinos and their music. The discos later became such a national phenomenon and disco music so formularized, with heavy simple drumming, soft, laid-back choral singing and an increasing air of prefabrication, that the movement's minority origins are often forgotten. But in the early days of the New York discos, three groups dominated: homosexuals, blacks, and Latins. As a result, gentled-up rhythm-and-blues singing and a great use of Latin (including Brazilian) percussion became a permanent part of the New York disco sound. Groups like Seguida, the more recent Nebula, led by guitarist Eddie Benitez, and Sabor (founded in 1973) were inevitably tempted to move away from Latin-rock, which did not do well in the East, to disco-oriented music.

But there were more fundamental reasons why Latin-rock has been mostly a West Coast phenomenon. The eastern market for Latin music has been largely Latin-Caribbean. Mainstream salsa has dominated, because the Latin population is large enough to support its own music industry, even though on short rations, and the potential non-Latino public has seen Latin music in overly ethnic terms. Eastern Latin-rock players had, essentially, nowhere to go. Ethnic and class snobbery hampered them until recently, and when Latin music did start to be widely accepted by non-Latins again, the currents had moved away from rock fusions.

Meanwhile, the salsa audience itself did not take to Latin rock—partly out of conservatism, and partly because young experimental bands got no encouragement from club owners and promoters, who preferred to play safe with hard-core salsa, especially since it was beginning to boom.

In any case, the talent and concepts of Carlos Santana overshadowed all his rivals, and Santana remained the only nationally accepted Latin-rock group when, in 1976, he formed a new salsa-oriented band and returned to the idiom in a series of albums—starting with the 1976 *Amigos*—that were an uncommonly equal balance of salsa and rock, with strong jazz elements in the keyboard work. Santana's own floating, ecstatic guitar style, Tom Coster's driving jazz-influenced keyboard playing, and a tight, Afro-Cuban nucleus in the percussion (focusing on congacero Armando Peraza) resulted in a richness that was augmented by Santana's penchant for lush romanticism in melodies such as "Europa," and his use of Spanish acuostic guitar in "Gitana," both on the *Amigos* album.

Despite Santana's popularity, Latin-rock showed no signs of becoming a generalized style in the late 1970s. Even the group Caldera, most of whose members come from Latin countries, played essentially a jazz-rock fusion with Latin touches.

On the other hand, just as happened with jazz, and in a rather different way with rhythm-and-blues, rock as a whole has been affected to an increasing extent by a Latin influence. This was of two kinds: Mexican and Chicano music became increasingly prevalent in the stylistic grouping variously called country-rock, California folk rock, and soft-rock; and salsa showed an increasing penetration of black-influenced rock groups.

The effect of Mexican and Chicano music was first felt in parts of the country where rock and country music co-existed: notably in Texas, where the town of Austin became a center of a kind of country music counterculture. An early enthusiast of Chicano music was Doug Sahm, who grew up in San Antonio and made a minor name in the 1960s as "Sir Douglas," with a cover of the Beatles' song, "She's About a Mover." Sahm returned to Texas in 1971, and took up Chicano music, recording an album called *The Return of Doug Saldaña* and being nominated "Chicano of the Year" by *Rolling Stone* magazine. He played and recorded with Chicano musicians in Texas, included a polka,

"Chicano," in pure norteño style with accordion player Flaco Jiménez on his Atlantic album *Texas Tornado*, and is said to have been responsible for bringing Freddy Fender back to public attention the 1963, after his jail term. Flaco Jiménez also appeared on *Chicken Skin Music*, the fifth album of acoustic guitarist Ry Cooder, and toured with Cooder's Chicken Skin Revue, leading a Tex-Mex quintet.

Less obvious, but infinitely more influential, is the Mexican influence on the highly successful country-rock singer Linda Ronstadt. Ronstadt, whose popularity can be gauged by an awesome five straight million-selling albums, was born in Tucson, Arizona. Her father is part-Chicano, and she has told an interviewer that Mexican music was the basis of her own style. "The kind of music I listened to as a child was Mexican music— rancheras, like Lola Beltrán. So country it is, but it just doesn't happen to be this country." Aside from a liking for the bolero rhythms that have become increasingly widespread in pop-country music, and occasional mariachi touches, the Mexican influence in Ronstadt's music is not readily apparent, but in their emotionalism, as well as their use of three-four and brisk two-four time, contemporary commercial rancheras are so similar to U.S. commercial country music that this is not surprising.

Whether or not Linda Ronstadt's example had been the major cause, the general area where folk, country, and rock idioms meet turned increasingly to Mexican music in the late 1970s. Most noticeable has been the use of mariachi rhythms to express a romantic (and sometimes slightly sleazy) atmosphere. An early and effective example was the Amazing Rhythm Aces' 1975 "Third Rate Romance, Low Rent Rendezvous," a song whose success may well have helped to spread the usage. Young satirical pianist-singer-songwriter Linda Hargrove used a similar effect in "Mexican Love Songs," in which mariachi trumpets, delicate Mexican guitar, marimbas, and a bolero beat interwove with real—though ironic—charm in a ballad about scented nights and hangover mornings.

But Mexican touches also became an increasingly common resource in any song needing a particularly beguiling melody or rhythm. Captain Hook's 1977 "Making Love and Music" was one example; Maria Muldaur used mariachi trumpets on her 1978 "Say You Will"; and touches of marimba and mariachi melodism, together with a bolero rhythm, underpinned the misty surrealism of Michelle Phillips's "There She Goes."

These examples of overt influence were matched by subtler and more integrated usages. Hoyt Axton had a particular liking for a Mexican tinge. His 1975 joke about drugs and alcohol, "The No No Song," used mariachi trumpets as an atmospheric novelty. His 1974 "When the Morning Comes" set mariachi-type melody with a bolero feeling in a straight country-rock context with no Mexican references in the lyrics. By contrast, his 1976 "Flash of Fire" used a rhythm assimilating country and Mexican strums to support a melody with no Mexican touches and a Dixieland frontline.

Except in the specific case of Latin-rock, salsa has had less effect on rock than Mexican music. Its influence started in the rhythm section, the first step in most groups being the acquisition of a conga drum, especially in groups influenced by black music. Since the conga has its own musical logic, this led to the importation of Latin *toques,* however ill-understood. But the most significant Latin influence on mainstream rock groups has come at one remove, through the effect of Latinized black styles.

As black music has become more *overtly* Latin-influenced in the late 1970s, specific salsa elements have begun to surface in rock numbers. An example is "A Long Time for a Little While," by BTO (formerly Bachman-Turner Overdrive). This makes use of the mid-paced, slightly ominous son montuno rhythm so popular with salsa-minded black groups, and a very Cuban-sounding *cencerro* (cowbell) pattern, though the piece's melody and instrumental approach is otherwise totally un-Latin.

Though country music has made occasional use of mariachi rhythms, the Mexican influence in Nashville-based commercial country music (in contrast to California and Texas country-rock) has only become strong in the late 1970s, probably owing to the success of Linda Ronstadt and other pop-oriented country singers. Crystal Gayle's 1978 *When I Dream* album contained several tracks with typical Latinized country rhythms, notably "Someday Soon," "Talking in Your Sleep," which is vaguely reminiscent of a son montuno throb, and "Too Good to Throw Away," and "Wayward Wind" both of which used a bolero. The same generalized Latin rhythms were used in several tracks on a 1968 album by Mel Tillis, *I Believe in You*. This generalized Latin rhythm, which was used mostly by the more commercial country singers, and almost exclusively for slow songs, seems to have been the result of a merging of the older bolero-ballad tradition of popular music dating from the 1940s, and the new Mexican influence.

Despite the growing Latin presence in country music, very few Latino singers appeared on the scene. Aside from Linda Ronstadt, only two made any kind of mark. One was Johnny Rodriguez, who recorded a number of best-selling singles and albums in a mainstream pop-country style. The other was Freddy Fender. Fender's 1973 album, *Fuera de Alcance/Out of Reach*, was described by *Rolling Stone*'s Chet Flippo as "the ultimate presentation of raunchy Tex-Mex rock-and-roll." But when he gained wider recognition in the mid-1970s, and switched to the Nashville-based Dot label (later bought by ABC), most of the qualities that made him original disappeared. Flippo had called Fender's first version of "Wasted Days and Wasted Nights," the song that had given him his first success in the 1960s, "a classic of South Texas rock." His version for Dot substituted the standard self-pity of three-beers-down country music for the high-octane singing with which Mexican ranchera singers skirt sentimentality and often achieve passion.

Fender's best work during the 1970s was done for the Houston-based producer, Huey Meaux, whose output and attitudes matched the eclecticism of a city strong in blues, Cajun music, rhythm-and-blues, as well as country singing.

While English-language styles were taking in Mexican elements, Chicano music itself continued to develop. Though the 1960s was perhaps its peak period, classic norteño music continued to be popular. Recent corridos have continued to reflect Chicano attitudes, especially the rise in political and ethnic consciousness. "El Corrido de Cesar Chavez" reflected this with its stanza,

No pedimos limosna
solo un pago mas decente
Les exige Cesar Chavez
Para ayudar la gente

(We don't ask charity, only a better wage. That's Cesar Chavez'
demand to help the people.)
The chorus of "Mexciano Americano" expressed a more
fundamental pride,

Yo soy de la raza de oro,
Yo soy Mexicano-Americano!

(I'm of the race of gold, I'm Mexican-American.)
Meanwhile the local fusion style of younger musicians like
Little Joe Hernandez was also affected by this political upsurge.
In 1970, Hernandez dropped the somewhat eccentric r&b image
of the Latinaires and renamed his group La Familia. Musically, he
reaffirmed his intention to stay with his Chicano roots rather
than looking for crossover success.

1970s' albums like Hernandez's *Para La Gente* were strongly
influenced by New York salsa in their brass arrangements, as
well as by mainstream dance-band techniques in the trap
drumming, the organ playing, and some of the ensemble writing.
Nevertheless, most of La Familia's numbers remained very
firmly rooted in Mexican music: not so much the north-of-the-
border corridos and polkas as the rancheras that had swept into
popularity during the 1950s. Interestingly, when La Familia did
venture into Latin-rock, as in their "La Tuna," they were as
heavily salsa-oriented as Azteca or Malo, even to the New York
salsa brass punctuating the heavy-metal guitar solos.

Meanwhile, other Chicano fusion groups were also building
a local base. Among them were Debbie "La Chicarita" Martinez
and the Sanchez Brothers, of Albuquerque, New Mexico, both of
whom ranged between American pop and rancheras. Martinez
often performed with a mariachi group, and the Sanchez
Brothers recorded rock as well as Chicano numbers on a family
label.

This general eclecticism has been a major feature of all 1970s Latin fusions. While Mexican music has predominated in country music and its rock offshoots, and salsa and Brazilian music in Latin-jazz, these categories have also intermingled within the major divisions. This intra-Latin blending has gone relatively unnoticed—in part because it has been strong in styles, like disco music, that do not draw much analytical attention, but also because it has been the work of individuals rather than groups.

The increasing importance of the Latin-jazz stream during the 1970s went equally unnoticed, at least until the latter years; while some individual talents were recognized, they were mostly regarded as oddities rather than part of a general trend.

On the West Coast, Stan Kenton's big band continued to play certain Latin-oriented numbers, and Cal Tjader's various small Latin-jazz groups worked constantly out of the San Francisco area. Tjader remained broadly faithful to the quintet style of the 1950s, but within that limitation his various recordings reflect a varied and acute perception of trends of Latin jazz. For his album *Agua Dulce,* he worked with various local Latin-rock musicians; several of his recordings made use of Brazilian rhythms; and he touched bases with New York salsa again in the 1974 *Primo,* which teamed him with Tito Puente and Charlie Palmieri. West Coast Latin-jazz also interconnected with the Latin-rock movement, notably through trumpeter Luis Gasca.

Though critical attention in the East was focused on free jazz, some of the decade's most interesting Latin jazz came out of New York. One example, Cortijo's brilliant *Time Machine* album, has already been mentioned. Another was the work of composer and vibraphonist Bobby Paunetto, who issued two outstanding albums of his compositions on his own Pathfinder label.

Paunetto, who took up his instrument with the encouragement of Cal Tjader, studied under Gary Burton at the Berklee School of Music. His two albums, *Paunetto's Point* and *Commit to Memory,* assembled an amazing aggregation of Latin and non-Latin players, all of whom combined Latin, jazz, and sometimes rock experience. Saxist Ron Cuber, bassist Andy Gonzales, and percussionists Jerry Gonzalez and Manny Oquendo were the backbone of Eddie Palmieri's most successful band. Colombian pianist Eddie Martinez has played with both Ray Barretto and Gato Barbieri; trumpeter Tom Harrell, soloist on several Horace Silver's albums, also did time with both Azteca and Malo; tenorist Todd Anderson with Cold Blood and the Loading Zone; reedman Bill Drewes worked with Jaki Byard and Gary Burton; and electric bassist Abraham Leboriel had played with both Henry Mancini and Herbie Hancock!

Under a singularly gentle surface, Paunetto's compositions encompass a remarkable range of influences. He touches virtually all the Cuban bases, from Afro-Cuban drumming to charanga violins, but he tinges the same strings with conservatory inflections, and his approach to jazz is very much colored by the modal and free-rhythm experiments of the late 1960s and early 1970s. The result is of a quietly exhilarating subtlety that provides a very rich frame for his soloists.

Though Argentinian tenorist Gato Barbieri reached a far wider public than Cortijo or Paunetto, his considerable popularity has obscured the importance of his Flying Dutchman and Impulse recordings. Taken together, the recordings he made between 1969 and 1975 represented a remarkable experiment in the blending of jazz with a range of Latin-American styles much wider than has been attempted by any other musician. As we have seen, *Third World* included variegated and important Brazilian elements. Barbieri next went back to the tango, playing two of Carlos Gardel's most famous themes, "Mi Buenos Aires Querido" (on *Pampero*) and "El Dia Que Tu Me Quieras" on *Fenix*, which also included "El Arriero" by Atahualpa Yapanqui, a politically oriented Argentinian folk singer. In the 1973 album *Under Fire*, Barbieri allowed full play to his lush but gutty ballad style, which he had until then somewhat repressed.

Barbieri has described his switch from Flying Dutchman to the Impulse label as a watershed and the three *Chapter* albums that resulted as "a retrospective of Latin America." In *Chapter One* and *Chapter Two* he set his playing against three very different South American styles: Andean Indian, Afro-Brazilian, and city tango. The tracks called "Encuentros," which mix Andean ethnic Spanish musicians with jazz players, are more interesting than successful. But the tracks lumped together under the name

"Encontros," which use Afro-Brazilian samba percussion, work well, and the number in which Barbieri solos over a típico piano-and-accordion tango group is delightful. (There is, of course, a reason: unlike jazz and Andean Indian music, jazz, the samba, and the tango—all urban styles built from European and African elements—have a good deal of common ground.) Remembering Chico O'Farrill's Latin-jazz charts of the 1940s, Barbieri hired him to write arrangements for the most powerful of all his albums, *Chapter Three*. Using such Latin sideman as Eddie Martinez and Tito Rodriguez's former trumpeter, Victor Paz, as well as several versatile jazzmen, Barbieri and O'Farrill succeeded in fusing the drive of the big Latin bands with a lush romanticism that, while an important part of Latin-American music, has almost never translated successfully into American terms.

The music of Paunetto and Barbieri alone would be sufficient to prove the continued creative viability of Latin-jazz. But they were not alone. A wide range of jazz, especially styles that also interrelated with black popular music, took on an increasing Latin edge. By the mid-1970s, several musicians associated with the Californian Milestone-Fantasy-Prestige group of labels— notably saxist Joe Henderson—were recording extensively in the by-now classic format of jazz soloing and ensemble over Latin or part-Latin rhythm sections. Percussionist Bill Summers's 1977 album *Cayenne* contained a track called "Latican Space Mambo" with far stronger salsa elements than the funk-jazz school had yet attempted. Summers, whose band included one Latino, Ray Obiedo (who played tres as well as guitar and sang coro), is an example of something new in Latin-jazz: an American, he is so adept at Cuban percussion, including the sacred *batá* drums, that he plays regularly in *lucumí* religious ceremonies.

The Latin elements in *Cayenne* went beyond the use of percussion, including strongly salsa-based piano. This break-away from a purely percussion role for the Latin tinge was becoming general by the late 1970s. Piano montunos were more frequently used, especially by the so-called funk-jazz or fusion-jazz groups: characteristic was the keyboard work on alto saxist David Sanborn's 1978 "Morning Salsa."

This fusion style, which blended Latin and jazz (and often other) elements in idiosyncratic ways, developed rapidly toward the end of the decade. Chick Corea made a notable contribution in his *My Spanish Heart* album, which in his words, "floats over my perception of the history of Spain, Africa and Latin-America." Chicano trumpeter Luis Gasca, whose experience included playing for Perez Prado, Mongo Santamaria, Stan Kenton, Woody Herman, and even Janis Joplin, recorded two thoroughgoing fusion albums, *Born to Love* and *Collage,* in the mid-1970s.

Almost as far-reaching as the return of the Cuban-based tinge was the influence of Brazilian elements in jazz and popular styles. This was undoubtedly due in significant degree to the presence of Airto and Flora Purim in various groups of the late 1960s and early 1970s. Besides playing for more than two years with Miles Davis, Airto recorded on the first Weather Report album, and both he and Purim were with Chick Corea's Return to Forever for a while.

Airto's percussion—a blend of Brazilian and contemporary free techniques—had a marked effect on jazz rhythm sections, as did several other Brazilian percussionists who began working regularly with jazzmen in the 1970s. Among them was Guilherme Franco, whose influences, besides Brazilian music, included Tito Puente, the great cuban congacero Tata Guines, Elvin Jones, Max Roach, and Gene Krupa. Franco has worked regularly with pianists Keith Jarrett and McCoy Tyner for several years.

Not all of the Brazilians working in the U.S. were percussionists. Among them was a guitarist-accordionist, Sivuca, who had been South Africa singer Miriam Makeba's musical director during the 1960s. Raul de Souza, a trombonist brought over by Airto in 1973, does not regard himself as a "Brazilian" musician (though he played with Sergio Mendes in Rio); but his work with Kenny Clarke, the Crusaders, Sonny Rollins, Azar Lawrence, and Cal Tjader, as well as with Airto, has helped to make the jazzmen of the 1970s more conscious of Brazil. A musician closely associated with Airto is Hermeto Pascoal, who has commuted between Rio and the U.S. for several recordings. On balance, Airto is probably the single most influential of

these Brazilian musicians. Not only did he introduce avant-garde
Brazilian percussion to American jazz—his use of percussion as
coloring is now standard procedure—and also bring over or
encourage several of the other musicians, but he also produced a
series of outstanding albums of his own. These began with the
1970 *Natural Feelings* and 1971 *Seeds on the Ground* by a group that
included Sivuca, Hermeto Pascoal, Flora Purim, and American
bassist Ron Carter. Both were very strongly Brazilian, though
one track on the former, "Terror," exemplified Airto's avant-
garde leanings, and "O Sonho," on the second album, was the
first of Flora Purim's experimental vocals on record.

By 1972, Airto was becoming more closely involved with
jazz musicians, and his next album, *Free*, included Chick Corea,
Keith Jarrett, and George Benson on various tracks. After the
rock-oriented 1973 *Fingers* and an interesting 1974 album with
Balkan influences, *Virgin Land*, Airto switched recording labels
and made what has been to date by far his most adventurous and
successful album, *Identity*, a remarkable blend of jazz and rock
with an extremely wide range of Afro-Brazilian music, all in the
service of a very personal vision. The texture of *Identities* was
extraordinarily dense. Driving Afro-Brazilian percussion, berimbau musical bow, bossa nova vocals, almost purely Congo-
Angola melodies, Amerindian wooden flutes, rich strings, rock
drumming and guitar, shimmering free-rhythm bells and
strikers, a kind of manic avant-garde scatting, were interwoven
through multiple tracking in a series of compositions so rich in
their references that they took on deeper meaning on every
listening. *Identities* was undoubtedly one of the finest single
recordings of all Latin fusion music.

This Brazilian nucleus intersected with the Latin-minded
West Coast jazzmen in the studios of Fantasy Records, with
whom Purim had a singing and Airto a production contract.
Among early results was the 1974 *Summer Solstice* album by Azar
Lawrence, McCoy Tyner's saxist, which included a long-term
New York resident, Almaury Tristao; Raul de Souza; and Guil-
herme Franco.

Though the Berkeley recording studios were the main
center of this Brazilian tinge for some years, it was becoming

increasingly widespread throughout the 1970s. An early sign of its importance was *Down Beat* magazine's establishment of a percussion category in its annual popularity polls, which was won by Airto several years running. A milestone of another sort was a 1975 recording by Wayne Shorter, of Weather Report: *Native Dancer*. This featured singer Milton Nascimento, Airto, David Amaro, and Roberto Silva, all Brazilian, as well as keyboardist Herbie Hancock, and included five tracks written by Nascimento. By 1977, the Brazilian influence was quite widespread. In that year, Dizzy Gillespie—who had never abandoned his love of Latin music—recorded an album, *Dizzy's Party*, which showed how well fringe-Brazilianisms could work in the hands of a musician who understood them. Both the title track and "Harlem Samba" had part-funk, part-samba rhythms whose Brazilian elements were strong enough to avoid the kind of cocktail-jazz garnish to which jazzmen have too often reduced Latin rhythms.

For some time, Gillespie worked with a young Brazilian percussionist, Paulinho da Costa, whose own 1977 album, *Agora*, included several remarkable tracks, including a magnificent piece of percussion chamber music; "Terra," an overdubbed work for berimbau; an unusually effective jazz-latin-disco track, "Belisco"; and a long reminiscence of Rio's samba schools, "Ritmo Number One." Da Costa's 1978 recording with guitarist Joe Pass and several Brazilian musicians, *Tudo Bem*, established something of the same jazz-Brazilian rapport as the early jazz-bossas of Charlie Byrd, but—characteristic of 1970s Latin-jazz—with much greater Brazilian participation.

Renewed interest also led to recordings by Brazil-based musicians flown in to the U.S. for the occasion. Notable among these were two more or less pure Brazilian albums on the Island label, *Samba Nova* and *Tropical*, by Jorge Ben, a major bossa nova composer, and Hermeto Pascoal's highly eclectic Warner Bros. album *Slaves Mass*.

Most of these Brazilian recordings kept their Latin and their jazz elements in some kind of balance. At the same time, there was a return of the kind of jazz-with-Latin-fringes that had always hovered on the outskirts of any major Latin-jazz movement. "Captain Marvel," in trombonist Urbie Green's album,

Señor Blues, which involved no Latin musicians (though its second trombonist, Sam Burtis, had played with salsa groups), was a fast samba made over by contemporary funk-jazz rhythm procedures. Further examples included two Brazilian-inspired numbers on guitarist Earl Klugh's well-received Blue Note album, *Finger Painting*—"Dr. Macumba" and "Cabo Frio."

By the mid-1970s, a Brazilian influence was also being felt in rock, though in far more tentative fashion than in jazz. Again, one significant influence was Airto. All of his later albums have blended Brazilian elements with both jazz and rock, but one particularly strongly rock-oriented album, *Fingers,* inspired an interesting group from Puerto Rico called Raices, whose Brazilian elements were much stronger than their salsa. Raices, which was formed in 1973, made one album in 1975 for the Nemperor label, but never gained much popular success.

More significant was Carlos Santana's second album after his return to Latin-rock, the 1977 *Festival,* whose opening number, "Carnaval," was a piece of almost-straight Rio carnival music played, so to speak, with a Cuban accent. Another cut on the same album, "Verão Vermelho," made use of classical-style acoustic guitar and a strong Brazilian feeling in the vocals. In 1978, the group Pablo Cruise had a considerable success with a cover of "I Go to Rio," by Peter Allen, which we shall meet again. But in rock proper, Brazilian inflections have shown no signs of becoming more than an occasional decorative feature.

Strong rock elements were meanwhile becoming a part of Brazilian music itself, in the hands of its younger artists. Neither singer Nascimento nor keyboardist Pascoal plays "Brazilian" music in any restrictively ethnic sense, though their strong combination of eclecticism and roots is typical of Brazil's highly experimental outlook. While making liberal use of the popular street-sound, as well as the African and Portuguese ends of the Brazilian ethnic spectrum, their albums also reflect strong rock and jazz elements, some English lyrics, a liking for avant-garde experimentation, and occasional lapses into artiness.

All these were individual examples of a trend also manifested in less obvious ways. One was the sudden popularity of the cuica, which from 1975 on began appearing in a wide variety of recordings, ranging from Willie Colon's album, *The Good, the Bad, the Ugly* to Ralph MacDonald's disco-oriented "The Only Time You Say You Love Me" and "Brazilian Skies."

Presumably by way of this funk-rock-jazz nexus, the Brazilian tinge has also shown signs of spreading into the cabaret field, in a rerun of the ebullient stereotypes common in the 1940s. In 1977, Peter Allen, a pianist-singer with a cult following on the younger supper-club circuit, recorded a remarkable version of his song, "I Go to Rio," whose ironically stereotyped Rio-as-earthly-paradise theme is set to a blend of disco, rhythm-and-blues, and Brazilian rhythms. Over it, Allen played a lengthy, marvelously eclectic paino solo that jumbled salsa montunos, "continental Latin" touches, ragtime, and jazz over samba-school percussion-and-whistles backing.

The tendency to mix rhythms and influences—common in American-Latin styles, but equally fundamental to Willie Colon's style and a standard procedure in 1970 salsa as a whole—is inherent in the New York disco music's combined salsa and Brazilian edge. A straight, though not necessarily clear, line links the Latin-black blends of the bugalú era and the particular combination of pseudo-mechanical trap drumming, salsa percussion, and samba-like lilt (with or without cuica) typical of the New York disco sound.

The reason is not far to seek. At least since the beginning of the tango era, individual dance crazes have invariably coincided with revivals of Latin styles in the U.S., for Latin dances have combined a danceability and an ebullience rare among their rivals. Moreover, coming from a culture in which people of all ages dance as a matter of course, they are not limited to any particular generation.

This general principle has been reinforced by the fact that the New York City discos are fairly heavily black and Latin in staff and public. Moreover, the city's two or three Brazilian discos have acted as a creative source for musicians since the mid-1970s.

The link between the bugalú and disco phenomena is symbolized by the career of Joe Bataan, who spent the beginning of the decade in limbo, his former Latin-soul successes apparently unrepeatable. Then in 1973, he recorded an album called *Salsoul* on the relatively insignificant Mericana label. This got airplay on New York's influential black radio station, WBLS, and Bataan found himself with a sizeable hit. After a national tour that included an appearance at the 1974 Berkeley Jazz Festival, he recorded a second album *Afrofilipino,* for the new Salsoul label. This was picked up for national distribution by Epic Records, and one cut, "La Botella," became a disco hit both in the U.S. and in Britain.

Bataan then went into eclipse again owing to a complex of disagreements with his record company, and spent 1976 developing the Brazilian sound that he was convinced was important to the developing disco style. The resulting album, *LaSo* (as in Latin Soul), appeared on MCA. Though this did not do particularly well commercially, it made exceptionally intelligent use of the typical mid-1970s New York musical quilt. The usual disco strings and "party-party" vocalizing was set off by good jazz solos, and an underlying rhythm-and-blues salsa blend in the rhythm section was freshened by Afro-Brazilian percussion. It was typical of the problems facing Latin musicians in breaking into the (from their point of view) separate "American" market that this mix—virtually unexplored when Bataan began working on it—was commonplace by the time his album appeared.

Developments in jazz, rock, and disco music were paralleled in the black popular music that had been called rhythm-and-blues and then soul. Aside from the fundamental shift to a Latinized rhythm, several groups created explicit fusions that gradually led to a marked and overt salsa content in black popular music—first in the earthy regions of what had come to be called funk music and then more generally.

A common denominator among these groups was a heavy commitment to rhythm. The enormously successful Earth, Wind and Fire developed an amazing percussive fire power based not only on leader Maurice White's five sets of timbales but on a trumpet section that doubled on congas! Aside from this generally Latin influence, they also made early use, in a number called "Evil," of the modified son montuno that seems to be contemporary black groups' favorite salsa rhythm, and returned to the same rhythm in the 1977 "Serpentine Fire."

Two other influential groups made even more specific reference to black-Latin blends. One was War, a band from Los Angeles whose highly successful 1974 *War Live* album included a widely played single with strong salsa elements, "Bailero." War had no Latin members, and the group's black-Latin blending was part of the general tendency to the use of Latin rhythmic patterns within black music. By contrast, Mandrill came by its fusions as of birthright. Its nucleus was three brothers from Panama, part of the large English-speaking minority of that country. The Anglo-Panamanians (many of whom, from Luis Russell to Billy Cobham, were important in jazz) have a dual musical heritage, since they come from a Latin country, but a community that still maintains strong ties with Jamaica and the United States. Since its first album, in 1970, Mandrill has developed a markedly personal sound out of radical and apparently effortless blends of jazz, r&b, and salsa, including a salsa-reggae fusion for solo trombone that is something of a trademark.

War, Mandrill, and Earth, Wind and Fire were precursors of an overt Latinization of black music which became more general around 1976. As it had done in the case of jazz, this soon spread out from the rhythm section. One track of an album by tenor saxist Willis Jackson made use of salsa inspirations in place of rhythm-and-blues brass riffs. Percussionist Ralph MacDonald (the son of Harlem calypso singer The Great McBeth, who frequently appeared on the same bill as Arsenio Rodriguez) has made use of conjunto brass.

A remarkable example of salsa influence in black music came in a 1978 album by Patti LaBelle, *Tasty*. This included one track, "Teach Me Tonight/Me Gusta Tu Baile," which was virtually pure salsa. A son montuno, its brass and sax sound was essentially that of the Fania All-Stars, its piano was Latin, it included a coro—and Patti LaBelle's own vocal combined soul and salsa ingredients and ended with an imitation of a *guarachera*'s improvisations.

Latin music's renewed influence during the 1970s raised the

question in Latino musicians' minds: would they benefit, either by reaching a larger audience with the pure salsa sound, or by "crossing over" themselves into American music?

Aside from the obvious and famous examples, whose market always had been American—notably Xavier Cugat, and, in a very different context, Mongo Santamaria—several musicians had maintained long, though low-profile, contact in the "American" music world. Ray Barretto had played conga as a sideman on hundreds of jazz, rhythm and blues, and latterly even rock recordings. Others, among them singer Sammy Davis, Jr., and pianist Chick Corea, were so thoroughly absorbed in "American" music that their Latin origins (musical or personal) were more or less forgotten. But most New York Latin musicians were essentially isolated from the mainstream in a separate and unequal market. Without an "American" recording contract, their chances of crossover in the contemporary music business were minimal. A handful of such contracts were therefore the first real signs that Latinos might move into the larger market.

Within a few months of each other in 1977, a skeletal version of the Fania All-Stars signed with Columbia Records and Ray Barretto with Atlantic Records. The Fania All-Stars, augmented by American guest musicians, made a series of essentially disco-oriented records. After an initial live salsa recording, Barretto explored a jazz-rock-salsa fusion, in an album produced by, and featuring, the Crusaders. Eddie Palmieri—perhaps the best known salsero outside the Latin market—joined Epic Records, and, after a long gestation, recorded an album with strong rhythm-and-blues elements as well as lucumí and Brazilian influences, *Lucumi, Macumba, Voodoo.*

These were all well-established musicians or groups. Given the fairly long-term nature of most major waves in popular music, the younger musicians—less set in their ways, with less to lose by risk-taking, and more likely to be temperamentally in tune with new developments—are particularly significant.

By 1977 there were clear signs that younger Latino musicians and bands were moving toward the general jazz-funk-disco-rock nexus. The immensely popular Bobby Rodriguez y la

Compañia experimented with English lyrics, as well as with a Dixieland jazz-like trumpet-clarinet-trombone lead in some numbers. Ricardo Marrero's The Group recorded an initial single, "Babylonia," which received play on the soul radio stations, and an eclectic 1977 album, *Time.* Angel Canales, leader of the group Sabor, had an interesting—because new to salsa—mannered, indeed almost decadent edge to his singing that probably stemmed from disco music.

Equally significant, younger Latin musicians were also finding work as studio sidemen. Notable among them were Nicky Marrero, a timbales player who became a star featured player with many groups, and a young flutist called David Valentin who moved freely between Latin and jazz-funk recording sessions.

Whether salsa itself can gain a wider audience is moot. Many Latin musicians believe that Spanish vocals are an inhibiting factor; yet English vocals would in themselves constitute a form of fusion, and no contemporary equivalent of the Latin bugalú yet shows signs of developing. More important than language, the recording industry has become almost entirely segregated. Even Fania records—by far the largest of the Latin companies—has no appreciable distribution outside the Latin markets. With the exception of Eddie Palmieri, salsa groups rarely play concerts before non-Latin audiences. Across-the-board distribution, airplay, and promotion—crucial to any crossover—are minimal, haphazard, and essentially accidental.

As a minority cult music, capable of inspiring great loyalty and enthusiasm, salsa has the esthetic depth and validity to gain a new non-Latin following like the *mamboniks* or Palladium holdovers who have remained loyal to Machito and Puente. Given that young Chicanos are discovering salsa for the first time, and that several cities are also beginning to support small Latin music markets of their own, such a cult-following could well develop on a national scale. But mass popularity is another matter. Pure jazz has never had it, nor have the authentic versions of any previously popular Latin styles. There is little reason to suppose that salsa will prove the exception.

NINE

Coda:
"Mundo Latino"

The popularity and influence of Latin-American music is an international phenomenon. In only one other area, Africa, has it had so far-reaching an effect as it has on the United States, but from the tango bass in many Greek *bouzouki* songs to Latin rock bands of Tokyo, its popularity has been worldwide.

To what extent 19th-century Europe was aware of Latin-American music is unclear. As we have seen, the famous habanera in Bizet's *Carmen* was possibly Havanese only in name, and though Juventino Rosas's "Sobre las Olas" (under the title "Über die Wellen") was hugely popular during the late 19th century, it was so Viennese in style that nobody believed it was Mexican. Toward the end of the century, however, the Orquesta Típica of Juan Torre Blanca did tour Germany specifically to spread knowledge of Mexican instrumentation and music, and there were doubtless many other scattered contacts.

The first indubitable major influence on Europe was the tango, which had crossed the Atlantic even before reaching the United States. By 1907, a group called Los Gobbi and Villaldo had recorded in France, and it was in Paris, in 1912, that Vernon and Irene Castle learned it. (Oddly enough, it did not become popular in Mexico for another decade.) The Brazilian maxixe, too, seems to have reached Europe before the U.S., though there it was a stage rather than social dance, to judge by a photograph in a 1906

Illustrierte Zeitung and a caption in an English magazine claiming it as the "1908 successor to the cancan."

Though the Castles claimed, in their *Modern Dance,* that the Parisians had toned the dance down, the tango caused at least as much scandal in Europe as in the U.S. The Vicar-General of Rome proclaimed that it "gravely outrages modesty," and the Cardinal Archbishop of Paris condemned "the dance imported from abroad known as the tango, which, by its nature, is indecent and offensive to morals, and in which Christians may not in conscience take part," adding that dancing the tango might well be a subject for Confession.

Such warnings daunted the French as little as the Americans. Indeed, the tango became, if anything, a *more* ingrained part of French than of American popular music, perhaps because one of its instruments was the accordion. It was still used by French music hall stars such as Line Renaud and Edith Piaf into the 1950s, and I recall my own astonishment during the same period at finding French teenagers dancing impartially to the tango and to the music of New Orleans jazzmen like Sidney Bechet.

The tango's influence was worldwide; its characteristic rhythm still sometimes surfaces in Greek *bouzouki* music, and I have even heard it in a recording of Malay *rongeng.* Though it, too, was discovered or rediscovered from time to time, Mexican music had much less impact, except via songs already popular in the U.S. The ballerina Anna Pavlova, who toured Mexico in 1918, added to her repertoire a ballet version of the *jarabe tapatico* (which had been described as Mexico's unofficial national dance), which helped to popularize some of its melodies, notably the so-called "Mexican Hat Dance." But in Europe as in the U.S., the next Latin style of major impact was the rumba. The rumba's effect, as it was summed up at the time by the London *Daily News,* was to "revitalize dancing as it has not been revitalized since the days when the American Foxtrot rescued us from those hops, parades and romps known as the polka, quadrille and lancers."

As in the U.S., the major vehicle of change was Don Azpiazú. The first British rumba band was formed in 1930 by one José Norman, who was engaged to a Cuban and had heard Azpiazú's recording of "The Peanut Vendor." In 1931, Queen Mary included the song in the music for the first Buckingham Palace ball since 1924, and Marion Sunshine sang it at a Royal Command Performance. According to Azpiazú's brother, Don Antobal, who had made a European sales tour in December 1930, it was through the British that the rumba spread to Europe. Neither Paris nor Berlin was interested in "The Peanut Vendor" until an English publisher bought it in January 1931 and had success with it. The resulting chain reaction was so strong that Antobal even claimed that American interest in the rumba, declining by early 1932, was revived by the sudden European enthusiasm. Don Azpiazú himself toured Europe that year playing the Casino at Monte Carlo, as well as Holland, Belgium, Spain, Italy, and Austria. The result was predictable. In Don Antobal's words, "Havana was denuded of musicians all flocking on our trail." Particularly popular was Ernesto Lecuona's Lecuona Cuban Boys, which toured Europe several times in the 1930s.

From then on, more or less every Latin wave that struck the U.S. also struck Europe, mostly by way of New York—though a British musician called Maurice Burman composed one of the earliest of non-Cuban congas, called simply "Conga," in 1935. In France, the rumba proved as durable as the tango. By 1952, Xavier Cugat's "Miami Beach Rumba" had received no fewer than twenty-seven different cover recordings under its French title of "Voyage à Cuba"! Internationally, simplified but unmistakable rumba rhythms became a permanent part of a remarkable range of music, including Greek *bouzoukia* (an example in an album widely offered to tourists in Greece is a piece called "Ipomoni," played by Stelios Zaphiriou).

Mexican music was never as influential as Cuban music with one notable exception: some German popular music of the late 1950s showed quite strong Mexican influences. The reason may have been a combination of the general popularity of Latin music as a whole, and the fact that the waltz and polka rhythms that were basic to Mexican music were Central European in origin. In any event, singers like the extremely popular Caterina Valente not only performed internationally popular numbers like "Andalucia" ("The Breeze and I") and the tango "Jalousie" but also

German songs plainly influenced by Mexican melody and, particularly, harmony.

Most Latin music, of whatever era, reached Europe second hand, via pop-American hybrids. But not all. In 1938, an all-woman group from Havana, La Anacaona Septet, topped the bill at Les Ambassadeurs in Paris, and played opposite guitarist Django Reinhardt at Chez Florence in Montmartre. One of its members was Graciela, who later became Machito's female lead singer, and it was trained by Alberto Socarrás. But such contacts were relatively rare, and there was no large permanent Latin community in any of the European cities to preserve a sense of authenticity or a base for Latin music. Latin musicians working in Europe were therefore largely out of touch with their roots, and under constant pressure to over-adapt their music to local tastes.

Britain's most famous Latin bandleader, Edmundo Ros, was a case in point. Ros, who came to London in 1937, began his musical career as tympanist with the Venezuelan State Symphony Orchestra. In London he switched to jazz drums, playing behind Fats Waller on one of his British tours, before founding his first sextet in 1940. This became a fixture at London's Coconut Grove during World War Two. (Queen Elizabeth is said to have danced for the first time in public to its music.)

At first Ros attempted to play fairly authentic smooth Cuban dance music. But like Cugat, he found that mass acceptance did not lie in that direction. On the advice of British musician friends he got rid of most of his percussion and emphasized the melody—a formula that brought him long-lasting success, at the cost of persuading the musically minded of two generations that Latin music was contentless and banal.

With the unique exception of Kenny Graham and his Afro-Cubists, a 1950s–60s group that combined Cubop with African drumming by Ghanaian percussionist Guy Warren, most British Latin music was indeed just that. Within very few years of Don Azpiazú's visit, it was mostly played by British musicians with lightly Latinized names, and rhythm sections devoid of Cuban percussion.

The same held broadly true for most parts of the world. Nevertheless, certain countries continued to have a public for Latin music until much later than others. Finland was one: Armando Orefiche and his Havana Cuban boys (a breakaway from the original Lecuona Cuban Boys) played in Helsinki in 1957, and a much altered version of the Lecuona Boys themselves several times in the 1960s and 1970s.

But the largest contemporary public for Latin music outside the New World—a public large enough to support a magazine devoted exclusively to Latin-American music—is Japan, with its large appetite for American music of all kinds. During the 1970s, the Japanese have developed a great enthusiasm for salsa. A large number of New York recordings have been released. The only Japanese salsa album released in the U.S.—*Joyful Feet*, by Matsuoka Naoya and his All-Stars—blends electric guitar à la Santana with fine post-bop ensemble wind writing as effectively as all but the best American fusion music. Other Japanese bands also exist, such as the Tokyo Cuban Boys.

For the most part, the Latin influence on the world's music has been both pervasive and slight; a faint tinge that has sometimes been apparently permanent, like the occasional *bouzouki* tangos and rumbas, sometimes a reflection of current American developments, like the transmuted Mexican bolero bass on which the Australian rock group Little River Band built their 1978 ballad "Light of Day."

In some parts of the world, however, this influence has been far from minor. Not surprisingly, these have been areas with strong cultural links to Latin America. The Trinidad calypso style of the 1930s was very strongly influenced by the Cuban septetos. While the singers remained purely Trinidadian, their accompanying bands adopted the distinctive septeto style of muted trumpet. In at least two cases, moreover, Cuban tunes were simply translated into the British West Indian canon. One of these was the Septeto Nacional's son, "La Chambelona," which was co-opted by Lord Power under the title of "Chambolina." The other was Miguel Matamoros's superlative "Olvido," of which a truncated version became a calypso called "Anacaona."

Outside the United States, however, infinitely the greatest impact of Latin music (and above all of Cuban idioms and New York salsa) has been felt in Africa, where the roughly coincidental arrival of the guitar and of recordings by Cuban guajiro groups such as the Trio Matamoros and the Guaracheros de Oriente brought about the birth of an entire new family of popular styles.

The adoption of the guitar by musicians all over Africa led to two main generic styles of modern popular music. The first usually involved a group consisting of one or two guitarists with some sort of percussion—almost always a bottle tapped with a knife to give a high chinking note: by a single guitar; or by a guitar with another instrument, usually African, with or without percussion. The second style came about through the addition of European instruments (usually, at first, guitar) to a traditional percussion dance ensemble.

Some African musicians began by playing on the guitar patterns much like the ones they had played on whatever stringed instruments were traditional for them. Others learned mainly by imitating whatever foreign models were available to them. At the opposite end of the scale from the semi-tribal "folk" songs were many recordings that were almost straight translations of foreign styles.

Among the most copied of recordings during the 1930s and 1940s were RCA Cuban discs pressed in London. Guitarists from Cameroon to Kenya—but most importantly, from the Congo—began to imitate the artists on these recordings, and in particular the Trio Matamoros and the Guaracheros de Oriente, the best-known guajiro groups. Mozambique examples of this early African acoustic guitar style show slight Portuguese and Brazilian traits. But the common Latin influence (direct or indirect) in other areas was practically always Cuban, though in the Belgian Congo there was some early biguine influence (the Congo being Belgian, and thus French-language, administered).

The influence of Latin music on later African dance bands was more varied. Ghanaian and Nigerian "high life" groups used local rhythms. The early band of E. T. Mensah, and particularly

Mensah's trumpet playing, owed much to the muted solo trumpet at one time featured by Perez Prado, and by Prado's British imitator, Eddie Calvert, whose version of "Cherry Pink and Apple Blossom White" is echoed frequently on Mensah's records from the 1950s to the 1970s. Ghanaian flutists are influenced by charanga flute-playing, but other frontline playing is mostly jazz-oriented.

The dance bands of the Congo—now Zaire—are a different matter. By the late 1950s their foreign ingredients were virtually all Cuban. Early discs of Congo music used fiddles in a response to the Cuban charanga ensembles. Until about 1958, Congo bands were playing in a fairly skilled Cuban-derived style, in which elements of a local guitar technique and an Africanization of melody lines were offset by fairly Cuban rhythm lines and sax or clarinet influence.

About 1960, however, Congolese musicians began to develop an idiosyncratic electric guitar style derived partly from local techniques and partly from the playing on guitar of lines that, in Cuban music, were carried by brass or sax. Congolese records from the early 1960s frequently used essentially Afro-Cuban brass phrasings in their guitar work.

The choice of the rumba had several important results for African pop music. First, the rumba has built-in possibilities for improvisation of its montuno, which gave Congo lead guitarists a chance to shine. Second, the use of a rhythm that was African in its roots but was not associated with any one part of Africa (as was Ghanaian highlife) accounted to some degree at least for the remarkable spread of Congo music. Highlife never caught on in East Africa, because it was too *West* African. The rumba—at least as reinterpreted by Central Africans—was, paradoxically, less foreign to East Africans.

East Africa was also considerably influenced by Cuban music. Tanzanian dance music in the early 1960s, as represented by groups like the Cuban Marimba Band with Salim Abdulla, modified the Cuban influence with an Arab element due to the Islamic civilization of the East Coast. Certain Tanzanian recordings of the early 1960s were almost purely Afro-Arab in singing style, and Salim Abdulla once brought off the stylistic *coup* of using an Arab-style bridge between two Cuban-type sections. The Arab content vanished later in the decade, except perhaps for a certain harsh but gentle quality in Tanzanian vocal tone, but Tanzanian bands continued to be affected by Latin elements imported by way of Kinshasa.

Kenya's pop music was less influenced by Cuba, though a much localized Latin beat given idiosyncrasy by the Kenyan two-voice, two-guitar formula and by a form consisting of three verses, each of a couplet repeated, was common until the late 1960s, when Zairean music's popularity virtually obliterated the local substyle.

Ever since the mid-1960s, the Latin element in African music has been growing smaller, until there is more difference between contemporary Zairean guitar playing and its Cuban sources than there is between Yoruba religious playing and the drumming of the Cuban lucumí that descended from it. Nevertheless, the creation of an Africa-wide nexus of styles from a largely Latin model is one of the most striking examples of Latin music's effect on the music of large parts of the world: an effect as important in this century (and as underestimated) as the impact of African music in the two that preceded it.

Glossary

Latin Rhythms

The basic meter of salsa is 4/4, organized by the two-bar clave pattern. The individual forms, of which the most common are listed below, are not simply "rhythms" that can be tapped with a pencil, but combinations of rhythmic pulse, melodic phrases, speed, song form, and so on.

Agogó

A percussion instrument of West African origin, the agogó is essentially a two-note clapperless double-bell, joined by a curved piece of metal and struck by a stick. Used in the African-derived religions of Brazil, it is one of several new percussion instruments introduced to the U.S. by Brazilian musicians during the 1970s.

Aguinaldo

Though they are sung around Christmas, Puerto Rican aguinaldos cover a wide range of social and topical as well as religious subjects. They are sung solo or by a choir and are based on the ten-line décima, which travelled from Renaissance Italy to Spain, and thence to virtually all of Latin-America.

Baião

One of many rhythms of the African-influenced Northeast of Brazil, the baião became popular in Rio de Janeiro around 1950 as a reaction against the increasingly international popular music of the time. Its most famous exponent, Luis Gonzaga, made the accordion-led *regional* group extremely popular. A few U.S. jazzmen experimented with the baião in the early 1950s, but it was too unsuccessful to be called a bridge between the samba and the bossa nova.

Bajo Sexto

A form of 12-string guitar used as an accompanying instrument by Chicano singers.

Barrio, El

"The district." The districts or areas of Latin American towns are called barrios, so when Latin immigrants settled in large numbers in New York's East Harlem, it became The district. The nickname has stuck even though many major U.S. cities now have barrios.

Batá Drums

Double-headed drums shaped like an hour-glass with one cone larger than the other. Sacred to Yoruba religion in Nigeria, they are also necessary to Cuban and U.S. lucumí worship. A number of salsa musicians have recently begun using batá drums in secular music.

Berimbau

A Brazilian musical bow of Congo-Angolan origin. An open gourd resonater is held against the chest, and the instrument's string is tapped with a stick.

Bolero

The Cuban bolero, originally a mid-paced form for string trios, became very popular internationally, usually in a slower and more sentimental form. The modern bolero is a lush romantic popular-song form, largely distinct from salsa, and very few singers are equally good at both.

Bomba

Originally a Puerto Rican three-drum dance form of marked west-central African ancestry, the bomba is especially associated with the Puerto Rican village of Loiza Aldea. In its old form it is still played there at the festival of Santiago, and New York Puerto Rican folk revival companies also perform it from time to time. Even in the dance band form introduced by Rafael Cortijo in the late 1950s, the bomba's melodies, as well as rhythmic pulse, are strongly African.

Bongó

Small double-drum played resting on the calves of a seated musician, called a *bongosero*. Its heads are tuned a fourth apart. Widely used in Cuban music of many sorts, especially the quartets and sextets playing sones, and an integral part of the salsa percussion section. In salsa, as in earlier string-based groups, the bongó tends to be played more ad lib than other drums and to provide a complex counterpoint to a number's main rhythmic pulse. The basic toque for the bongó, called the *martillo*, can be rendered onomatopoeically as "Dicka-docka-dicka-ducka."

Bossa Nova

A Brazilian fusion of cool jazz elements with various Brazilian rhythms, including the baião but particularly the samba. Often wrongly considered Afro-Brazilian, it is a sophisticated and recent form developed by hip musicians and avant-garde poets. Most were white, though Bola Sete, a leading bossa nova guitarist, is an exception.

Bugalú, Latin

The Latin bugalú was a somewhat simplified and more sharply accented mambo with English lyrics, singing that combined Cuban and black inflections, and r&b influenced solos. For a few years the bugalú, and a less known Puerto Rican rhythm, the jala jala, were staples of the "Latin soul" movement.

Cencerro

Large hand-held cowbell played with a stick, producing two notes according to where it is struck. In Cuban music and salsa, usually played by the bongó player when the band goes into the "ride" or mambo, after the main vocal sections.

Chachachá

The chachachá is said by some to have derived from the second section of the danzón, by others to be a slower mambo. It was sometimes called a "double mambo" in New York, because its basic dance step was the mambo with a double step between the fourth to first beats. The chachachá developed around 1953 in the hands of Cuban charangas, most notably the Orquesta Aragón.

Charanga

A Cuban dance orchestra consisting of flute backed by fiddles, piano, bass, and timbales. Charangas tended to play different dances from the Afro-Cuban conjuntos, the most characteristic being the danzón. Charangas ranged from large society units to small street-bands. Modern charangas use bongó and conga in the rhythm section and have taken on many more Afro-Cuban elements than their predecessors.

Cierre

Essentially a break, the cierre ranges from a two-note bongó phrase to a complicated pattern for a full band more like a bridge-passage. Good cierres are fundamental to salsa structure, but they are so varied and used in so many ways that closer definition would be misleading.

Clave

An offbeat 3/2 or 2/3 rhythmic pattern over two bars, the basis of all Cuban music, into which every element of arrangement and improvisation should fit. Clave is an African-derived pattern with equivalents in other Afro-Latin musics. The common 3/2 Cuban clave varies in accentuation according to the rhythm being played. Clave seems to be part of the inspiration for the two-bar bass patterns in modern black music. 2/3 reverse clave is less common, though the guaguancó uses it.

Claves

Twin strikers of resonant wood used less frequently in salsa than in earlier Cuban music. The claves player usually plays the basic clave pattern (q.v.), which is normally implied rather than stated by modern bands. Many variants of claves exist throughout Latin America.

Conga Drum

A major instrument in the salsa rhythm section, the conga is literally the "Congolese drum," and it began life in the Afro-Cuban cults. Arsenio Rodriguez is said to have introduced it to the conjuntos on a regular basis, and Machito's Afro-Cubans were the first to use it on New York bandstands. There are several types of conga, including the small *quinto,* a solo improvising the instrument; the mid-sized *conga;* and the large *tumbadora.* Played by an expert, the conga is capable of a great variety of sound and tone, not only from the different ways of striking or rubbing the head, but through raising the instrument from the ground when it is played held between the knees. A conga-player is called a *conguero* or *congacero*.

Conga Rhythm

The Cuban conga was originally a carnival dance-march from Santiago de Cuba, with a heavy fourth beat, but the rhythm is common to carnival music in many parts of the New World. The conga rhythm is more easily simplified than most Cuban rhythms and was a natural for nightclub floorshows. It never became permanent in mainstream Latin music, though Eddie Palmieri introduced a modified version called the *mozambique* in the late 1960s.

Conjunto (lit. "combo")

Cuban conjunto sprang from the carnival marching bands and combined voices, trumpets, piano, bass, conga, and bongó. Arsenio Rodriguez ran a seminal Cuban conjunto that used the smokey tone of the tres (q.v.) to balance the brass, and over the years conjuntos began adding a trombone or even in New York substituting trombones for trumpets.

The *Chicano* conjunto consisted of an accordion lead, guitar and/or bajo sexto (q.v.), often bass, and sometimes spoons, with the addition of bongó or other Cuban-derived percussion during the 1960s. Used strictly for instrumental dance music until the 1930s, during the 1940s it became the standard backing for corridos, rancheras, and other vocal forms.

The *Puerto Rican* conjunto, the basic group of jibaro country music, consisted of cuatro, guitar, and güayo scraper, though trumpet and/or clarinet were added at various times, and accordion-led conjuntos playing danzas and waltzes for dancing were not uncommon.

Contradanza

17th and 18th century dance of French origin from which many Latin American ballroom dances derive via mainland Spain, including the danzón and the danza.

Coro

The "chorus." In salsa, the two or three-voice refrains of two or four bars sung during montunos. The lead singer improvises against the refrains. Coros are used in various ways in arrangements; as reprises or, by an alteration of the refrain, to establish a change of mood.

Corrido

This Mexican and Chicano ballad form developed during the 19th century and reached its peak during the first half of the 20th. Pure folk ballads in their simplicity, their detail, their deadpan performing style, the corridos were the history books, news reports, and editorials of the illiterate. They chronicled the whole of the Mexican civil war, almost all notable crimes, strikes, and other political events, and a hundred other subjects besides.

Cuatro

A small, ten-stringed guitar, one of the many guitar variants to be found in Spain and Latin America. The cuatro is a major instrument in Puerto Rican jibaro country music.

Cuica

A small Brazilian friction drum with a tube fastened to the inside of the drumhead, which is rubbed to produce a squeaky sound on the same principle as children use with a wetted finger and a window pane, but infinitely more varied. The cuica became a familiar sound in 1970s disco music, jazz, and salsa.

Danzón

A Cuban ballroom dance derived from the contradanza in the late 1870s. It was regularly played by flute-and-fiddle charangas until the early 1950s. The danzón bears the mark of Europe and its first section was usually a promenade, but its charm is not merely nostalgic. Its melodies echo from time to time in modern salsa.

Descarga

The word means "discharge" and is a Latin musician's slang term for a jam session. Descargas occupy a position midway between salsa and Latin-jazz, since they tend to preserve the Cuban structures yet contain far more jazz soloing than does salsa.

Guaguancó

The mid-paced guaguancó has African roots and was originally a drum form related to the rumba. Though often played 4/4, it has a strong 6/8 feel. The basic rhythm is traditionally carried by three congas and usually includes a good deal of solo drumming. The theme of a modern guaguancó is a somewhat loose melody line. It is one of the few 2-3 reverse clave forms.

Guajeo

A riff in the charanga style, especially for violin. Functionally, guajeos tie the melodic and rhythmic elements of a number together, acting as a sort of trampoline for flute and other solos. They are melodic patterns firmly based on the basic clave and tumbao.

Guajira

The slow guajira came from the Spanish-Cuban music of the guajiros. Much of its feeling comes from Hispanic melodies and guajeos that were originally, and often still are, played on the tres. The guajira is similar to the slow son montuno but is more delicate and less driving. Its lyrics frequently deal with rural nostalgia.

Guajiro Music

The Spanish-derived idiom of the Cuban farmers. The main instruments are the tres, guitar, and percussion, and the main form includes the décima, a ten-line verse from 17th-century Spain.

Guaracha

The original Cuban guaracha was a topical song form for chorus and solo voice, with improvisation in the solo. It was presented in 3/4 and 6/8 or 2/4 time signature. The guaracha developed a second section, employed for much improvisation, as in the son montuno. It appeared to have almost died out in Cuba by the 1930s, yet it is now one of the forms commonly used by salsa groups; a fast rhythm with a basic chicka-chicka pulse. Its last section is the probable source of the instrumental mambo. The guaracha is said to have originated in 18th-century *maisons d'assignation* and its lyrics are still often racy and satirical.

Güayo. See *Güiro*

Güiro

A scraper. The Cuban and Puerto Rican güiro, often called güayo in Puerto Rico, is made from a notched gourd and played with a stick. Poor players produce a steady ratchet-like sound. Skilled ones provide endless, crisp counter-rhythms against the rest of the percussion section.

The güiro, like the maraccas, is usually played by a singer. In the Dominican Republic, the güiro, also called the güira there, is made of metal and played with a kind of metal fork. The metal instrument's harsh sound adds a zest to country merengue playing, but it is rarely used in salsa.

Habanera

Cuban dance of Spanish origin, the first major Latin influence on U.S. music around the time of the Spanish-American War. Provided the rhythmic basis of the modern tango, which makes its influence in 20th-century American music difficult to trace.

Inspiración

"Inspiration," an improvised phrase by a lead vocalist or instrument.

Jíbaro Music

The jibaros are the mountain farmers of Puerto Rico, and their music is the most strongly Hispanic part of the island's folk tradition. Mostly string-based, jibaro music uses many Spanish-derived forms, including the ten-line décima verses—which a good singer must be able to improvise. A notable instrument is the small cuatro guitar. Many fine jibaro musicians, including singers Ramito and Chuitin, and cuatro player Yomo Toro, live in New York. Though various Puerto Rican salsa singers had used occasional jibaro inflections, Willie Colon brought the style into salsa by hiring Toro for a Christmas album in 1972.

Latin Jazz

A hybrid of jazz and Latin music. The term could cover anything from a Cuban number with a couple of Louis Armstrong phrases to a straight jazz number with a conga, but is best confined to crosses with a more or less full Latin rhythmic section, or one combining several Latin and jazz elements, and an instrumental frontline.

Latin Rock

A hybrid of rock and Latin elements. Most commonly rock-oriented guitar and keyboard solos are played over salsa-derived rhythms, but often rock and salsa rhythmic elements are blended; bands may use sections with a salsa coro, and build rock solos out of a Latin guajeo.

Latin Soul

Hybrid style from the late-1960s, combining salsa and rhythm and blues elements. Latin soul, which was based on early rhythm-and-blues and the bugalú, grew up among East Harlem and Bronx teenagers, who used both Spanish and English lyrics over a music that was somewhat more Latin than black.

Lucumí

Cuba's most widespread African-derived religion. Its theology is based on the faith of the Nigerian and Dahomeyan Yoruba people, and Yoruba is the liturgical language of Cuban lucumí. In Latin-American terms, lucumí is one of many African-derived faiths, and is widespread in Puerto Rico (and the Latin U.S.) under the general name of "santeria." Lucumí gave important elements to modern salsa, including much of its rhythmic basis, several songs, and a great deal of African melodic flavor. Many modern salsa musicians, especially in New York, are adherents of lucumí, or santeria, and the sacred batá drums are coming back into use in secular music.

Mambo

An Afro-Cuban form that came out of the Congolese religious cults. The big band mambo of the 1940s and 1950s developed characteristic contrasting brass and sax riffs, which many musicians regard as stemming from the last section of the guaracha.

Mambo Section

A section of contrasting riffs for salsa frontline instruments, setting trumpets against saxes or trombones, for example, sometimes under an instrumental solo. The section was said to derive from the guaracha, and got its name during the late 1940s and early 1950s.

Maraccas

A tuned pair of rattles made from gourds filled with pebbles or seeds, one of a wide range of Amerindian-derived rattles. A skilled maracca-player such as Machito plays a subtle role in the polyrhythmic counterpoint.

Mariachi

Mexican strolling groups of (usually) semi-professional musicians. Originally string orchestras, since the 1940s they have become trumpet-led ensembles. Their name stems from a corruption of the French *mariage,* since they were frequently hired for weddings.

Marimba

A form of xylophone with wooden slats over resonators. The name is African, but the marimba is widespread in western Colombia, parts of Mexico, and in particular Guatemala. Marimba groups were very popular in the U.S. during the 1920s.

Marimbula

A bass descendant of the African finger-piano, the marimbula consists of a wooden box with prongs of metal fastened to it, tuned to play a series of bass notes. The marimbula was common in Cuba and the Dominican Republic, as well as in several non-Latin Caribbean islands.

Maxixe

An old Brazilian dance derived from an earlier local ballroom dance heavily influenced by the early 20th century tango. It was briefly popular in the U.S. around the First World War, but never caught on to any permanent extent.

Merengue

Though dances by this name are found in many countries, the merengue is originally from the Dominican Republic, where it dates back at least to the early 19th century. The modern merengue has a notably brisk and snappy 2/4 rhythm, with a flavor very different from the somewhat more flowing Cuban and jaunty Puerto Rican dances. The country form, for accordion, tambora drum, metal scraper, and voice, is heard everywhere in the Dominican Republic. The big band version of Dominican bands like Johnny Ventura's and Felix del Rosario's is often heard at New York concerts.

Montuno Section

A vehicle for improvisation in Cuban and salsa numbers, based on a two or three-chord pattern repeated ad-lib under the instrumental or vocal improvisations. The piano often maintains a repeated vamp of guajeos, a process known as *montuneando.*

Orquesta Típica

A "Typical Orchestra." In Cuba, a now extinct type of group combining a flute and two clarinets, with timbales prominent in the rhythm. In Mexico, a group organized by "trained" musicians to present cleaned-up versions of folk and popular music.

Pachanga

The pachanga was a rage among New York Latin teenagers around 1961, as played by the then hugely popular charangas. There is some dispute as to its origins. It seems to be Cuban, but it never reached the popularity there that it enjoyed in the eastern U.S. It had a fast, syncopated ta-tum ta-tum pulse. The pachanga died out because the dance involved proved to be too energetic for most.

Plena

An Afro-Puerto Rican urban topical song form said to have been developed in Ponce during World War I. The plena has four or six-line verses, with a refrain. Lyrical content is social comment, satire, or humor. Instrumentation has ranged from percussion through accordion or guitar-led groups to various dance band formats. Its most famous composer and exponent was Manual Jiménez, known as Canario. It has been a minor influence on salsa through the work of Rafael Cortijo in the late 1950s and Willie Colon in the 1970s.

Ranchera

The ranchera, developed in the nationalist theater of the post-1910 revolution period in Mexico, became very much the equivalent of U.S. commercial country music. Professional singers developed an extremely emotional style, one of whose characteristics is a held note at the end of a line, culminating in a "dying fall" that could drop a third or more. Rancheras became an important part of Chicano music from the 1950s onward as moved from a folk-popular form to a greater professionalism.

Rumba

Most of what Americans call rumbas were forms of the *son* which swept Cuba in the 1920s. The Cuban rumba was a secular drum form with many variants, including the guaguancó and the columbia, though modern musicians tend to regard all these as separate. Its descendent variations can be heard in New York parks any summer weekend played by groups called rumbas or rumbones. By analogy, a percussion passage in a salsa number, or a percussion-only jam session, is sometimes called a rumba or rumbón.

Salsa

A contemporary word for hot, up-tempo, creative Latin music, it means "gravy" or "sauce." Originally, it was used as a descriptive such as "swinging" or "funky." The origins of the current usage are obscure, but it began to circulate in the late 1960s.

Samba

An Afro-Brazilian dance with several variations in different parts of Brazil. The best-known are the urban sambas, said to derive from the maxixe and the highly percussive sambas of the carnival "schools" of Rio. The characteristic shuffling 2/4 rhythm, fused with jazz, was part of the bossa nova.

Septeto or Sexteto

The Cuban septetos and sextetos of the 1930s played mostly sones and boleros. They were trumpet-led string groups, usually with tres, guitar, maraccas, bass, and bongó. Famous groups included the Septeto Nacional and the Sexteto Habanero. The music they played fell somewhere between the guajiro string groups and the brassier conjuntos. Septeto trumpet style is singularly lyrical, moving between 19th-century brass-band cornet and jazz in its inspiration. The septeto style as a whole is subtle, crisp, and charming.

Shekere

An African-derived rattle made of a large gourd with beads held by a string net on the outside. It is one version of a rattle common in Africa and Afro-Latin America and works on the opposite principle from maraccas.

Son

The son is perhaps the oldest and certainly the classic Afro-Cuban form, an almost perfect balance of African and Hispanic elements. Originating in Oriente province, it surfaced in Havana around World War I and became a popular urban music played by string-and-percussion quartets and septetos. Almost all the numbers Americans called rumbas were, in fact, sones. "El Manicero" ("The Peanut Vendor") was a form of son derived from the street cries of Havana and called a pregon. The rhythm of the son is strongly syncopated, with a basic chicka-CHUNG pulse.

Son Montuno

A reverse clave (2-3) form, usually mid-paced or slow, with a pronounced CHUNG-chicka feel. The son montuno developed as a separate form from the general con tradition. It was, like the guaracha, one of the first forms to include a second, improvised section, the montuno. Though it is not fast, the Afro-Cuban son montuno has an intense, almost relentless quality.

Sonero

In the strict sense, a man who sings or plays the Afro-Cuban son, but now the improvising lead singer in the salsa style. A good sonero improvises rhythmically, melodically, and verbally against the refrain of the coro. The word guarachero is a synonym, though less used.

Tambora

A double-headed drum, basic to the Dominican merengue. It is played with a single stick, while the other head is damped by hand to give tonal variety.

Tango

Probably the world's best-known dance after the waltz, the modern tango developed in Argentina at the beginning of the 20th century. It took its rhythm from the Cuban habanera and the Argentinian milonga, and its name probably from the Spanish *tango andalúz*.

Timbales

A percussion set-up consisting of two small metal drums on a stand, with two tuned cowbells, often a cymbal and other additions. The timbales descended from small military dance and concert bands. They were originally confined to the charangas and orquestas típicas, to which they imparted a distinctive, jaunty, march-like rhythm, but during the 1940s they came into wider use. The timbales are played with sticks, with the player striking heads, rims, and the sides of metal drums. All this plus cymbal and cowbells make for a varied instrument. A standard timbales beat, the *abanico*, is a rimshot-roll-rimshot combination.

Tipico

An imprecise but extremely important concept in modern salsa. Literally it means "typical" or "characteristic," but it is more generally used to identify the downhome, rural, popular styles of the Latin countries. Thus, the Cuban tipico music that became so important in New York in the 1960s and 1970s was basically conjunto and charanga music. But the septetos are also típico, since their style is simple and popular rather than bourgeois.

Toque

A "beat," but essentially a standard rhythmic phrase for percussion. Many toques derive from African religious drumming, in which particular rhythmic patterns were used to summon individual gods. A Latin percussionist is judged not by his energy level, but by his knowledge and use of standard toques and variations in his improvisations and in support of the band.

Tres

A nine-string Cuban guitar; a mainstay of guajiro music and of the Afro-Cuban septetos. The tres was established as an important part of the Cuban conjunto by Arsenio Rodriguez, himself a fine player. The instrument came into New York salsa during the Cuban típico revival of the late 1960s and early 1970s.

Tumbao

A repeated rhythmic pattern for bass or conga drum. Based on the fundamental clave, the bassist's tumbaos provide the scaffolding for the constant rhythmic counterpoint of the percussionists.

Select Discography

Note The number and obscurity of available Latin l.p.s makes a full listing impossible. This discography includes relevant or typical current albums and some important deleted items still to be found in some stores and many rummage sales.

Though no 78 rpm recordings are listed, I have picked up almost all of those I discuss in antique or thrift shops. Many from the 1940s, especially Xavier Cugat and popular American-Latin songs, are plentiful in such places.

Collections

Afro-Bahian Religious Songs. Library of Congress AFS-L13.
Bomba! Monitor MFS 355.
Brazil, Songs and Dances of. Folkways FW 6953.
Danzas de Puerto Rico. SMC-1026.
Mexico: Corridos. Folkways FW 6913.
Spanish and Mexican Folk Music of New Mexico. Ethnic Folkways FE-4426.
Texas-Mexican Border Music, Vol. 1, An Introduction, 1930–1960. Folklyric 9003.
Texas-Mexican Border Music, Vol. 2, Corridos, Part 1. Folklyric 9004.
Texas-Mexican Border Music, Vol. 4: Norteño Accordion. Folklyric 9006.
Understanding Latin Rhythms. LP Ventures, LPV 337.

Groups and Individual Musicians

Afro-Cuban Band: *Rhythm of Life.* Arista AB 4188.
Alegre All-Stars, Vol. 4. Alegre SLPA 8440.
Alpert, Herb's Tijuana Brass: *Whipped Cream and Other Delights.* A&M SP-4110.
Aragón, Orquesta: *Original de Cienfuegos.* Cariño DBLI-5011.
Arcaño y Sus Maravillas: *Danzón Mambo.* Cariño DBM1-5806.
Azteca. Columbia KC 31776.
Barbieri, Gato: *Fenix.* Flying Dutchman FD-10144.
Barbieri, Gato: *Chapter Two, Hasta Siempre.* ABC/Impulse AS-9263.
Barbieri, Gato: *Chapter Three, Viva Emiliano Zapata.* ABC/Impulse ASD 9279.
Barretto, Ray: *Carnaval.* Fantasy PR-24713.
Barretto, Ray: *Acid.* Fania SLP-346.
Barretto, Ray: *Charanga Moderna.* Tico SLP 1087. (Contains "El Watusi.")
Bataan, Joe: *Subway.* Fania LP 345.
Bataan, Joe: *Salsoul.* Mericana XMS-124.
Bechet, Sidney: *Bechet of New Orleans.* RCA Victor LPV-510. (Contains "Egyptian Fantasy.")
Ben, Jorge: *Samba Nova.* Island ILPS-9361.
Ben, Jorge: *Tropical.* Island SLPS 9390.
Bola Sete: *Bossa Nova.* Fantasy 8349.
Bravos del Ritmo, West Side Latino LT-LA 192-E2. (Collection of big bands and conjuntos.)
Broadway, Orquesta: *New York City Salsa.* Coco CLP-140X.
La Calandria, Vol. 2. Ansonia ALP 1399. (Puerto Rican jíbaro music.)
Canario y Su Grupo: *Plenas.* Ansonia ALP 1232.
Cha Cha Chá, La Gloria del. West Side Latino LT-LA 084-L2.
Chango. ABC ABCD-872.
Colon, Johnny: *Soul & Latin.* Cotique CS-1087.
Colon, Willie: *El Malo.* Fania SLP 337.
Colon, Willie: *Cosa Nuestra.* Fania SLP-384.
Colon, Willie: *The Good, the Bad, the Ugly.* Fania XSLP 00484.
Colon, Willie, w. Yomo Toro: *Asalto Navideño.* Fania SLP-399.
Concepción, Cesar: *La Plena y El Bolero de Puerto Rico.* Cariño DBMI-5807.
Cortijo y Su Combo: *Bombas para Bailar.* Tropical TRLP 5172.
Cortijo: *Maquina de Tiempo/Time Machine.* Coco CLP-108.
Cuba, Joe Sextet: *Wanted Dead or Alive.* Tico SLP-1146. (Contains "Bang Bang.")
Cuban Jam Session, Vol. 2. Panart 3055.
Cugat, The Best of: Mercury SR 60870.

Curbelo, José: *Los Reyes del Mambo*. Carino. DBMI-5809.
DaCosta, Paulinho: *Agora*. Pablo 2310-785.
Damiron y Chapuseaux: *Los Reyes del Merengue*. Seeco SCLP 9260.
De Souza, Raul: *Colors*. Milestone M-9061.
Fajardo: *Sabor Guajiro*. Caliente CLT-7084.
Gardel, Carlos. Arcano DKL1-3149.
Gardel, Carlos: *Memorias de Carlos Gardel*. Arcano DKL1-3146.
Garland, Red: *Rediscovered Masters*. Prestige P-24078.
Getz, Stan. (See also Gillespie.)
Getz, Stan, w. Laurindo Almeida. Verve VLP-9150.
Gilberto, João & Jobim. Capitol ST 2160. (Reissue of *Brazil's Brilliant João Gilberto*, first bossa nova album released in U.S.)
Gillespie, Dizzy, w. Machito: *Afro-Cuban Jazz Moods*, Pablo 2310-771.
Gillespie, Dizzy: *Pleyel Concerts*. Vogue DP-18 (import).
Gillespie, Dizzy: *Dizzy's Party*. Pablo 2310-784.
Gillespie, Dizzy, and Stan Getz: *Diz and Getz*. Verve VE-2-2521.
Gottschalk, Louis Moreau: *A Gottschalk Festival*. Turnabout TV-S 34440-42.
Guaracheros de Oriente. Panart LP-2015.
Harlow, Larry: *Tribute to Arsenio Rodriguez*. Fania SLP 00404.
Harlow, Larry: *Hommy*. Fania 00425.
Hernandez, "Little Joe": *Arriba!* Buena Suerte BSR 1001.
Hernandez, "Little Joe," and La Familia: *Para La Gente*. Buena Suerte BSR 1038.
Huerta, Las Hermanas: *Interpretan a Felipe Valdes Leál*. Caytronics CYS 1410. (Rancheras)
El Indio de Nabori. Panart LP-2052. (Guajiro music.)
Jiménez, Flaco. Arhoolie 3007.
Kenton, Stan: *New Concepts of Artistry in Rhythm*. Creative World ST-1002. (Contains "23°N-82°W.")
Kenton, Stan: *Cuban Fire*. Creative World ST-1008.
Kenton, Stan: *Collector's Choice*. Creative World ST-1027. (Contains "Artistry in Tango," "Viva Prado.")
Kenton, Stan: *By Request*. Creative World ST 1036. (Contains "Machito.")
Kenton, Stan: *Milestones*. Creative World ST 1047. (Contains "The Peanut Vendor.")
Kenton, Stan: *The Formative Years (1941–1942)*. Creative World ST 1061.
Kirk, Roland: *Slightly Latin*. Limelight LS 86033.
Lopez, Trini: *At PJ's*. Reprise R9-6093.
Machito and His Orchestra: *Latin Soul Plus Jazz*. Tico CLP 1314.
Machito: *Afro-Cuban Jazz*. Verve VE-2-2522.

Malo: *Ascencion.* Warner Bros. BS-2769.
Mann, Herbie: *Latin Mann.* Caliente CLT-7073.
Mann, Herbie, w. Machito: *Super Mann.* Trip TLP-5031.
Marrero, Ricardo, and the Group: *Time.* Vaya JMVS-64.
Martinez, Narciso: Folklyric 9017.
Martinez, Sabu: *Jazz a l'Espagnole.* Alegre LPA-802.
Matamoros Trio: *Ecos de Cuba.* Kubaney MT-116.
Morales, Noro: *Bailemos Con Noro Morales.* Tropical TRLP-5027.
Moreira, Airto: *Natural Feelings.* Buddha BDS-21-SK.
Moreira, Airto: *Seeds on the Ground.* Buddah BDS5085.
Moreira, Airto: *Identity.* Arista AL-4068.
Nascimento, Milton: *Milton.* A&M SP-4611.
Orquesta Novedades: *Danzones Antiguos.* Maype 179.
Pacheco, Johnny: *The Best of Pacheco.* Alegre CLPA 7011. (Charanga)
Pacheco, Johnny: *Los Compadres.* Fania SLP-00400. (Conjunto)
Palmieri, Charlie: *Charanga Duboney: Echoes of an Era.* West Side Latino
    WS-LA-240-I.
Palmieri, Eddie: *Live at Sing Sing.* Tico CLP 1303.
Palmieri, Eddie: *The Best of Eddie Palmieri.* Tico CLP 1317.
Palmieri, Eddie: *Sentido.* Coco CLP 103.
Palmieri, Eddie: *The Sun of Latin Music.* Coco CLP 109XX.
Palmieri, Eddie, w. Cal Tjader: *Bamboleate.* Tico SLP-1150.
Parker, Charlie: *The Verve Years, 1950–51.* Verve VE-2-2512.
Pascoal, Hermeto: *Slaves Mass.* Warner Bros. BS 2980.
Paunetto, Bobby: *Paunetto's Point.* Pathfinder PLP 1775.
La Playa Sextet w. Tito Rodriguez. Alegre SLPA-8870.
Prado, Perez: *Patricia.* Carino DBLI-5019.
Prado, Perez: *Havana, 3 a.m.* RCA Victor LPM-1257.
Prado, Perez: *Concierto Para Bongó.* West Side Latino L 31005.
Puente, Tito: *Cuban Carnival.* Cariño DBLI1-5153. (Includes original
    "Para Los Rumberos.")
Puente, Tito: *Dance Mania.* Cariño DBLI-5017.
Puente, Tito: *The Best of Tito Puente (1964–69).* Tico SLP-1203.
Puente, Tito: *Para Los Rumberos.* Tico CLP 1301.
Purim, Flora: *Stories To Tell.* Milestone M-9058.
Ramito: *Sabor Boricua.* Tropical TRLP 5156. (Puerto Rican jíbaro music.)
Rodriguez, Arsenio: *El Sentimiento de Arsenio.* Cariño DBMI-5802.
Rodriguez, Bobby, and his Company
Rodriguez, Pete: *The Best of Pete Rodriguez.* Alegre SLPA-878. (Includes
    "Pete's Boogaloo.")
Rodriguez, Tito; *Estoy Como Nunca.* West Side Latino LT-LA 129-D.

Rodriguez, Tito: *Live at the Palladium.* West Side Latino L31067.

Romeu, Antonio Maria: *El Danzón.* Panart L-3037.

Santamaria, Mongo: *Afro-Roots.* Prestige PR-24018.

Santamaria, Mongo: *Drums and Chants.* Tico LP-1149.

Santamaria, Mongo: *El Bravo.* Caliente CLT-7074.

Santamaria, Mongo: *Sabrosa!* Fantasy 8058.

Santana: Columbia KC-31776.

Santana: *Abraxas.* Columbia KC 30130.

Santana: *Three.* Columbia KC 30595. (Contains "Para Los Rumberos.")

Santana: *Amigos.* Columbia PC 33576.

Seguida: *Love Is . . .* Fania XSLP 00478.

Septeto Nacional: *Como Se Baila el Son.* Bravo 104.

Sexteto Habanero: *Collección de Oro.* CD-1201.

Shearing, George: *Latin Escapade.* Capitol SM 11454.

Tjader, Cal: *Latino.* Fantasy 8079.

Tjader, Cal: *Los Ritmos Calientes.* Fantasy 24712.

Tjader, Cal: *Primo.* Fantasy 9422. (With Charlie Palmieri and Tito Puente.)

Tjader, Cal. (See also Eddie Palmieri.)

Toro. Coco CLP-106.

Ventura, Johnny: *Superhits.* Mate 017. (Big band Dominican merengue.)

Viloria, Angel, and His Conjunto Tipico Cibaeño. Ansonia ALP 1206.

Bibliography

Note Almost the only source of material on New York salsa is *Latin New York* magazine, whose articles by Max Salazar and others are too numerous to mention individually.

ALVARENGA, Oneida, *Musica Popular Brazilena*. Mexico City: Fondo de Cultura Economica, 1947.

ARNAZ, Desi, *A Book*. New York: William Morrow, 1976.

BASCOM, William, *Shango in the New World*. Austin: African and Afro-American Research Institute, University of Texas, 1972.

BASTIDE, Roger, *Les Amériques Noires*. Paris: Payot, 1967.

BLESH, Rudi, and Harriet Janis, *They All Played Ragtime*. New York: Knopf, 1950; Oak Publications, 1971 (revised).

BMI, "Pop Hits, 1940–1974" (monograph).

BORNEMANN, Ernest, *A Critic Looks at Jazz*. London: Workers' Music Association, n.d.

CARPENTIER, Alejo, *La Música en Cuba*. Mexico City: Fondo de Cultura Economica, 1972.

CASTLE, Mr. and Mrs. Vernon, *The Modern Dance*. New York: Harper and Brothers, 1914.

CHASE, Gilbert, *America's Music*. New York: McGraw-Hill, 1966.

CHASE, Gilbert, *The Music of Spain*. New York: Dover, 1959.

COURLANDER, Harold, "Musical Instruments of Cuba." *Musical Quarterly*, April 1942.

CRUZ, Francisco Lopez, *La Musica Folklorica en Cuba*. Sharon, Conn.: Troutman Press, 1967.

DE LA TORRE, José Maria, *Lo Que Fuimos y Lo que Somos*, or *La Habana Antigua y Moderna*. Havana, 1857.

DEMORIZI, Emilio R., *Musica y Baile en Santo Domingo*. Santo Domingo: Librería Hispaniola, 1971.

ENCYCLOPÉDIE de la MUSIQUE et DICTIONNAIRE du CONSERVATOIRE, Vol. 4: Music of Spain and Portugal.

EWEN, David, *American Musical Theater*. New York: Holt, Rinehart, 1958.

FEATHER, Leonard, *The Book of Jazz*. New York: Horizon Press, 1965.

GEIJERSTAM, Claes af., *Popular Music in Mexico*. Albuquerque: University of New Mexico Press, 1977.

GILBERT, Louis Wolfe, *Without Rhyme or Reason*. New York: Vantage Press, 1956.

GOMEZ-SANTOS, Marino, *Xavier Cugat*. Barcelona: Ediciones Clipper, 1958.

GONZALEZ-WIPPLER, Migène, *Santeria*. Garden City, N.Y.: Anchor Books, 1975.

GREEN, Stanley, *Ring Bells! Sing Songs!*. New York: Arlington House, 1971.

GREEN, Stanley, *The World of Musical Comedy*. New York: Grosset and Dunlap, 1960.

GRENET, Emilio, *Popular Cuban Music*. Havana: Ministry of Education, 1939.

HAGUE, Eleanor, *Latin American Music*. Santa Ana, Cal.: Fine Arts Press, 1934.

HANDY, W. C., *Father of the Blues*. New York: Macmillan, 1941.

HISTORIA de la ORQUESTA TÍPICA, *Evolución Instrumental del Tango*. Buenos Aires: Ed. A. Peña Lillo, 1966.

HOWARD, Joseph H., *Drums in the Americas*. New York: Oak Publications, 1967.

KMEN, Henry A., *Music in New Orleans: The Formative Years*. Baton Rouge: Louisiana State University Press, 1966.

KOLB, Carolyn, "Expo/1884." New Orleans: *New Orleans* magazine, 1970.

LEON, Argiliers, *Musica Folklorica Cubana*, Havana: Biblioteca Nacional Jose Marti, 1964.

LINARES, Maria Teresa, *La Música Popular*. Havana: Instituto del Libro, 1970.

LOGGINS, Vernon, *Where the Word Ends: The Life of Louis Moreau Gottschalk*. Baton Rouge: Louisiana State University Press, 1958.

LOMAX, Alan, *Mister Jelly Roll*. New York: Duell, 1950.

LUPER, Albert T., *The Music of Brazil*. Washington: Music Division, Pan-American Union, 1943.

MALONE, Bill C., *Country Music U.S.A.* Austin: University of Texas Press, for American Folklore Society, 1968.

MARKS, E. B., *They All Sang*. New York: Viking Press, 1935.

MARQUIS, Donald M., *In Search of Buddy Bolden*. Baton Rouge and London: Louisiana State University Press, 1978.

MATTFELD, Julius, *Variety Music Cavalcade*. New York: Prentice-Hall, 1952.

MUÑOZ, Maria Luisa, *La Musica en Puerto Rico*. Sharon, Conn.: Troutman Press, 1966.

OLIVER, Paul, *The Story of the Blues*. Philadelphia: Chilton, 1969.

ORTIZ, F., *La Africania de la Musica Folklorica de Cuba*. Havana: Cardenas, n.d.

PAREDES, Americo. *With His Pistol in His Hand*. Austin: University of Texas Press, 1958.

ROBB, J. D., "Spanish Mexican Folk Music of New Mexico." Notes to Ethnic Folkways FE4426, 1952.

ROBERTS, John Storm, *Black Music of Two Worlds*. New York: Praeger Publishers, 1972.

ROSE, Al, and Edmond Souchon, *New Orleans Jazz Family Album*. Baton Rouge: Louisiana State University Press, 1967.

SALDIVAR, Gabriel, *Historia de la Musica en Mexico*, Mexico City. SEP, 1934.

SCHULLER, Gunther, *Early Jazz*. New York: Oxford University Press, 1968.

SERRA, Otto Mayer, *Panorama de la Musica Mexicana*. Mexico City: Colegio de Mexico, 1941.

SHAFER, William J., and Johannes Riedel, *The Art of Ragtime*. Baton Rouge: Louisiana State University Press, 1973.

SHAPIRO, Nat, and Nat Hentoff, eds., *Hear Me Talkin' to Ya*. New York: Rinehart, 1955.

SHAW, Arnold, *Honkers and Shouters: The Golden Years of Rhythm and Blues*. New York: Macmillan, 1978.

SLONIMSKY, Nicholas, *Music of Latin America*. New York: Crowell, 1945.

SOUTHERN, Eileen, *The Music of Black Americans*. New York: Norton, 1971.

STEARNS, Marshall W., *The Story of Jazz*. New York: Oxford University Press, 1956.

STRACHWITZ, Chris, Booklet accompanying album "Texas-Mexican Border Music Vol. 1," Folklyric Records, 9003.

VALLANCE, Tom, *The American Musical*. New York: Castle Books, 1970.

Index